Through Belgian Eyes

Belgian Eyes

Charlotte Brontë's Troubled Brussels Legacy

A wonderfully fresh and informative book, seeing the connection between Charlotte Brontë and Brussels in the round for the first time. Helen MacEwan's acknowledged expertise on both the place and the author comes together perfectly in this packed and fascinating study of Brontë's mixed feelings about the city that formed her as a writer – and its equally ambivalent responses to her.

CLAIRE HARMAN, author of *Charlotte Brontë: A Life*

Once again, Helen MacEwan writes eloquently about Charlotte Brontë in Brussels, bringing together her expert knowledge of the city Brontë inhabited and of the great works that drew on this experience. She balances Charlotte's critique of Brussels against the impressive counterweight of her legacy: her astute social observation of Brussels in the 1840s – its education, its park, its king, its manners and food – her placing the city at the centre of a great work of literature.

LYNDALL GORDON, author of *Charlotte Brontë: A Passionate Life*

Helen MacEwan has achieved something very unusual: she has found a fascinating area of Brontë studies untouched by previous writers. The impact of Brussels on Charlotte Brontë is well-documented, but MacEwan is the first writer to ask what impact Charlotte Brontë had on the Belgians.

Impeccably researched from a huge range of sources, from the 1840s to the present day, and from city guide books to academic studies, this scholarly but engaging and readable book investigates every aspect of Charlotte's Belgian legacy. Charlotte's opinion of Belgians (apart from her beloved teacher) was negative in the extreme, but MacEwan, in fourteen varied chapters, shows us that Belgians have not only been, on the whole, very forgiving, but that they attach immense value to her fiction. One surprise for non-Belgian readers is the importance of *Villette* and *The Professor* as a unique record of a vanished Brussels, since razed by relentless redevelopment. MacEwan illustrates Belgian appreciation of Charlotte's uncanny accuracy in bringing to life its lost urban landscapes, its cosmopolitan population, its art exhibitions, concerts, boarding-schools, churches, its park and public celebrations – even its royalty. The best description of King Leopold I, according to his Belgian biographer, MacEwan tells us, is Charlotte's, in *Villette*. Beyond verisimilitude, Belgians find romance in that lost Brussels as the site of Charlotte's unhappy love, recognising that her anguished sense of being alone in a foreign land crucially heightened her imaginative creativity. MacEwan's remarkable book, by enabling us to read through Belgian eyes, sheds surprising new light on novels we think we know.

PATSY STONEMAN, Emeritus Reader in English, University of Hull, and Vice-President of the Brontë Society

Through Belgian Eyes

Charlotte Brontë's Troubled Brussels Legacy

HELEN MACEWAN

sussex
ACADEMIC
PRESS
Brighton • Portland • Toronto

2 4 6 8 10 9 7 5 3 1

First published in Great Britain in 2017 by
SUSSEX ACADEMIC PRESS
PO Box 139
Eastbourne BN24 9BP

Distributed in North America by
SUSSEX ACADEMIC PRESS
ISBS Publisher Services
920 NE 58th Ave #300, Portland, OR 97213, USA

British Library Cataloguing in Publication Data
A CIP catalogue record for this book is available from the British Library.

Library of Congress Cataloging-in-Publication Data
Applied for.

Paperback ISBN 978 1 84519 910 4

Typeset and designed by Sussex Academic Press, Brighton & Eastbourne.
Printed by TJ International, Padstow, Cornwall.

Contents

Acknowledgements

I would like to thank the following people for their help with research for this book: Brian Bracken for assistance with numerous research enquiries; Anne Quiévreux, daughter of Louis Quiévreux, for information on her father and for alerting me to Marie Gevers' article *The Brontës in Africa*; Sophie De Schaepdrijver and Leen Huet for their thoughts about Charlotte Brontë and her novels; Kristien Hemmerechts for permission to quote from her articles; Claire Billen of the Université Libre de Bruxelles for information on points of Brussels history; Jean Heyblom and Jean-Jacques de Gheyndt of the *Cercle d'Histoire de Bruxelles* for answering various queries; Vanessa Gemis of the Université Libre de Bruxelles for providing Valérie Piette's article *Un réseau privé d'éducation des filles*; Johan Hellinx for his thoughts on Flemish history and culture. I would also like to thank Brian Bracken and Paul Gretton for reading the book and making comments.

Thanks are due to the following for assistance with the illustrations: Gina Deneckere and Bram Delbecke for help in locating the *Gardeuse des Dindons* cartoon; Annie Terlinck for information on Louis Ghémar's lithographs of the Tour de Rocher and of Edouard de Biefve's *Une Almée*; Wilfred Vandervelde for providing scans of these lithographs; Selina Busch for her map of Brussels; Elena Lauwers for help in locating the picture of the Palais Granvelle; the staff of the Prints Department of the Royal Library of Belgium for assistance with and information on numerous nineteenth-century prints of Brussels; the BELvue Museum for the photo of the subterranean rue Isabelle in the Coudenberg archaeological site.

I am grateful to my husband for his patience while I was absorbed in this project. Last but not least, my thanks to Anthony Grahame, Editorial Director at Sussex Academic Press, for taking on this book and for his patient guidance, and to Boyd Schlenther for coming up with the title of the book!

List of Illustrations

Cover

Front: The Boulevard du Jardin Botanique by Paul Lauters, 1844 (Royal Library of Belgium, F2008 326).

Back: Charlotte Brontë by J.H. Thompson, probably painted after her death (© Brontë Society).

Colour plates

Charlotte Brontë, chalk drawing by George Richmond, 1850 (National Portrait Gallery, London).

The Coudenberg Palace. Attributed to Jan Brueghel the Younger, 1627 (Museo del Prado, Madrid).

Panoramic view of Brussels by Paul Lauters, c. 1850. (Royal Library of Belgium, S II 39544).

Mme Reuters. Illustration by Edmund Dulac for *The Professor*, Dent, London, 1922.

Rosine, the portress at Mme Beck's Pensionnat. Illustration by Edmund Dulac for *Villette*, Dent, London, 1922.

La Vie d'une Femme by Fanny Geefs, 1842. Private collection.

Arcadie Claret, Leopold I's mistress for the last 20 years of his life. Paul Fearn/Alamy Stock Photo. Reproduced with permission from Alamy.

Lucy has a sighting of the ghostly nun. Illustration by Edmund Dulac for *Villette*, Dent, London, 1922.

Rue Isabelle and the gateway to the Jardin des Arbalétriers. Watercolour by Jacques Carabain, 1890s (Musée de la Ville de Bruxelles).

The Brussels Ommegang in 1615 by Antoine Sallaert. Paul Fearn/Alamy Stock Photo. Reproduced with permission from Alamy.

The grave of Constantin and Zoë Heger in Watermael-Boitsfort cemetery.

The Heger family in 1847, by Ange François. Reproduced by kind permission of the owner.

Map of Brussels

'Oh it is certain that I shall see you again one day'

ON 14 February 1842 the 25-year-old Charlotte Brontë, accompanied by her sister Emily, arrived in Brussels to complete her education. As an escape route from the hated *métier* of governess, she, Emily and Anne had hit on the idea of opening a school; it was to prepare themselves for this project that the two eldest, at Charlotte's instigation, decided on a stay abroad to perfect their French and generally enhance their qualifications. Running a school was a poor second best to the sisters' dream of being published writers, but it was at least an improvement on looking after spoiled children in other people's houses.

Brussels was an obvious choice because Belgium was cheaper than France and they had friends and contacts there. The British chaplain's wife recommended a suitable boarding school; Yorkshire schoolfriends of Charlotte's, Mary and Martha Taylor, were already studying in Brussels at another establishment, too costly for the cash-strapped Brontës.

Apart from a break in Haworth at the end of 1842 after the death of their Aunt Branwell, Charlotte was to remain in Belgium for almost two years, finally leaving on 1 January 1844. Emily did not accompany her back to Brussels, opting instead to take her aunt's place as housekeeper at the Parsonage.

What drove Charlotte to Brussels, with the less enthusiastic Emily in tow, was not just ambition but restlessness and curiosity. Tired of schoolroom drudgery, she longed not only to qualify herself for a more independent life professionally but also to see something of the world. Before crossing the Channel, her excited talk was of the churches and art galleries she would visit.

The sisters were installed at the *Pensionnat de Demoiselles* Heger-Parent, run by Zoë Parent with her husband Constantin Heger,[1] who taught the boys at the *Athénée Royal* next door as well as the young ladies at his wife's school. In her second year, Charlotte gave English classes at the Pensionnat to pay for her studies. Her account of the unruliness of the Belgian pupils in

The Professor and *Villette* has the ring of painful truth. Charlotte had no vocation for teaching, and did not gain control in the classroom with the same ease as her fictional schoolteachers William Crimsworth and Lucy Snowe.

Her return to Brussels without Emily, despite the homesickness she had battled there, was not driven solely by considerations of the French and German she still had to learn. Constantin Heger, who had been tutoring the sisters in French, had written to their father lauding their progress and urging at least one of them to pursue her studies for another year. It was a kind and affectionate letter and Charlotte was not reluctant to act on his proposal, braving the perils of the journey from Haworth to make her way alone to the Pensionnat in January 1843, drawn, she said later, by an 'irresistible impulse'.

From the start, Charlotte had been fascinated by the directress's husband. He occupies a large part of one of her first extant letters from Brussels to her best friend Ellen Nussey: a choleric, 'black, ugly being' with extraordinarily mobile features (like an 'insane tom-cat' or 'delirious hyena' was her comparison), who, she told Ellen, was 'very angry with me at present because I have written a translation which he chose to stigmatise as *peu correct* – not because it was particularly so in reality but because he happened to be in a bad humour when he read it'. She informed Ellen, gleefully, that her tutor wrote 'stern' comments in the margins of her *devoirs*, the French compositions set by him as homework assignments. Charlotte's youthful fiction was full of brooding Byronic heroes, and she seems to have revelled in Heger's sternness and mood changes. In this she was unlike her sister. 'Emily and he don't draw well together at all – when he is very ferocious with me I cry – and that sets all things straight.'[2] Charlotte's fictional heroes were masterful, even despotic, and there was a masochistic element in her heroines' relationships with these men. The shedding of tears, when prompted by the man she came to call her 'master', was pleasurable. He was an inspirational teacher who won his pupils' devotion, and when his displeasure drew their tears he would melt at the sight and become all affability again. It is a trait Charlotte captures in his fictional counterpart, Monsieur Paul Emanuel in *Villette*.

In a school full of girls and mistresses with whom she found nothing in common, Charlotte lived for her tutorials with Heger and for the comments he wrote on her work. They were not always stern. They engaged her in interesting dialogue: debates, for example, about the relative importance, in literary composition, of inspiration, intuition and personal experience as opposed to craftsmanship honed through imitation of great writers. She was excited by the use of a foreign language, French, as the medium for this intellectual tête-à-tête. She bared her soul to him in an essay supposedly written by a poor painter who suffers from feelings of solitude and social failure but is convinced of his own genius. Her imaginary painter is called George Howard. It is not very difficult to perceive that the twenty-five-year old George Howard has rather a lot in common with Charlotte Brontë, twenty-five when she first went to Brussels.

This was the last essay she composed for Heger, at any rate the last of the twenty or so that have survived. By the time she wrote it, in October 1843, her initial happiness at being back in Belgium had given way to depression. For a time she had given Heger English lessons, an experience she had very much enjoyed, but these were discontinued and she saw less and less of him. Occasionally her day was brightened by a surprise present from him, but in letters home she spoke increasingly of the monotony and solitude of her life abroad, and of a growing *froideur* on the part of Madame Heger. She told her brother Branwell that she was becoming 'exceedingly misanthropic and sour'. She lamented her lack of affinity with her Belgian fellow inmates, whom she viewed as uninteresting, passionless, insincere. 'The black swan Mr Heger is the sole ... exception to this rule (for Madame, always cool and always reasoning is not quite an exception).'[3]

Much has been written about Charlotte's visit to the church of St Gudule in the summer of that year, and the fact that despite her rabid anti-Catholicism she persuaded a Catholic priest to hear her confession, an episode narrated in detail in *Villette*. Judging from her letters home and her description of Lucy Snowe's sufferings during a solitary summer in the city of Villette, Charlotte seems to have experienced what was virtually a nervous breakdown in the school vacation of 1843, spent almost alone at the deserted Pensionnat. Biographers have often linked her visit to the confessional with her feelings for Heger, then holidaying with his heavily pregnant wife and their four young children on the Belgian coast.

Charlotte's four surviving letters to her former teacher, spanning the two years after she returned to Yorkshire, reveal the extent of her infatuation with her 'master'. Torn up by him, retreived and stitched together by his wife, and eventually, in 1913, presented by the couple's children to the British Museum and published in *The Times* for the world to read, they have generally been viewed as evidence that Charlotte was 'in love' with her Belgian professor. What we know for certain is that in her last novel, *Villette*, through her characters Lucy Snowe and M. Paul she lived out in fiction a love affair with Heger, or at any rate with a character inspired by her perception of and fantasies about her teacher.

Although it is inevitably Haworth and the moors that predominate in popular images of the Brontë family, those familiar with Charlotte's story have always recognised the significance of Brussels for her life and work. However, the focus in accounts of her stay in Belgium has been on Heger and his impact on her. The importance of that relationship is clear from *Villette*, but the novel also reflects many other aspects of the Brussels environment in which two years of her life were passed. From the vantage point of a Brussels boarding school she was a keen observer of life in the Belgian capital in the 1840s. Although many of her observations were made within the walls of the Pensionnat, she was equally attentive when she was out and about in the city's streets.

The Brontës were great walkers. During their time in Brussels, tramps on the moors were replaced by long walks along the newly-completed boulevards encircling the city, first laid out under Napoleon's rule on the site of the old ramparts, as well as rambles in the narrow, winding streets of the town centre. On these walks, and on occasional outings to concerts or art galleries, Charlotte mentally stowed away her impressions. Some of her remarks about the city's culture and society were caustic, but there is much more to explore in her relationship with Belgium than her sardonic remarks about the Belgians. Her recording of numerous features of Brussels and of every detail of events such as a concert attended by the cream of the Brussels bourgeoisie, her psychological analysis of a range of characters, from the school portress to King Leopold I, provide numerous snapshots of Belgian life. Comparison of her impressions with those of other foreign visitors and of native observers serves to round out and balance her picture.

When writing *Villette* almost ten years after leaving Belgium, 'she had only to close her eyes for things and people of Brussels to reappear'. Her descriptions of the city's life 'reflect a reality observed and conveyed with startling fidelity', in the words of one Belgian scholar.[4]

In one respect at least, the relationship with Belgium was one that Charlotte endeavoured to keep alive after returning to Yorkshire. Her letters to Heger represent a desperate attempt to maintain a link with Brussels, to preserve a closeness of communion with the one Belgian in whom she believed she had found a soulmate. It was a call to which Heger could not or would not respond. In the face of a barrage of appeals for his support and an announcement that she intended to return to see him, Heger, never a diligent correspondent, fell silent, doubtless judging it safest for her sake as well as his own to break off the connection. 'Oh it is certain that I shall see you again one day – it really has to be – for as soon as I have earned enough money to go to Brussels I shall go – and I shall see you again if it is only for a moment,' she wrote in July 1844.[5]

Charlotte never did return to Brussels, but she did so in imagination in *The Professor* (written in 1845–6 but not published until after her death) and, some years later, in *Villette* (started in 1851 and published in 1853). The two novels have established a lasting link between Charlotte Brontë and Brussels, and the story of her unrequited love is one of the city's literary legends. Although Heger proved unresponsive and cut short her dialogue with him, her interaction with her Belgian readers continues to this day. This book is an exploration of their responses, of those continuing echoes of Charlotte's stay at the Pensionnat.

Belgian reactions to *Villette* and *The Professor* provide new ways of looking both at the novels and at Charlotte Brontë herself, a view 'through Belgian eyes'. In the process of examining these, the book delves into the Brussels world that Charlotte portrayed in the two novels, some understanding of which is needed in order to assess her portrayal and the responses of her Belgian readers.

The different aspects of Charlotte Brontë's legacy discussed in this book are discussed by theme rather than chronologically (with the exception of Chapter 2, which examines the early reception of her work in Belgium). For reference, a chronological summary of events that have focused attention in Belgium on Charlotte, such as translations, biographies and film or stage adaptations, can be found at the end of this book. These events are frequently referred to in the different chapters, since they prompted many of the Belgian commentaries cited. The publication of Charlotte's letters to Heger in 1913, the appearance of the first complete French translation of *Villette* in 1932 and the two-year exhibition on Charlotte Brontë held at the Charlier Museum in Brussels in the run-up to the centenary of her death (1953–55), are examples of events that have drawn attention to her time in Brussels and her 'Brussels novels'. More recently, her Belgian stay was given prominence in publications and other events marking the bicentenary of her birth (2016).

My main focus is on Belgian reactions to Charlotte's time in the country and to *Villette* and *The Professor*, the two novels that grew out of her experiences there, rather than to her other fiction. However, Chapter 2 looks at the first reception not just of *Villette* of her best-seller *Jane Eyre*, which in Belgium, as elsewhere, has always been the most widely read of her books and was the work that first introduced her to Belgian readers.

1 French speakers generally use the spelling 'Héger' with an accent. However, Constantin Heger spelled his surname without an accent, presumably owing to its German origin; his granddaughter Simone Beckers-Heger confirmed that this was the correct spelling. Later generations of the family have tended to use the accent.

2 Letter to Ellen Nussey believed to have been written in May 1842. Smith, *The Letters of Charlotte Brontë*, Volume II, pp. 284–5.

3 Letter to Branwell Brontë, 1 May 1843. Smith, *The Letters of Charlotte Brontë*, Volume I, pp. 316–17.

4 Charlier, *La vie bruxelloise dans 'Villette'*, p. 78. (Unless otherwise indicated, translations are my own.)

5 Letter to Constantin Heger. Smith, *The Letters of Charlotte Brontë*, Volume I, p. 359.

CHAPTER ONE

'Bruxelles, la mal-aimée'

B RUSSELS is not a city rich in literary associations. Its name conjures up few romantic images. In the opinion of the editors of *Écrire Bruxelles/Brussel Schrijven*, a collection of essays on how the Belgian capital has inspired writers through the ages, it suffers from the lack of a clear identity – certainly of a clear literary identity – and has not given birth to any great literary myths.[1] The writer Jacques De Decker, in the foreword to a cultural history of Brussels, acknowledges that it has fired the imagination of few Belgian authors, let alone foreign ones.[2] It seems strangely appropriate that probably the most celebrated work of literature to take Brussels as its setting not only fails to give the city its real name, but disguises it under the inglorious one of 'Villette', 'little town'.

Today, Brussels is dubbed the 'capital of Europe', but its role as the main seat of government of the European Union gives it a somewhat negative image as a capital of bureaucracy. The impressions of those actually acquainted with it, its visitors and residents, are mixed. It is a city of considerable charms, not least of which is its manageable size; it is also a city all too often marred by uninspiring urban development and an air of neglect.

Charlotte Brontë, too, had mixed impressions of the Brussels she knew in the 1840s. It was 'a beautiful city',[3] 'a brilliant capital'.[4] She waxed enthusiastic about the splendour of its neo-classical buildings and of a concert hall she visited. At the same time, she was scathing about the limitations of her fellow students and teachers and of the Brussels burghers she observed at events in the city. She derided the mediocrity of the paintings she saw at a Brussels art exhibition and the performances at a concert she attended. For Belgian readers, her picture mercilessly reveals the provinciality of their capital in her time.

Brilliant capital or a town of provinciality and mediocrity? The accounts of other nineteenth-century observers paint a similarly mixed picture. The city was a much smaller place then than it is today. It had only recently acquired the status of capital of the new state which came into being

1

with the 1830 Revolution that brought separation from the northern Netherlands. It could not compete in attractions with London or Paris or Rome, but guide books of the period testify to its appeal, as does the fact that large numbers of Britons chose to make their home there after the Battle of Waterloo.

The Brussels of Thackeray's *Vanity Fair*, depicted on the eve of that battle, was a 'brilliant little capital'. Frances Trollope, mother of the more famous Anthony, visited it in 1833, shortly after Independence. In her travel book on Belgium she urged British travellers to explore the country in depth rather than treating it as the 'high road to the Rhine', a mere place of passage on the way to Germany and Switzerland. She found Brussels 'delightful' while pointing out that, post-Independence, high society life in the capital was less sparkling than before the Revolution. The new King, Leopold I, presided over a lacklustre court boycotted by the many aristocratic families whose allegiance was still to William I, the ousted Dutch King, while the city bore the physical scars of the four days of bloody conflict of the Revolution. But Mrs Trollope still found Brussels 'one of the prettiest little capitals in Europe'.[5] An 1843 guide book by Henry Robert Addison also sings its praises: 'A more cheerful and inviting looking City is not to be met with on the Continent of Europe'.[6]

In the first flush of independence, Belgian writers, too, sang the praises of the city which found itself, for the first time, the capital of a nation called Belgium. In the opinion of Henri Moke, a historian writing in 1844, it was a town that had always captivated foreigners and was now rapidly turning itself into a modern city. He highlighted recent improvements, extolling the elegant boulevards and the smart new *faubourgs* springing up beyond them.[7] In the view of Roel Jacobs, a Brussels historian of our own time, Charlotte and Emily Brontë were fortunate to have the experience of living in the capital of the country with the most liberal constitution and highest rate of industrialisation on the Continent, an excellent place in which to experience the bourgeois *art de vivre*.[8]

However, Brussels had long lost the glittering image it enjoyed in its seventeenth-century Golden Age, when the court at the Coudenberg Palace was presided over by the Archdukes Isabella and Albert, the popular governors of the Spanish Netherlands. The writer Louis Quiévreux, one of the Brontës' most ardent fans in Belgium as well as a connoisseur of Brussels and its history, relates how he first fell in love with his native city when looking at a painting representing it as it was in that prosperous era, which saw a flowering of art, architecture and learning. Writing in the 1940s, he referred to the Belgian capital as 'a *grand seigneur* that had been luxuriously arrayed in its days of glory and still retained a few jewels of value'.[9]

By the nineteenth century, after the centuries of often indifferent foreign rule under Spain, Austria and France that succeeded that of the Archdukes, much of the city's medieval sumptuousness, the 'rich old remains of Brabant splendour', in Frances Trollope's words,[10] had faded, preserved intact only in the Grand Place and Hôtel de Ville. The Coudenberg Palace had burned down in 1731. In its place, the city's Austrian governors had, in the late eighteenth century, built a new quarter around the park and royal palace in the Haute Ville, the highest part of the city. Although this new district was distinctly Parisian in flavour, Brussels was on a very much smaller scale than the French capital. All too often it was seen as the miniature capital of a miniature country, slightly ludicrous in its pretensions to be taken seriously. A 'villette', in fact. It was seen in terms of what it was *not* – as a city that was not Paris, but a mere counterfeit of Paris on a smaller scale. Such perceptions have not been held by foreign visitors alone. The Belgian historian Carlo Bronne, a biographer of Leopold I, describes Brussels as a city that became the capital of Belgium by chance, thanks to its central location (on the boundary between Dutch-speaking Flanders in the north and francophone Wallonia in the south). It was a city without a real port, without a river worthy of the name, without a bishop: the river Senne was so polluted that it was covered up in the 1860s for hygiene reasons, and the Church of St Michel and St Gudule where Charlotte Brontë went to confession did not officially become a cathedral (though often referred to as such) until 1962, when it became co-cathedral of the Archdiocese of Mechelen-Brussels.[11]

Bronne might have added that the Brussels of Leopold I was a city without a literature of any note. Belgian literature was then in its infancy, and in any case, the Low Countries have always excelled in the visual rather than literary arts. Bruges and Ghent and Antwerp have produced great painters rather than internationally renowned writers, and through the centuries Brussels has distinguished itself as a producer of commodities such as lace and tapestries rather than great works of literature. As for literary classics in which the city itself makes a really significant appearance, Jacques De Decker identifies only two, neither of which is by a home-grown writer. One is Goethe's play *Egmont*, set in the sixteenth-century Low Countries during the anti-Spanish unrest. The other, says De Decker, is Charlotte Brontë's *Villette*.[12]

He is by no means the only Belgian commentator to name *Villette* as the novel that gave Brussels a place in world literature. And yet a literary tourist seeking traces of Charlotte – and Emily – in the city may feel that little is done to advertise the Brontë connection. In 1979 the Brontë Society, a British literary society, placed a plaque commemorating the sisters' stay in Brussels, but the *Bruxellois* themselves have never erected a memorial or named a street after Charlotte Brontë.

It might be supposed that one explanation for this could be Charlotte Brontë's attitude to Belgium and the Belgians. *Villette* not only relegates Brussels to the status of a 'small town' but nicknames Belgium 'Labassecour', 'the farmyard', and both *Villette* and *The Professor* are full of disparaging remarks about the Belgians. It would be quite understandable if they were to feel some reluctance to honour an author who lost no opportunity to cast aspersions on the appearance, intellect and character of the people of her host country, reading 'intellectual inferiority' in the Flemish physiognomy and expressing the view that the Belgian climate was 'such as to induce degeneracy of the mind and body'.[13]

What the Belgians feel towards Charlotte will be discussed in subsequent pages of this book. But a glance at the attitudes of some of the other foreign writers who passed through the capital would suggest that she was not alone among celebrated visitors in making derogatory remarks about her host country. One of her literary heroes, Thackeray, visited around the time of her stay. Reporting on his impressions in *Little Travels and Roadside Sketches* (1845), Thackeray, a toweringly tall man with all the sense of superiority of the Englishman abroad, laughed at the 'Lilliput look' of the Belgian capital just as Charlotte, who was diminutive in stature, tended to look down her nose at 'Villette'.

If Charlotte suffered acutely from homesickness in Brussels, for many other literary visitors to the city in the nineteenth century it was, literally, a place of exile. Fleeing political persecution at home, French exiles or *proscrits* found refuge in the Belgian capital. Other visitors, seeking refuge from persecution of a different kind, went there to escape from their creditors. All too often, their response in return for the city's hospitality was to denigrate it as a dull backwater and complain of *ennui*.

One exile who did not spend long enough in Brussels to suffer from *ennui* but did experience annoyances there was another literary hero of Charlotte Brontë's. Lord Byron spent a few days in the city in April 1816 on his way to Italy, in flight from scandal about his failed marriage and affairs with various women, including his half-sister, as well as from creditors. This did not deter him from running up further debt by travelling in style, in a carriage built in imitation of that of his hero Napoleon and fitted out with every convenience; rather in the manner of a modern camper van, it contained both sleeping accommodation and dining equipment.

Although the sight of the Waterloo battlefield inspired Byron to write some stanzas of *Childe Harold*, his stay in Belgium was overshadowed by the breakdown of a second carriage for his luggage and servants. A new one ordered in Brussels also proved unsatisfactory. After a dispute with the carriage-maker Byron made an abrupt departure with much of the bill still unpaid. Despite this, Brussels guidebooks and history books treasure the memory of his lightning visit.

Most of the exiles who spent time in Brussels were French. While Thackeray's mockery of the Belgian capital was at least good-humoured, the same cannot be said of some of its French visitors. Of these, the worst offender by far was the poet Charles Baudelaire, who like Charlotte Brontë spent two years living in Brussels. The main reason why he ended up in the Belgian capital in 1864 was one that becomes predictably familiar to anyone reading a guide to literary visitors to the city, namely debt. Like Byron, Baudelaire was no stranger to scandal either; bourgeois disapproval of his verse collection *Les Fleurs du Mal* published some years earlier was such that he was prosecuted for offending public decency.

As he was soon to find out, his renown in Belgium was not nearly as great as he imagined. He went there with dreams of making money through a lecture tour and of publication by the publisher who had made Victor Hugo rich. Hugo spent part of his exile from Napoleon III's regime in Brussels and made a fortune when *Les Misérables* was published there in 1862.

Like Charlotte Brontë, Baudelaire had viewed Brussels as a promised land,[14] but his hopes soon faded. Hugo's publisher was uninterested in him and the lectures were poorly attended. Baudelaire was disgusted by what he saw as Belgian indifference to literature; the promoters of his lectures, for their part, were unimpressed by his performance as a speaker. The talks were Baudelaire's first experience of speaking in public. At the second of them he managed to scandalise the young ladies of Mme Goussaert's Pensionnat in Koekelberg, the school that had been attended in the 1840s by Charlotte's friends Mary and Martha Taylor. At a sign from their teacher, the demoiselles exited the room *en masse* when Baudelaire began his talk with a comparison:

fear of public speaking, he explained to the audience, was a kind of virginity. He had lost it when he gave the first of the talks, and no more regretted it than he did the loss of the other kind.

Almost penniless, Baudelaire spent his two years in Brussels in a badly-lit room in the Hôtel du Grand Miroir near St Gudule. (Sadly, like some of the legends in Brussels about Charlotte Brontë, there appears to be no foundation for the story in some guide books that the French poet kept a pet bat in a cage for company, feeding it on bread and milk.) Disappointed in all his plans for Brussels and in poor health, he vented his *ennui* and frustration by filling pages with notes for a savage attack on Belgium, which were published after his death under the title *Pauvre Belgique*. He denounced what he saw as the mediocrity of everything in the country. He wrote of the Belgians' 'menacing stupidity' and blind 'spirit of obedience and conformity'. 'If you go to Belgium you'll be less severe about your own country. You'll thank God He made you French and not Belgian . . . . Having long searched for the reason for the existence of the Belgians, I have come to imagine that they were perhaps souls reincarnated, in punishment for horrible vices in past lives, in hideous bodies that are their physical image . . . . A Belgian is a living Hell on earth. He is his own Hell.' Charlotte's own criticisms of things Belgian seem positively mild in comparison. Even the good things of Belgian life, such as the cuisine and the beer, brought no pleasure to this Parisian dandy. For Baudelaire's palate, Belgian food was too salty, while drinking *faro*, the Brussels lambic beer, was tantamount to drinking urine given that it was brewed in the valley of the Senne, a river used as a sewer.

A charitable interpretation is that he projected his growing disgust with humanity in general onto the Belgians in particular. In the words of the Belgian novelist Camille Lemonnier, 'Baudelaire was an exile from the world; in Belgium he was twice an exile.'[15] And the Belgians have largely forgiven him. His stay in the city is much commemorated and his embittered musings read without rancour; due respect is paid to his genius and allowances are made for his sufferings in Brussels – the disappointments he encountered and his wretched physical and mental state at the time. He had long been suffering from syphilis. As if in punishment for his assaults on Belgium, while there he had a stroke that brought on paralysis. He died a year later back in France, aged only 46.

Baudelaire was the most extreme of the French writers who criticised Belgium, but he was by no means alone. A century before him, Voltaire had complained of the *ennui* of life in Brussels and its dearth of intelligence, knowledge and wit.[16] In Charlotte Brontë's own period the impressions of the Romantic poet and essayist Gérard de Nerval, who visited in 1840, were published in his travel books *Lorely: Souvenirs d'Allemagne* and *Notes de Voyage*. Nerval left a fascinating and detailed description of the city that Charlotte knew. While his account was a balanced one, it does reflect his countrymen's general view of the Belgian capital as a poor copy of Paris. Take its river, for example. Paris had the Seine, with all its wealth of historical and literary associations. Brussels had the Senne. In Nerval's time this polluted and malodorous river had not yet been redirected underground and covered over for reasons of sanitation; it still made its sluggish way through the centre of the city, but it was a poor apology for a river, Nerval said, no more than a 'stream': 'What kind of capital is a city where you can't drown yourself?'[17]

Charlotte does not mention the Senne, and she was impressed by the elegance of the Haute Ville. Nerval was considerably less so. Not even the smart streets of the Upper Town could impress a visitor accustomed to Paris. Brussels was a mere 'satellite' of Paris and, moreover, by imitating it had lost much of its original Flemish flavour. It could offer no more than 'Parisian life in a narrow circle'.[18] For the Parisian *flâneur*, the opportunities for *flânerie*[19] offered by Brussels, with its poor paving, dim street lighting (except in the Haute Ville) and hilly topography, fell far short of those in the French capital.

The tradition of denigrating Brussels was continued by French literary visitors in the twentieth century. The iconoclastic writer Octave Mirbeau, one of the first tourists to arrive by car, recorded his feelings about the city in his 1907 travologue *La 628-E-8*, named after his car's licence plate. Mirbeau claimed that Brussels was so unexciting one could litererally die of boredom there. In Ixelles Cemetery, he visited the tomb of Georges Boulanger, a French general who fled to Brussels with his mistress Marguerite de Bonnemain when threatened with arrest for conspiracy in France. After Marguerite's death in 1891 he shot himself on her grave and was buried with her. The story had become one of the city's romantic legends. Yet Mirbeau's comment was that Boulanger must have been driven to suicide by the tedium of life in Brussels.

If some French visitors seem to have gone there only to feel suicidal, others became homicidal. It was in Brussels in the summer of 1873 that the stormy, on-off relationship between the poets Rimbaud and Verlaine came to a dramatic head. Verlaine had left his wife and infant son to run away with the 19-year-old Rimbaud for what proved to be a turbulent stay in London. After a row, Verlaine departed alone for Brussels, but was soon asking Rimbaud to join him there. Once Rimbaud complied, it was not long before the pair had fallen out again. When the younger man threatened to leave, Verlaine, in a drunken rage, bought a revolver, shot his companion in their hotel room and slightly wounded him. After the wound had been dressed Rimbaud once more announced his intention of catching the next train out of Brussels. As Verlaine and his mother, who had also joined him, accompanied Rimbaud to the station a fresh quarrel broke out, in the course of which Verlaine drew his revolver again. This time Rimbaud took the matter to the police. Although he later withdrew the charge of attempted murder, Verlaine was sentenced by a Brussels court to a fourteen-month prison sentence which he served mainly in Mons, an experience he recorded in *Mes Prisons*.

The unhappy stays in Brussels of *poètes maudits* are duly commemorated in its streets. A plaque marks the site of Baudelaire's hotel in rue de la Montagne and another has been placed on the site of the hotel in rue des Brasseurs where Verlaine shot Rimbaud.

Happily, not all literary visitors came to Brussels only to criticise it or at any rate be unhappy there. Victor Hugo had every reason to be grateful to the Belgian capital. Not only did he make a fortune from the publication of *Les Misérables*, but he was much fêted during his stays in the city. He praised it as a place where political exiles like himself could find freedom, including freedom from censorship – as Karl Marx had done before him when expelled from Paris for seditious articles. It was only in the wake of the 1848 revolution in France that the Belgian government, fearful for the country's security, found it necessary to ask Marx to leave.

Hugo's close association with the Belgian capital – he made frequent visits and had a house there – is a source of pride and satisfaction to the city. Yet almost equal importance is given to associations with literary guests who showed scant gratitude towards their host city. A guide book published in 1990, Marcel Van Nieuwenborgh's *Literaire wandelingen door Brussel*, is an account of foreign writers, including Charlotte Brontë, who have spent time in Brussels. At times it reads like a litany of insults levelled at the city by its literary visitors.

This appears to afford Van Nieuwenborgh more entertainment than offence. Such failure to take umbrage is typically Belgian, but in this case it might also be explained by an observation made by Octave Mirbeau, who noted that even the Belgians themselves often seem to have scant love for their capital city. Many acknowledge that they have never taken Brussels to their hearts. Apart from its less lovable features (it is remembered by the American writer John Dos Passos, who spent part of his childhood there in the 1890s, as a city of hard grey paving stones and grey skies),[20] there are political and linguistic reasons for this indifference. The Dutch-speaking population of the country – the Flemish – do not embrace it as their capital. Before Belgium became a nation state in 1830, Brussels had been largely Dutch-speaking, but after Independence it became the francophone centre of government, with French the language of administration. The Flemish are more likely to identify emotionally with Antwerp or Ghent.

Thus, Brussels has suffered from being a somewhat unloved capital. It has been called 'Bruxelles la mal-aimée',[21] a city that even the *Bruxellois* themselves frequently fail to appreciate. Its dearth of really significant literary associations is one result of this lack of affection. London has Dickens and a host of other chroniclers. It teems in our imagination with fictional Londoners: Oliver Twist, Sherlock Holmes, Jeeves and Wooster. Paris is associated with Balzac, Hugo and scores of other writers. But Brussels has no Dickens, no Balzac. While Dutch-speaking Belgians turn for inspiration to Flemish towns, francophones have often taken France as a reference point. In some cases, with French readers in mind, they have set their works in France rather than Belgium. Simenon's novels, to take an example, almost never refer to Brussels. Admittedly he himself was from Liège, but one reason for ignoring the Belgian capital in his fiction was that it was Paris and not Brussels that inspired him as a setting.[22]

The Brussels of Charlotte Brontë's day was rarely chosen as a setting by the Belgian novelists of her own time, when the vogue was for historical novels, while of the foreign authors who lived in the city it was Charlotte who drew the greatest literary inspiration from her time there. Two of her four novels are closely based on her experiences in the city, a fact not always reflected in the space dedicated to her in its guide books. The escapades, trials and tribulations of her male contemporaries are often found more colourful than the vicissitudes of a *sous-maîtresse* (assistant teacher) at the Pensionnat Heger.

Charlotte is the only female writer named among the celebrated nineteenth-century literary visitors in the Brussels guide books. Unlike her male counterparts, most of whom were already published writers when they arrived in Brussels, at the time of her stay she was a complete unknown.

While they spent much time out and about in the city in cafés, restaurants and taverns, drinking, talking, womanising, getting into debt, she spent most of hers closeted within the walls of a girls' boarding school. Yet it is to her work and not theirs that Belgians turn to find a picture of their capital in the nineteenth century.

Charlotte Brontë called it 'Villette', a less than respectful name for a capital city. But it is to 'Villette' that her novel owes its title, surely an indication of the city's importance in the book.

1   Acke and Bekers, *Écrire Bruxelles/Brussel Schrijven*, pp. 34, 245.
2   Foreword by Jacques De Decker, of the Belgian Academy of French Language and Literature, to De Vries, *Brussels: A cultural and literary history*.
3   Letter to Ellen Nussey, May 1842. Smith, *The Letters of Charlotte Brontë*, Volume I, p. 285.
4   Letter to Ellen Nussey, June 1843. *Ibid.*, p. 325.
5   Trollope, *Belgium and Western Germany in 1833*, p. 50.
6   Addison, *Belgium as she is*, p. 102.
7   Baron, *La Belgique Monumentale, Historique et Pittoresque*, pp. 147–211.
8   Interview in *Brussel Deze Week*, 14 April 2008.
9   Preface to Quiévreux, *Bruxelles, guide de la capitale et de ses environs*.
10 Trollope, *Belgium and Western Germany in 1833*, p. 71.
11 Bronne, *Léopold Ier et son temps*, p. 159.
12 De Vries, *Brussels: A cultural and literary history*, pp. ix–x.
13 *The Professor*, Chapters 8 and 12.
14 Charlotte called Brussels her 'Promised Land' in a letter to Ellen Nussey, 9 December 1841. Smith, *The Letters of Charlotte Brontë*, Volume I, p. 274.
15 Preface to Morice, *L'Esprit Belge*.
16 In a poem written in 1740.
17 Nerval, *Œuvres*, p. 811.
18 *Ibid.*, p. 813.
19 The term *flâneur* (stroller or lounger, urban observer curious about everything he sees) became particularly fashionable in Paris in the nineteenth century. Baudelaire, who defined the *flâneur* as a 'passionate spectator', extolled *flânerie* as a way of life.
20 Quoted in Van Nieuwenborgh, *Literaire wandelingen door Brussel*, p. 118.
21 Notably by the poet Armand Bernier in his 1959 verse collection of that name.
22 According to Jacques De Decker in his Foreword to De Vries, *Flanders, a cultural history*, p. x.

CHAPTER TWO

'Good gracious, Madame, où avez-vous appris la speak French?' The Early History of *Jane Eyre* and *Villette* in Brussels

T HE work that first introduced Charlotte Brontë to Belgian readers, however, and for which she has always been best known in Belgium as in every other country, was not Villette but Jane Eyre.

Charlotte died on 31 March 1855. On 21 April the daily newspaper *L'Etoile Belge* devoted half its front page to an obituary of 'Currer Bell', who is also identified by her real name. It consists largely of passages translated from an obituary by Harriet Martineau published on 6 April in *Daily News*. It makes no mention of Charlotte's stay in Brussels even though Martineau's article does allude to it; the obituarist is interested not in Charlotte's Continental sojourn but in the tragedies of her life and the isolation and remoteness of her Haworth existence. There is, however, a brief reference to *Villette*, in a passage lifted from Martineau. At the time of Charlotte's death, French and Belgian readers had not yet had an opportunity to read more than a first instalment of the novel in French translation.

There was something inexpressibly affecting in the aspect of the frail little creature who had done such wonderful things, and who was able to bear up, with so bright an eye and so composed a countenance, under such a weight of sorrow, and such a prospect of solitude … In so utter a seclusion as she lived in – in those dreary wilds, … in that retreat where her studious father rarely broke the silence – and there was no one else to do it; in that forlorn house, planted on the very clay of the churchyard, where the graves of her sisters were before her window; in such a living sepulchre her mind could not but prey upon itself; and how it did suffer, we see in the more painful portions of her last novel – *Villette*.[1]

Most of the obituary refers to what its author calls the 'charming and pensive' novel *Jane Eyre*, 'a masterpiece that has been in everyone's hands.' Evidence of its popularity came at the end of that year of Charlotte's death, when there was eager anticipation in Brussels at the prospect of a stage version of the novel.

Announcing this stage adaptation, the quarterly *Revue Trimestrielle* observed that there was no need to explain the subject matter of the work, since it was 'known to most of our readers'. The journal described *Jane Eyre* as a thrilling novel, full of interest, that 'had become popular even on the Continent'.[2] The Belgian bourgeoisie of the period were not known for their interest in literature, preferring music, the theatre and art, but some novel-reading did go on. Some of it went on amid the heavy draperies of the ladies' apartments, despite the disapproval of their confessors, portrayed in *Villette's* Père Silas as omnipresent Jesuitical figures controlling every aspect of the lives of those they directed. Mme Beck's young ladies are not encouraged to read novels, and certain aspects of Charlotte's best-seller would doubtless have been frowned on by the real-life Père Silases of Brussels.

Published in England in 1847, 'Currer Bell's *Jane Eyre* had been serialised in French in 1849 in the *Revue de Paris* and *L'Indépendance Belge* as *Jane Eyre: memoires d'une gouvernante*. That translation, or rather free adaptation, by Emile Dauran-Forgues, a prolific French journalist, critic and translator who signed himself 'Old Nick', was published in book form the same year. By the time of the stage adaptation, some Belgian readers might have read a much more faithful translation by the Frenchwoman Noëmi Lesbazeilles Souvestre, published in 1854.

'Adaptations' of foreign works took huge liberties with the text, and those reading 'Old Nick's translation of 1849 were given a heavily abridged version of the novel. Much of Jane's early life is omitted, but the novel's appeal could not be lost in translation. It would have kept the pages turning feverishly in stuffy Brussels drawing rooms and given its crinoline-clad readers many an agreeable *frisson*, a suggestive word that recurs at regular intervals in the French text.

Unlike 'Old Nick', Noëmi Lesbazeilles Souvestre provided a full and faithful rendering of the novel. It was her only published work. At the time she produced it she was a very young woman, only twenty, not much older than *Jane Eyre* when she takes up her post as governess. Like Charlotte she was one of three sisters and the daughter of an intellectual father, a writer with enlightened ideas on women's education. He deplored the lot of women without fortune in the society of his time, a subject close to Charlotte's heart, and wished his daughters to be prepared for a career and independence. One of Noëmi's sisters, Marie, was a women's educator and a feminist. Lesbazeilles Souvestre's translation, which she claimed in her introduction had been authorised by Charlotte, is still used in some editions of the novel available today.

By the time of the stage adaptation of *Jane Eyre* in November–December 1855, some of the playgoers who went to see it might have been aware of Charlotte's later novel *Villette*, first published in January 1853. Her earlier and sketchier tale set in Brussels, *The Professor*, was not published until after her death, in 1857, and in French translation in 1858. *Shirley*, published in 1849, had come out in French translation in 1850.

Villette, with its Brussels setting, might have been expected to arouse particular interest in Belgium. The first French translation did not appear until 1855, but before it did, the novel was brought to the attention of Belgian readers in the second quarter of 1854, when the *Revue Trimestrielle* published a review of '*Villette* by Currer Bell, author of *Jane Eyre*'.[3]

The author begins by explaining why his review is appearing some time after the novel's publication. 'If we are a little late in talking about this book, let no-one accuse us of negligence. A more commendable motive held back our pen. Agitated by unjust attacks, and fearing to apply the law of "an eye for an eye" too rigorously, we preferred to wait until the little wounds to our self-esteem had healed. Now, time has so completely calmed our anger that all our impartiality is restored.' The reviewer is charmed by the first part of the book set in England, but once Lucy crosses the Channel his enthusiasm evaporates rapidly. 'In which country does she disembark? That is what she does not want to tell us in so many words. The port of arrival is called Boue-Marine [Sea Mud], the country, Labassecour, the capital, Villette. Villette has an upper town and a lower town, a park, boulevards, a béguinage[4]. The main school is called an Athénée. French is spoken in Villette. Can you guess? Don't search too far; it's not difficult.'

The reviewer finds the novel full of 'mockery, invectives and calumnies'. Belgian schoolgirls are portrayed as 'insolent, cold, frivolous, hypocritical, greedy, lazy and lying'. Even more objectionable is Charlotte's sneering reference to the Belgian Revolution of 1830, only 12 years before her arrival. The monument to the 466 fallen insurgents in the Place des Martyrs had been erected only four years earlier,[5] and Heger himself is thought to have been among the patriots who fought in the revolt. But the English miss seems to

▲ The Place des Martyrs and the monument to the fallen Belgian insurgents in the 1830 Revolution.

◄ Fighting in the *Passage de la Bibliothèque* leading down to rue Isabelle during the 1830 Belgian Revolution.

question whether it was worthy of the name of revolution and even whether it had actually taken place: 'In past days there had been, said history, an awful crisis in the fate of Labassecour, involving I know not what peril to the rights and liberties of her gallant citizens. Rumours of wars there had been … a kind of struggling in the streets – a bustle – a running to and fro, some rearing of barricades, some burgher-rioting, … much interchange of brickbats, and even a little of shot. Tradition held that patriots had fallen: in the old Basse Ville was shown an enclosure, solemnly built in and set apart, holding, it was said, the sacred bones of martyrs.'[6]

It is worth wondering whether the story that Constantin Heger fought at the barricades is actually true. Charlotte would surely have heard of it and would have been likely to be less disrespectful in her allusions to the uprising – though, naturally, her fictional Labassecour cannot be assumed to be Belgium in every particular.

Everything in Labassecour, says the reviewer, is a target for Lucy's mockery, 'from the courageous efforts of its citizens to secure their independence to the way in which floors are cleaned, "with damp coffee-grounds", as Lucy tells us solemnly, "used by Labassecourien housemaids instead of tea-leaves" as in England' – just as, the reviewer points out, 'a travel book about China would give us a recipe for bird's nest soup'.[7]

While Belgian irritation at Charlotte's belittling of the revolution is understandable, it comes as something of a surprise that much of the reviewer's indignation is reserved not for Currer Bell's views on Belgium but for her use, or rather misuse, of the French language. 'Everyone speaks French in this English novel,' he laments, singling out some of the phrases put into the mouth of Ginevra Fanshawe as examples of how French was *not* spoken, whether by young ladies or anyone else. Like more than one reviewer on the British side of the Channel, he found instances of 'coarseness' in Charlotte's writing. Some of the French expressions were *de mauvais ton* – vulgar, unfitted for polite society; others were simply *franglais*, expressions translated literally from English. He found it unacceptable that the characters say in bad French what could be said in good English. What would Currer Bell have thought, he asks, if he had couched his comments on her novel not in his own language, French, but in *franglais*, as in 'Good gracious, Madame, où avez-vous appris la speak French?'

The reviewer was perhaps unduly severe. After her two years of diligent study, Charlotte in fact left Belgium with a good command of French. Her French biographer Ernest Dimnet went as far as to consider the 'firm and supple' French of her letters to Heger superior to Heger's own style.[8] In one of those letters, written two years after leaving Brussels, Charlotte told her 'master' about her love of his language – and the reason for that love. 'I read all the French books I can get, and learn daily a portion by heart – but I have never heard French spoken but once since I left Brussels – and then it sounded like music in my ears – every word was most precious to me because it reminded me of you – I love French for your sake with all my heart and soul.'[9] She adored using it and, as pointed out by her irritated reviewer, lost no opportunity of doing so. In *The Professor*, Crimsworth regrets not being able to reproduce entire conversational exchanges in French; the flow of Zoraïde Reuter's conversation, in particular, 'loses sadly by being translated into English'.[10]

Notwithstanding the reviewer's irritation, by the end of the piece he had recovered sufficiently from the 'wounds to his self-esteem' dealt by Lucy Snowe to conclude with praise of Currer Bell's 'energetic talent, vigorous and perfect style and rich imagery' and acknowledge her powers of feeling and discernment.

He describes *Villette*, however, somewhat dismissively, as a 'little novel of manners'. He felt that the subject of a girls' boarding school was not worthy of Charlotte's talent (particularly as he thought satire was not her forte), which deserved to be deployed in a 'wider and nobler' field. But the fact that *Villette* was reviewed in the *Revue Trimestrielle* at all was a compliment that must be attributed to the popularity in Belgium of the much better-known *Jane Eyre*. The journal, then in its first year of publication, fast became a highly respected one covering literature, the arts, politics and science.[11] That it had a high regard for Charlotte Brontë's work is shown by the interest it took the following year in the stage adaptation of *Jane Eyre*. It is worth noting that other major British novelists, such as Dickens and George Eliot, do not make it into its pages.

Despite this, the *Revue Trimestrielle*, in common with other Belgian journals, did take an interest in British affairs, publishing articles extolling the virtues of British society. Anglophilia was in the air in Belgium at the time, with many admiring looks cast in the direction of its neighbour across the North Sea. There had been numerous reports on the Great Exhibition at the Crystal Palace in 1851. Britain was seen as a country of liberty and progress, its values not infrequently compared favourably with Belgium's other main country of reference, the France of King Louis-Philippe and (from 1852) Napoleon III. In fact the many Anglophiles in Belgium at that time were pretty much in agreement with Charlotte's estimation of the virtues of her country, if not with her criticisms of their own.

The following year, 1855, Belgian readers had the opportunity to read *Villette* in French when it was serialised in the monthly *Revue Britannique*, published both in Paris and Brussels. The first instalment appeared in March, shortly before Charlotte's death. The novel soon came out in book form in both France and Belgium; curiously, one of the Belgian editions was printed in rue Villa Hermosa, a street close to the Pensionnat.

More curiously still, this free French translation or rather adaptation of *Villette*, published under the title *La Maîtresse d'anglais ou le Pensionnat de Bruxelles*, not only gave the author's real name as well as her *nom de plume* on the title page ('Curer Bell/Charlotte Bronti') but, as the title indicates, did away with her half-hearted attempts at disguising the novel's Brussels setting. In this translation, Villette is Brussels, and Labassecour and the Labassecouriens have become Belgium and the Belgians. In *La Maîtresse* Mme Beck, described in *Villette* as a typical Labassecourienne, is 'a *Bruxelloise* from top to toe'.

◀ *La Maîtresse d'anglais ou le Pensionnat de Bruxelles.*

The French translator makes a guess, not always successfully, at the Brussels places that Charlotte was likely to have had in mind. In *Villette* Charlotte often borrowed actual Brussels place names but used the name of one place to refer to another, or combined elements of more than one of them. Her church of St Jean Baptiste, whose bells Lucy can hear from the Pensionnat garden, appears to be inspired, not by the church of that name in the Béguinage down in the old town, but in part by St Gudule and in part by St Jacques sur Coudenberg in Place Royale; the Pensionnat was roughly equidistant between the two. In *Villette*, as Lucy and M. Paul stroll back to the Pensionnat after declaring their love for each other, on the eve of his voyage to the West Indies, 'Jean-Baptiste's clock tolled nine'; in *La Maîtresse d'anglais*, however, when they part for the last time at the Pensionnat door, the hour is tolled by the bells of St Gudule, never named in *Villette*. The Hôtel Crécy in *Villette* where Paulina de Bassompierre lives is believed to have been inspired by the Hôtel Cluysenaar in rue Royale where the Brontës' friends the Wheelwrights had an apartment, but in *La Maîtresse* it has become the better-known Hôtel Bellevue in Place Royale, today the BELvue museum. Charlotte's hero Wellington stayed there at the time of Waterloo.

Sometimes the use of real names in place of Charlotte's fictional ones is to be regretted. It is rather disappointing to find that Mme Beck's physician, Dr Pillule ('Pill'), who in *Villette* is called away to attend to a patient in the old university town of Bouquin-Moisi ('musty book'), has become a less picturesque Dr Mathys who has to make a trip to Leuven. For Louis Quiévreux, 'There is something piquant and amusing about the fictional names used by Charlotte Brontë.'[12]

Although rue Isabelle, where the Pensionnat Heger stood, is not named as such, with the translator merely modifying Charlotte's fictional 'Rue Fossette' to 'Rue des Fossettes', the indications of the location of Mme Beck's Pensionnat – 'a five-minute walk from the park and ten minutes to the royal palace'; the palace is not mentioned in *Villette* – were precise enough to make Mme Beck's Pensionnat easily identifiable as Mme Heger's for readers familiar with it. This exposure of the Pensionnat caused Mme Heger much distress.

Belgians reading the French translation, however, were spared some of Charlotte's worst assaults on them. The anonymous translator not only cuts and embellishes at will, but tones down or completely re-writes some of Charlotte's most stinging comments.

Thus, Ginevra's remark that 'the natives [of Labassecour] are intensely stupid and vulgar' becomes 'The Belgians are not as witty as the French and don't waltz as well as the Germans', and the sneering tone has been expunged from the passage on the 1830 uprising. Nevertheless, enough of Charlotte's comments about Belgium remain to leave her readers there in no doubt as to her sentiments.

Whereas 'Old Nick's similarly free translation of *Jane Eyre* in 1849 was succeeded a few years later by a much more faithful one, *La Maîtresse d'anglais* was the only French translation of *Villette* available until 1932 (of course, some in Belgium would have read the novel in English). This suggests that at that period the general verdict on the novel of readers in France and Belgium was that expressed in the *Revue Trimestrielle*: it was a slight work, a mere novel of manners, and unworthy of the author of *Jane Eyre*. It would not have been as widely read as the latter novel, but one place where it *was* read was at the Pensionnat Heger. The copy of *La Maîtresse* owned by Constantin and Zoë Heger is still in the possession of one of their descendants today, with pencilled comments in the margins, probably by one of the Hegers' children; Charlotte's allusions to Mme Beck's character are annotated with an occasional exclamation mark or interjection such as 'indigne!' ('shameful'). It is not difficult to imagine Mme Heger's own reaction on reading the book. Charlotte Brontë and her time at the Pensionnat became a taboo subject. The British writer Frederika Macdonald, who recorded her time as a pupil at the Pensionnat in 1859–61 in *The Secret of Charlotte Brontë*, said that she never heard Charlotte's name mentioned there and did not learn of the Brontës' stay until years later.

The name of the translator responsible for *La Maîtresse d'anglais* is not known. A hundred years after its publication, a singular theory about the identity of this anonymous translator was put forward by Robert Goffin, a prolific writer and member of the Belgian Royal Academy of French Language and Literature. His idea was mooted in an article about the exhibition on Charlotte Brontë at the Musée Charlier in 1953–55.[13] Goffin's imagination was fired by exhibits such as photos of Charlotte's torn-up letters to Heger, and a sprig of heather, supposedly from the Haworth moors, that had been laid on his grave by an unknown hand.

Goffin speculated that Charlotte's affection for Heger had been reciprocated. He was particularly excited by a copy of *La Maîtresse d'anglais*, having previously been unaware of the existence of this early French translation. Who was the translator? Goffin's reply to this hitherto unanswered question was, bizarrely, that it could only have been Heger himself! Who else in Brussels, argued Goffin, knew that Currer Bell was Charlotte Brontë?

Who else could have known the real identity of the places referred to in *Villette*, and replaced the fictional names with the real names? Charlotte must have remained secretly in touch with 'the man who was the reason for her life' and sent him copies of her works, including *Villette*, in which Heger must have found 'the burning words of a hopeless love'.

Goffin was forced to admit that his theory posed some problems. If Heger was the translator, how to explain that he was responsible for the publication in French of a book that caused his wife so much grief? Goffin was unable to answer this question but nevertheless offered his hypothesis for what it was worth.

His suggestion was based on an imperfect knowledge of facts such as that by 1855 Currer Bell's real identity was common knowledge in literary circles. His theory is surely one of the wildest to have come out of Belgium, a country not normally associated, as Charlotte pointed out in *The Professor*, with the romantic and the poetic.[14] The Brontës, though, have always been the subject of mystery, speculation and romantic fantasies wherever they are known. It is hardly surprising that Belgium should be no exception.

'You have to shake them hard to get a tear or applause out of them'

To return to the stage adaptation of *Jane Eyre*.

During her time in Brussels Charlotte, from within the walls of the Pensionnat Heger, could hear the sound of horses' hooves and the wheels of carriages conveying the real-life Bassompierres and Brettons of the city to the plays and concerts of which she herself had only occasional tastes. It was 1842–3 and she was an obscure parson's daughter unknown in the capital outside a tiny circle of friends and acquaintances. Twelve years later, the carriages rumbling over the Brussels paving stones were bearing the bourgeoisie of 'Labassecour' to see a performance of her own work, already known to the city's literati. Dead eight months earlier, Charlotte did not live to hear of this Brussels stage adaptation of her best-seller.

The play premiered in the Théâtre Vaudeville, rue de l'Evêque, before moving to a newer venue. The second theatre to which the carriages conveyed the Brussels burghers was an elegant new one in the Galeries St Hubert. Charlotte Brontë just missed seeing the Galeries, a splendid marble and gilded glass-vaulted shopping arcade that opened only four years after her departure, in 1847. It was the city's pride and joy at the time and is still one of its major attractions today, one of the few places in Brussels where

◀ The Galeries St-Hubert.

time seems to have stood still. The first of its kind on the Continent, unrivalled even in Paris, it was built by the fashionable architect Jean-Pierre Cluysenaar, some of whose early creations Charlotte saw during her time in Brussels. She attended a concert in his opulent Salle de la Grande Harmonie, and her friends the Wheelwrights lived in an apartment building designed by him.

With her naïve love of luxury and brilliant interiors, Charlotte would surely have relished the glittering displays of the shops in the Galeries St Hubert. It was the shopping mall of its time, offering smart cafés and the wares of jewellers, watchmakers, glovers, wig-makers, printers and engravers. On rainy afternoons she could have wandered through this emporium, known as 'the umbrella of Brussels' because of its ribbed roof and offering an opportunity for *flânerie* in a wet climate, instead of taking her *ennui* and homesickness to the streets of the old city centre (the lower town or 'Basse Ville'). In that case, the Galeries might have figured in *Villette*. But Charlotte was in Brussels just before the start of the developments from the mid-century onwards that transformed it into a modern city. The arcade, close to Grand Place, was the first incursion of this new city into the old Basse Ville. It was to be followed rapidly by other transformations of central Brussels such as the construction of new boulevards on the site of the Senne when the river was covered up in the 1860s. By the time *Jane Eyre* was staged, the city was fast expanding, too, with the building of new quarters beyond the boulevards such as the Quartier Leopold, which today houses many of the European Union institutions. By 1855 it had 3,000 affluent residents and a railway station.

In Charlotte's time, the site for the Galeries was already being cleared in an area of narrow streets and alleys; the opposition of the locals who lost their homes and businesses to the scheme was so bitter that a barber cut his throat with his best razor in protest at the impending demolition of his shop. A few years after it opened, the Galeries, described by a Belgian historian as 'a charming vanity fair, a meeting point for old gentlemen, journalists and actresses',[15] also became a rendezvous for French exiles. In 1852 Victor Hugo's mistress, the actress Juliette Drouet, lodged there, around the corner from Hugo in Grand Place.

As they settled into their seats, the theatre-goers attending the stage version of *Jane Eyre* were looking forward in pleasurable anticipation to *frissons* galore in the warmth of the Théâtre Royal des Galeries Saint-Hubert. The play had been announced as a fresh and exciting work, particularly its *dénouement*, said to depart considerably from the novel's. Mlle Magnan, a popular new actress, was taking the title role. Nothing like *Jane Eyre* had ever been staged in Belgium, the journals said, and the star role was a part like no other that Mlle Magnan had played.

There had already been a London stage adaptation of *Jane Eyre* by a certain John Courtney, which was performed at the Victoria Theatre in 1848 within a few months of the novel's publication. Charlotte, who did not see the play, was right in supposing it to be an exaggerated and vulgarised version 'to please the populace'.[16] The action was absurdly compressed and much of the time was taken up with a comic subplot involving servants. The French-language adaptation staged in Brussels was in fact based on a German one called *Die Waise aus Lowood* (The Orphan of Lowood), which had premiered in Vienna in 1853. The author was Charlotte Birch-Pfeiffer, an actress and prolific adaptor for the stage of novels by authors including Dickens, Hugo and Dumas. Birch-Pfeiffer's adaptation of Charlotte's novel was her greatest stage success, and continued to play throughout the century.[17]

The Belgian journals referred to the difficulties of dramatising the novel, which unlike those of Dumas, for example, did not lend itself readily to the stage. It would be interesting, they said, to see how well the Belgian co-writers Pierre Royer[18] and Victor Lefèvre, the latter a new young playwright, had tackled the task, since there were differences between their version and *Die Waise aus Lowood*. Everything, said the previews – the novel's popularity, the choice of artistes, the *mise en scène* – promised a brilliant evening's entertainment. Highlighting the fact that the play's authors were Belgian, the journals appealed to audiences to abandon their habitual preference for Parisian productions and generally lukewarm reception of home-grown ones.

Apart from a prologue showing the child Jane's unhappiness at her Aunt Reed's, all the action of the play is set at Thornfield Hall. In between appearances by Grace Poole and the odd blood-curdling burst of laughter backstage, Jane makes the acquaintance of her master, who in this adaptation has been ennobled and become 'Lord' Rochester (in the German one he is splendidly re-christened 'Lord Rowland Rochester').

A change in both the German and Belgian adaptations startling for those familiar with the novel is the arrival at Thornfield, not of Blanche Ingram and her entourage, but of Jane's old enemy Aunt Reed and her daughter Georgina, whom Rochester is pretending to woo. Another innovation is that 'Lord' Rochester has ordered a pink dress for Jane to wear in the company of these grand guests which she refuses to put on, preferring to adhere to her usual sober look. This is evidently inspired by the scene in the novel where she feels humiliated when he takes her shopping for brightly-coloured dress materials. But curiously it is in *Villette*, not *Jane Eyre*, that specific reference is made to a pink dress, one worn by Lucy Snowe, which M. Paul disapproves of as a sign of vanity. It is just possible that Birch-Pfeiffer deliberately incorporated this element from the later novel; *Villette* was published in January 1853, the year that *Die Waise aus Lowood* premiered in Germany.

Mrs Reed has been ruined by her son and sees Georgina's marriage to Rochester as the only alternative to destitution. Aware of Rochester's love for Jane, she asks Jane to give him up, a request which Jane grants since she believes that in any case Rochester intends to marry Georgina.

From this point on, the plot developments of the German and Belgian plays part company. In Birch-Pfeiffer's play, when Rochester reveals his secret to Jane, the nature of this secret comes as a surprise not just to her but to those familiar with Charlotte's novel. It turns out that the madwoman is not his wife but his sister-in-law! Having originally been betrothed to Rochester, she deserted him to marry his richer elder brother but then eloped with a Polish officer, going mad when Rochester's brother killed her lover and took her daughter Adèle from her. The brother died repentant for his deed and entrusted his mad wife to Rochester. The revelation of Rochester's secret therefore reveals him as saint rather than sinner, rather like M. Paul who, Lucy discovers, is supporting his dead fiancée's relatives. Jane's belief in Rochester is such that she never believed the rumours that the maniac was his wife. She is, however, determined to leave and let him marry Georgina. A scene ensues based on the proposal scene in the novel. Rochester having assured Jane he cares nothing for Georgina, the play ends abruptly with her throwing herself into his arms crying (to cite the English translation of the play) 'Oh, Rowland, my lord, my love, I am thine' as the curtain falls.

In the Lefèvre/Royer version, as Jane is preparing to leave Thornfield for her Aunt Reed's sake, the Reeds are informed of the existence of Rochester's wife by a friend and fellow guest who turns out to be the brother of Rochester's lawyer. Rochester is forced to own up and the Reeds and Jane leave Thornfield.

A final act follows that was written specially for the Belgian adaptation. The dénouement is closer to the novel's than Birch-Pfeiffer's, and turned out to be as action-packed and fast-moving as promised by the previews; it sent the Brussels playgoers home excited and happy. A year has passed since Jane's departure. Between claps of thunder, Rochester, alone in the drawing room as a storm gathers outside, announces his intention of taking his own life, while Mrs Fairfax tries to dissuade him with hints that Jane may return. It is not Jane, however, who enters at this point but a thoroughly crushed and repentant Mrs Reed. Her son having ruined the family and then killed himself, she wishes to make amends to Jane for past cruelty by giving her the news that her uncle has died leaving her his fortune. As Rochester explains that Jane is no longer at Thornfield, the manic laugh of Lady Rochester, who has broken free of her chains, is heard offstage and he goes to investigate. Mrs Fairfax reveals to the Reeds that she has been in contact with Jane, who is alive and well and staying with the 'St John family'.

Re-enter Rochester. After an unsuccessful tussle with the madwoman, he is resolved to put an end to his misery, but a fresh clap of thunder makes him drop the pistol he has just put to his head. Enter Jane, who has heard of his anguish and come to comfort him – though only as a friend, since, she tells him, she is now 'Mrs St John'. In his despair at this news Rochester seems about to strike her, but instead falls to his knees and sobs. A servant reports that Bertha, agitated by the storm, has climbed onto the roof with a flaming torch. As Rochester rushes off again after her, Mrs Reed in her turn falls to her knees and ask Jane's forgiveness, which is readily granted. As the tumult outside grows ever louder, Jane, at the window, relays a breathless report of events on the battlements. When Bertha hurls herself from the roof, Jane faints in the belief that Rochester, too, has fallen to his death. The master of the house, however, enters unhurt with the news of his lady's death. He is now free to marry but since Jane, by her own account, is not, he declares his resolution of going abroad to die of grief. At this juncture Mrs Fairfax reveals that Jane was only pretending to be married in order to guard against temptation. As Jane and Rochester are united, everyone sinks to their knees again, at Jane's instigation, to pray for the soul of the dead Lady Rochester.

Despite the plot changes, the play preserves at least some of the flavour of the original in the characters of Jane and Rochester and their exchanges. The reviews were enthusiastic. Eugène Van Bemmel, the editor of the *Revue Trimestrielle*, which had reviewed *Villette* the previous year, wrote that it was a long time since he had witnessed the public so enthralled by a drama. 'It is many years since the public have taken so much interest in any play and passed so easily from anxiety to tears or been so passionate for a persecuted heroine.'[19]

This description of a Brussels audience moved to tears by Charlotte Brontë's *Jane Eyre* is at odds with her own account, in *Villette*, of the audience at a concert attended by the King. She writes that the concert-goers, particularly the female part of them, looked as if nothing would stir them; typical, in her view, of Labassecourien bourgeois, their faces showed nothing but an 'expressionless calm'.[20] Her impression was corroborated by a Belgian observer who claimed that Brussels theatre-goers prided themselves on not displaying emotion: 'You have to shake them hard to get a tear or applause out of them'.[21] If Charlotte had lived only a few months longer she might have heard of the emotion provoked in an audience of stolid 'Labassecourien' burghers by the dramatisation of her own work on the Brussels stage.

How many of those attending knew that the author of *Jane Eyre* had lived in Brussels only ten years earlier? Probably not many outside the Hegers' circle, but that circle was an ever-widening one and there must have been pupils and ex-pupils of the Pensionnat at the performances. Might Constantin Heger, who was a theatre-lover, have attended? By this time the Hegers are likely to have read the novel. We know that Heger was gratified by his portrayal as M. Paul; whether or not he would also have recognised some of his own traits of personality and physique in the character of the rakish Rochester, and what he would have made of this, must remain an intriguing but unanswered question.

Although *Jane Eyre* remains the most popular of Charlotte's novels in Belgium to this date, *Villette* and *The Professor* have always been read with interest there for their Brussels setting, as will be seen in the following chapters.

1   Martineau's obituary is reprinted in Miriam Allott, *The Brontës: The Critical Heritage* (London: Routledge & Kegan Paul Ltd, 1974), pp. 301–5.
2   *Revue Trimestrielle*, 1856, Vol. 9, pp. 368–9.
3   *Ibid.*, 1854, Vol. II, pp. 279–83.
4   Lay religious community for women.
5   In 1838.
6   *Villette*, Chapter 38.
7   *Ibid.*, Chapter 22.
8   Dimnet, *The Brontë Sisters*, p. 106.
9   Smith, *The Letters of Charlotte Brontë*, Volume I, p. 435.
10 *The Professor*, Chapter 18.
11 Founded by the distinguished university teacher and man of letters Eugène Van Bemmel, it ran from 1854 to 1868.
12 *Le Soir*, 14 July 1957.
13 Goffin, Robert, 'Le Grand Amour de Charlotte Brontë', *Le Figaro Littéraire*, 16 May 1953.
14 'Belgium! name unromantic and unpoetic ...' *The Professor*, Chapter 7.
15 Bronne, *Léopold Ier et son temps*, p. 220.
16 Letter to W.S. Williams dated 5 February 1848 in Smith, *The Letters of Charlotte Brontë*, Volume II, pp. 25–7.
17 Both John Courtney's play and an English translation of Birch-Pfeiffer's can be read in Patsy Stoneman, *Jane Eyre on Stage, 1848–1898* (Aldershot: Ashgate Publishing, 2007).
18 I am indebted for this detail to Brian Bracken, who has identified one of the co-playwrights as Pierre Royer.
19 *Revue Trimestrielle*, 1856, Vol. 9, pp. 368–9.
20 *Villette*, Chapter 20.
21 Hymans, *Bruxelles à travers les âges*, Volume III, p. 231.

CHAPTER THREE

'Miss Baudelaire': Charlotte and the 'Labassecouriens'

'Singularly cold, selfish, animal and inferior'

CATEGORISED in 1854 by its first Belgian reviewer as a *petit roman de moeurs*, a 'little novel of manners',[1] *Villette* has been described by readers in Belgium as a *tableau de moeurs belges*: a picture of Belgian manners. This is not, of course, how it is generally read outside Belgium. The country is not even named as such; without explanatory notes or knowledge of Charlotte Brontë's life it is perfectly possible to read the novel without knowing that its setting was inspired by Belgium. Most readers are gripped by aspects such as the depth of Charlotte's psychological analysis, her treatment of the situation of women in her time and the richness of her prose, rather than her observations on 'Labassecour'. But, understandably, for 'Labassecourien' readers these observations have a particular interest. Understandably, too, many Belgians find the picture of them in both *Villette* and *The Professor* unduly negative and often downright insulting.

At the time that Charlotte Brontë crossed the Channel in the early 1840s there was considerable goodwill towards Belgium in many sections of British opinion. For one thing, Leopold I, who had accepted the throne of the young country in 1831, was approved of as an enlightened constitutional monarch. He was well liked in Britain because of his marriage many years earlier to the popular Princess Charlotte (as the daughter of the Prince Regent, the future George IV, she was in line for the throne), who had died in childbirth in 1817. The English had taken the Anglophile Leopold to their hearts; he had become a kind of honorary Englishman. At the time of the 1830 Revolution there had been widespread scepticism that Belgium, with its lack of experience in self-government, could go it alone, but by the 1840s, even conservative opinion in Britain regarded the new country as being established on a reasonably firm footing. As a liberal and highly industri-alised nation, Belgium was sometimes perceived as 'a little Britain on the Continent.'[2] Thomas Roscoe, the author of an 1841 guide book, considered

27

that among the reasons for these warm feelings towards Belgium were the positive results of Flemish emigration to England in past centuries (a phenomenon that was at a height with settlements of Flemish Protestants fleeing religious persecution in the sixteenth century):

> There is perhaps no country in Europe which, from a variety of concurrent circumstances, presents so many points of interest and attraction as Belgium at the present period. Intimately connected with England in regard to her history, character and position, in regard to the progress of useful science, and the facilities of communication; the consolidation of her monarchy and free institutions under the auspices of a prince deservedly dear, from former associations, to the English people, is alone calculated to produce a community of feeling, with that respect and attachment derived from mutual benefits, which independent and institutional states never fail to entertain towards each other ...
>
> But there are other and more enduring claims which Belgium might fairly prefer upon our gratitude and affection. She pointed us the way to commercial enterprise; she instructed us in manufacturing skill; she colonised our incipient towns with experienced industrious artisans; and she sent us colonists of a higher grade – her great painters, architects and sculptors, who raised and who adorned royal palaces and noble mansions ...[3]

This general approval does not appear to have impinged on the 25-year-old Charlotte Brontë, viewing the country and its inhabitants with a sardonic eye from within the Pensionnat Heger. Her views on Belgium are made all too clear, whether in *The Professor*, in which Belgium is identified as such, in *Villette*, in which it is thinly disguised as the 'farmyard' or 'poultry yard' ('Labassecour' can mean either of these), or in her letters home from Brussels. At best, the Belgians were unintelligent, stolid, lacking in passion; at worst, they were insincere, deceitful. As the 1854 reviewer of *Villette* complained, the book is full of mockery and invectives.[4]

The Belgian character was 'singularly cold, selfish, animal and inferior'.[5] This view, voiced here in a letter and reflected in her novels, was largely based on what Charlotte observed within the Pensionnat. The Brontës had no Belgian friends outside those walls. They spent most of their time in the classroom and their acquaintances in the city were British. Charlotte had a keen eye for the minutiae of Brussels bourgeois life, which she put to good use on her outings in the capital, but always as an outsider, an onlooker.

If she had had, or had made, more opportunities to meet the inhabitants of the city where she lived, it is possible that her view of Belgians would have been more balanced. In the scene in *Villette* where Lucy Snowe attends a night-time fête in the park, she is provided with a chair from which to enjoy the festivities by a M. Miret, a shopkeeper she knows whom she bumps into in the crowd. She tells us that he is the short-tempered but intelligent and kind-hearted bookseller in whose shop M. Paul likes to chat, relax and smoke his cigar, lounging on the counter as he reads the latest instalment of a novel hot from the Paris press.[6] M. Miret bears the stamp of being a real-life Brussels acquaintance. The pen-sketch of him and his shop illuminates the face of a Villette burgher for a brief moment as if by the light of one of the lanterns in the park, opening a window on the bustling life that was going on around the Pensionnat.

Charlotte's views of the Belgians she observed within its walls are voiced by both Crimsworth and Lucy Snowe. Crimsworth reports that the general tone of the pupils in Mlle Reuter's establishment is 'marked by … an eager pursuit by each individual of her own interest and convenience, and a coarse indifference to the interest and convenience of everyone else'.[7] He also acknowledges, however, that a teacher tends to see the worst side of his pupils, the 'wrong side of the tapestry'.[8] As both a pupil and teacher at the Pensionnat, Charlotte had ample opportunities, as in any such closed community, to see the more objectionable sides of her fellow inmates. 'If the national character of the Belgians is to be measured by the character of most of the girls in this school … their principles are rotten to the core,' she said in a letter to Ellen Nussey in July 1842.[9] And that was exactly what she did: she extrapolated her observations of the pupils and teachers to Belgians in general, measuring the national character of Belgium by that of Mme Heger's pupils – and that of Mme Heger herself. Some of the directress's traits or perceived traits were almost certainly drawn on by Charlotte to create the character of Mme Beck and were presented by her as representative of the Belgian character. Mme Beck is 'Labassecourienne from top to toe'.[10]

Charlotte's views as set out in *The Professor* were commented on by a female journalist writing under the name of René Gange, in an article entitled *Une Anglaise à Bruxelles* in *Le Soir* in 1890.[11] The author takes issue with Charlotte for basing her impressions of an entire country on a bunch of badly-behaved pupils, quoting a remark by Crimsworth in *The Professor*:

'"The boy is father to the man," it is said; and so I often thought when I looked at my boys and remembered the political history of their ancestors. Pelet's school was merely an epitome of the Belgian nation.' This conclusion comes at the end of a passage in which Crimsworth discourses on the obduracy and dullness of understanding of the 'youth of Brabant'.

> Their intellectual faculties were generally weak, their animal propensities strong; thus there was at once an impotence and a kind of inert force in their natures; they were dull, but they were also singularly stubborn, heavy as lead and like lead, most difficult to move.

Crimsworth observes that a teacher who showed these youths too much indulgence would 'speedily receive proofs of Flemish gratitude and magnanimity in showers of Brabant saliva and handfuls of Low-Country mud'.[12] Crimsworth establishes his authority with his pupils by drawing a line beyond which he will show no more indulgence and will become a despot requiring submission. The system he describes seems a common enough way of ensuring discipline in the classroom, yet he attributes its success with his Belgian pupils to Belgium's history of enforced subservience to foreign rulers. All of which prompts a protest from the author of the article:

> Isn't this more like a moral description of a wild people of the Congo? It is an attempt to judge a whole nation from a class of noisy, lazy and disobedient young misses, who probably tormented Charlotte. She sets out to judge the spirit and intelligence of the whole of Belgium on the basis of a handful of naughty pupils in a girls' boarding school in an obscure street in Brussels.
> What if we did what Charlotte does, and claimed that an English workhouse, with all its misery, pauperism and cruelty, provided an exact image of the whole of the country?

As for Charlotte's slurs on the political history of Belgium, if she was so well acquainted with history she could not be unaware, in the writer's opinion, that 'the Flemish were already great in the past when the English were still nothing'.

The poet and essayist Lucien Christophe, in an article entitled *Le roman bruxellois de Charlotte Brontë* (1939), also objects to Charlotte's generalisations and conclusions, pointing out that 'When we Belgians read the opening chapter of *Jane Eyre* and see a rich family making life miserable for the poor relation in the house, we don't leap to the conclusion that these are specifically English ways of behaviour. Yet when Mme Beck covertly inspects Lucy Snowe's belongings, the author's remark is: 'All this was very un-English'.[13]

A great deal is said in *The Professor* and *Villette* about such behaviour. Distrust of others and hypocrisy are rife in the fictional schools in both novels, giving rise to the methods of espionage employed in these establishments. However, in this respect Charlotte's criticisms were directed as much at the Catholic mindset and Catholic ideas of education as at Belgians. Moreover, she does not attribute deceitfulness and hypocrisy only to Belgians. While it is true that the Belgian Mlle Reuter and the Labassecourienne Mme Beck are skilled in the art of subterfuge, among the pupils in Charlotte's fictional pensionnats it is the aristocratic girls who are the most deceitful owing to the admixture of 'quick French blood' in their veins,[14] and in all probability her comments in this regard would have been very similar in a boarding school in Paris. Crimsworth attributes Mlle Reuter's lack of sound principles and sacrifice of honesty to expediency to her Catholic upbringing rather than her Belgian origin, believing that a Protestant husband might instil the virtues of integrity in her.[15]

'The honest aboriginal Labassecouriennes had an hypocrisy of their own too; but it was of a coarse order, such as could deceive few.'[16] Mme Beck's 'Labassecourien' pupils may not be scrupulous about telling the truth, but in some ways they are very direct. The girls are 'blunt', 'brusque' and 'boisterous'. Lucy Snowe parries their rough, if friendly, ways with frosty reserve.

> A constitutional reserve of manner had by this time told with wholesome and, for me, commodious effect, on the manners of my co-inmates; rarely did I now suffer from rude or intrusive treatment. When I first came, it would happen once and again that a blunt German would clap me on the shoulder, and ask me to run a race; or a riotous Labassecourienne seize me by the arm and drag me towards the playground: urgent proposals to take a swing at the 'Pas de Géant' [a pole with ropes attached to it, in the playground], or to join in a certain romping hide-and-seek game called 'Un, deux, trois,' were formerly also of hourly occurrence; but all these little attentions had ceased some time ago – ceased, too, without my finding it necessary to be at the trouble of point-blank cutting them short.[17]

▲ Manneken Pis.

'Coarseness' is a word often applied to Belgians by Charlotte's English observers. Several weeks into his stay in Belgium, Crimsworth observes that he has yet to see 'any appearance of sensitiveness in any human face'.[18] Belgians are jocund, unthinking.[19] The jovial Mme Reuter in *The Professor*, Mlle Reuter's mother, with her leer and licentious speech, epitomises Crimsworth's perception of 'continental, or at least Belgian old women'.[20] Charlotte's choice of 'Labassecour', the farmyard, as her fictitious name for Belgium has been interpreted by some of her Belgian readers as a reference to what she saw as the Belgians' coarse manners.[21] Earthy, jovial humour can indeed be seen as the spirit of the little figure who has long been the emblem of Brussels: Manneken Pis, dubbed by the fastidious Baudelaire 'le pisseur'.

'Two young wolves who found themselves shut up with a litter of greedy, noisy puppies.' Thus a Belgian journalist, writing about the Brontës in 1929, drew the contrast between the aloof English sisters and their Belgian classmates.[22]

The Labassecouriens of 'La Basse Ville'

In *The Professor*, some of Charlotte's uncomplimentary remarks are directed against what she calls the 'Flemish' or 'flamands'. This is generally taken by readers in Belgium to refer specifically to Flemish rather than French-speaking Belgians, though arguably Charlotte frequently uses the terms 'Belgian' and 'Flemish' interchangeably.

Marysa Demoor, a professor at Ghent University, complains in *The Fields of Flanders*, a book about British views of Flanders and Belgium, that Charlotte depicts the Flemish as an un-evolved or degenerate race, appearing to view a 'Netherlander', someone from the Low Countries, much as she would a 'Neanderthal'.[23] Often cited by Flemish commentators is Robert Moore's description of the Flemish physiognomy and physique in *Shirley*: 'The clumsy nose standing out – the mean forehead falling back ... All body and no legs ...'.[24] In the view of these commentators, Charlotte was echoing francophone prejudices about the Flemish. In her recent novel *De Meester* (The Master, 2013), published in English as *Charlotte Brontë's Secret Love*, the writer Jolien Janzing suggests that Charlotte must have caught such prejudices from the Hegers. In fact there is no actual evidence of this. Janet Harper, a later pupil at the Pensionnat, had affectionate memories of the school's Flemish cook,[25] and a few years after the Brontës left a teacher was hired to give Dutch lessons.[26]

Since the separation from the Netherlands in 1830, French had been the language of administration in the Dutch-speaking north of the country as well as the French-speaking south. (In fact the predominance of French as the language of the nobility and bourgeoisie dated back to before Independence and even before the annexation of the Low Countries by France in 1794–1814.) Dutch remained the language of the working class, and most of the Dutch speakers encountered by foreign travellers were servants or peasants; the chambermaid Crimsworth meets in the hotel where he spends his first night in Brussels, wearing wooden shoes and a short petticoat and speaking only Dutch, is a case in point.[27] (In an 1871 guide book to Brussels, servants are described as still wearing short petticoats and wooden shoes.)[28] Mme Walravens' servant speaks only the 'aboriginal tongue of Labassecour' and does not understand French, as was the case with the majority of servants in Brussels.[29]

In the capital, the Flemish, who accounted for almost two-thirds of its population, inhabited the Basse Ville rather than the predominantly French-speaking Haute Ville. The majority were illiterate. They spoke various regional dialects of Dutch, and in Charlotte's time the Flemish movement, promoting literature in Dutch, was still in its infancy. Dutch literature had languished in the southern Netherlands under foreign rule. A little later in the nineteenth century, particularly after rules were drawn up standardising

Dutch spelling and grammar in Flanders, a new generation of Flemish writers started to write in their own language.

In her novels Charlotte makes reference to just one Dutch term, meaning a cake or cookie and spelled 'koek' in Dutch and 'couque' in the French version of the word (Charlotte misspells it 'couc'), when Crimsworth goes into a shop in rue de Louvain to buy a *couque aux raisins*, a currant bun. Today, these pastries are still sold in every baker's shop and café in Belgium. Crimsworth's comment on his one venture outside the comfort zone of French is, 'It is a Flemish word, I don't know how to spell it'.

If Crimsworth finds his pupils slow to learn and 'difficult to move', could this not have been because they were being forced to learn in French, not their first language? That is the opinion of some Flemish readers. Furthermore, Crimsworth was attempting to teach them a third language, English. The writer Geert Van Istendael suggests linguistic problems as the reason for the perceived stupidity of Crimsworth's pupils. Did it not occur to him, marvels Van Istendael, that if the boys were difficult to get into motion this was likely to be due to a failure in communication? Crimsworth didn't know a word of Dutch, and his pupils probably didn't have a clue what he was saying to them in English.[30] Against this it could be argued that Crimsworth and his pupils did in fact have a common language, French, since middle-class children like the ones he was teaching generally had a good grasp of French even when Flemish in origin. It might also be pointed out that Charlotte Brontë was not a patient teacher and had as low an opinion of her pupils' abilities when teaching at an English school as she did in Belgium. 'Stupidity the atmosphere, schoolbooks the employment, asses the society' was how she summed up life at Roe Head, the Yorkshire school where she taught some years before going to Brussels, describing her pupils as 'fat-headed oafs' and complaining of their 'idleness, apathy and ... asinine stupidity.'[31]

The title of a talk on Charlotte Brontë's attitudes to the Belgians given in Britain by Marysa Demoor was 'The Flemish maid replies', a reference to the servant Crimsworth bumps into in his hotel: 'Her face was broad, her physiognomy eminently stupid; when I spoke to her in French, she answered me in Flemish, with an air the reverse of civil ...'[32] Demoor started her talk with an historical exposition of the situation of the Flemish after the Belgian Revolution.

In her novel *Charlotte Brontë's Secret Love*, Jolien Janzing, who is of Dutch parentage but has lived for most of her life in Flanders, also gives the Flemish an opportunity to have their say. In the novel, the imaginary character Emile is a Flemish workman whom Charlotte meets when accompanying Heger to the French evening classes he gives for workers. Emile is learning French because he wants to become a foreman in the factory where he is employed. He tells Charlotte he needs to speak the language of 'the masters' if he is to be promoted. Countering Charlotte's unfavourable descriptions of the Flemish physiognomy, Janzing stresses Emile's good looks and the nobility of his features. In a quayside tavern in a working-class district of Brussels – doubtless one of those Belgian taverns so smoke-filled that, complained Théophile Gautier, you could barely see your own feet let alone distinguish the forms of your fellow drinkers[33] – Emile gives Charlotte the Flemish view on life in 1840s Belgium. For the working classes, it was a time of economic hardship. If you were Flemish, the francophone bourgeoisie (to which the Hegers of course belonged) were oppressors. Emile believes the country had been better off when united with the Netherlands. He was not alone in holding this belief. The separation from the Netherlands, a commercial, seafaring and colonial country with plenty of outlets for the products of Belgium's burgeoning industries, posed difficulties for its economy.

Economic conditions in Flanders were so bad, in fact, that many Flemish emigrated. At a subsequent meeting Emile asks Charlotte to marry him and emigrate with him to Wisconsin. It is an offer slightly reminiscent of St John Rivers' request to Jane to accompany him to India, where she can be a useful helpmate. Charlotte, who only hours earlier has indignantly rejected a proposal by M. Heger to become his mistress, turns down Emile's offer as well, thereby losing an opportunity to study the Flemish perspective at even closer quarters.

Sense and insensibility...

Even when not accusing the Belgians of hypocrisy or stupidity, Charlotte complained of their stolidity. They had no feelings, no passion, she lamented. Nothing moved them. They had 'marsh phlegm'[34] or 'lymph'[35] in their veins. 'The phlegm that thickens their blood is too gluey to boil'.[36] Phlegmatism, frequently attributed to the British, was not a quality calculated to appeal to the Brontë temperament.

Charlotte found it particularly exasperating as displayed by the female part of the Belgian population. Mme Beck is described as 'passionless',[37] as are the placid Labassecourien bourgeoises Lucy observes at a concert, who appear to be incapable of being stirred by any intellectual or emotional excitement.[38]

As we saw in the preceding chapter, if press reports of audience reactions to the dramatisation of *Jane Eyre* were accurate, Belgians were not always as impassive as Charlotte claimed. Yet her impressions are borne out by the comments of the Belgian observer cited in that chapter who tells us that 'You have to shake them hard to get a tear or applause out of them':

> Belgian audiences ... have a thick skin and a steady pulse ... Their coldness and scepticism are a result of their temperament and education; they pride themselves on their placidity, which they regard as a virtue. They think that if they don't applaud loudly or often, it's because they are demanding, and if they are demanding, this means that they are connoisseurs. Thanks to their *sang-froid* they often display good judgement, but this *sang-froid* is at times no more than indifference or insensibility.[39]

The Abbé de Pradt, a Frenchman who was a close observer of the Belgians as Archbishop of Mechelen in the years of French annexation of Belgium, similarly commented on their phlegmatic demeanour, but wrote that it was a mistake to conclude from this that they were cold-hearted:

> Belgians make a religion of habit, of a succession of days all equally peaceful. They equate calm with happiness. Their life is a straight line, their affections have no emotion in them, their joys no animation. Don't judge them, however, by their coldness and the awkwardness of their manners. Their hearts don't lack warmth, particularly when it comes to charity.[40]

In *Villette*, M. Paul is the only Labassecourien who displays any kind of passion. When he makes a fiery patriotic speech about his country at a prize-giving ceremony for the pupils of the Athénée, Lucy's comment is: 'Who would have thought the flat and fat soil of Labassecour could yield political convictions and national feelings, such as were now strongly expressed?'[41] In fact, at a time when the Revolution was still fresh in the memory, there was no shortage of patriotic fervour in the new kingdom of Belgium, yet Charlotte recognises such fervour only in the character in *Villette* who is presented as the least typical example of a Labassecourien.

However, comments made by the historian Carlo Bronne on his countrymen in the mid nineteenth century bear out many of Charlotte's observations of Labassecouriens. Enumerating the characteristics of the Belgian bourgeoisie at the time of Charlotte's stay – in the same pages in which he cites admiringly her appraisal of the character of Leopold I, whom she saw at the concert she describes in *Villette* – he calls the citizens of Brussels, the burghers whom Charlotte had occasion to scrutinise at that concert, 'a people without imagination ... without hate and without love, incapable of passion for what is just or beautiful. Belgian hearts had no dreams.'[42] He writes of their 'apathy' and the *ennui* of their lives. 'Comfort and material well-being were all that was aspired to, nothing intellectually or morally elevated.'[43] More positively, Bronne quotes the verdict of the French critic and historian Hippolyte Taine. While admitting that the average Frenchmen would find the Belgian lifestyle stultifyingly boring – custom-bound, incurious, heavy and vulgar – Taine considered that the placid Belgians had attained a contentment and wisdom their lively neighbours to the west lacked.[44]

The Belgian writer Charles d'Ydewalle opined that under Leopold I his countrymen were 'the happiest people in Europe'.[45] After centuries of subjection to foreign domination and foreign wars, it was perhaps hardly surprising that having finally gained independence they aspired to nothing higher than a quiet life.

Lucy Snowe's pupils are described as undisciplined, refractory and indolent. Such comments are not just made about middle-class Belgian girls; in a reference to the workmen who sometimes carry out repairs in the classrooms, Lucy notes that, 'Foreign artisans and servants do everything by couples: I believe it would take two Labassecourien carpenters to drive a nail.'[46] Charlotte was a shrewd observer. A similar remark is made by Henry Robert Addison, who knew Belgium well. 'If you wish to fit up a single room, the probability is, that you must employ half a dozen workmen: the man who makes your blind, will not put it up, nor the man who puts it up make the roller: a third man must be sent for to adjust the spring, and a fourth to make the window go up and down; like the natives of the East, every one adheres so closely to his particular branch of trade, that he refuses, although well able to do so, to stir in the slightest degree beyond its exact limits.' Addison observed, moreover, that while Belgian workmen worked hard enough when they did work, the national fondness for the fêtes and fairs marking the saints' days of the Catholic calendar meant that they would often toil only four days out of the seven, not returning to their labours until all their cash had been spent at the fair.[47] Moreover, a Belgian commentator, the historian Alexandre Henne, characterised Belgian workmen as somewhat undisciplined and rebellious.

The recalcitrance noted by Henne and other observers could be seen as a positive trait, denoting a sturdy independence. An observation of Charlotte's often cited approvingly by her Belgian readers is her reference to the egalitarian spirit that reigns in 'Labassecour'. The girls at both her fictional Pensionnats appear not to be divided by rigid class barriers. Lucy observes that 'Equality is much practised in Labassecour; though not republican in form, it is nearly so in substance, and at the desks of Mme Beck's establishment the young countess and the young bourgeoise sat side by side'.[48] *La Maîtresse d'anglais*, the early French adaptation of *Villette*, makes this reference more specific to Belgium: 'There is political equality in Belgium; though a monarchy, social organisation is democratic'. Alexandre Henne described the Belgians as natural Republicans, an undeferential race who refused to kow-tow to monarchs or to their social superiors generally.[49] The French traveller Edmond Texier noticed how senators who had just been in the presence of the King ate their *tartines*[50] and downed their tankards of beer in the pot-houses just like everyone else.[51]

Belgians prided themselves on being an egalitarian society and compared themselves favourably with the British in this respect. Although Britain was approved of as a country of liberty and human rights, the cradle of many of the ideas that had inspired social and political progress on the Continent, there was disapproval of the fact that these ideals sat, anomalously, alongside a rigid class system, with undue subservience to the upper classes. The London correspondent of one of the main Belgian newspapers, writing in the 1860s, noted on the one hand that England was 'a monarchy in form yet a republic in substance' (a remark almost identical to Charlotte's observation on 'Labassecour'), while, on the other, deploring the British fondness for titles and the aristocracy.[52]

The author of the 1890 article *Une Anglaise à Bruxelles* cited earlier speaks with distaste of the British contempt for inferiors that could make the lives of lowly employees a misery, a national characteristic she also attributes to the French. Noting the Frenchman M. Pelet's treatment of the

Flemish ushers he employs at his school, she observes that in both England and France there was a much more crushing sense of social superiority than in Belgium. 'The spirit of liberty that penetrates this nation to the core gives it respect for others even when that other is an inferior.'[53] This observation was borne out by the British traveller Henry Smithers, who noted that Belgians treated their servants as equals, without the haughtiness that often made him blush to be English. Lucy Snowe notes the 'freedom of manner' of the pert Rosine, the portress at Mme Beck's. Rosine is French, not Labassecourien, but Lucy describes her manner as 'not altogether peculiar to herself, but characteristic of the domestics of Villette generally'.[54]

Smithers also noted that Belgians were free from that 'formality, reserve and pride which is oftimes observable in the English character, and which is so repulsive to strangers'.[55] Charlotte, however, appears to approve of British reserve and pride. She and Emily were disliked for their standoffish- ness during their time at the Pensionnat. The attitude of the British pupils in Mlle Reuter's school towards their non-British compeers is a lofty one, although it can be justified in this context as a response to the hostility of the other pupils: 'They warded off insult with austere civility and met hate with mute disdain; they eschewed company-keeping, and in the midst of numbers seemed to dwell isolated.' Charlotte acknowledges that the stiff English girls would appear 'repulsive' to many,[56] and in *Villette* M. Paul attacks the 'insufferable pride'[57] of British women, which he sees as a char-acteristic of their religion. But the half-English Frances Henri in *The Professor* prefers 'English pride to Flemish coarseness'.[58] In *The Professor*, Charlotte even imagines English pride as also having an appeal for a Belgian: Mlle Reuter is attracted by Crimsworth's 'haughty air'. 'How well disdain becomes him!'[59] In the fictional character of William Crimsworth, Charlotte is expressing a personal preference for heroes who are proud and sardonic; the arrogance of her countrymen abroad did not tend to make them popular with other nationalities.

Nevertheless, while Charlotte's and Emily's aloofness at the Pensionnat may not endear them to Belgian commentators, it is sometimes excused by them as being part and parcel of the English character. 'Completely isolated in the midst of numbers' was Charlotte's description of their position at the school, as British and Protestants.[60] 'Si l'Angleterre est une île, chaque Anglais est un îlot (if England [i.e. Britain] is an island, each Englishman is an islet),' is the comment of the author of a 1939 newspaper article about the Brontës. Their standoffishness is also often excused on the grounds that they were sufferers from culture shock. 'Protestant, provincial, northern, they felt isolated in this Catholic, more worldly and more southern culture, and did their best to increase the distances still further.'[61] Charlotte's hostility to some aspects of the culture in which she found herself transplanted is attributed to her uneasy situation as a *déracinée*, uprooted from her natural environment. That she was aware of the negative impression she made on those around her at the Pensionnat is suggested by some of the criticisms she puts into the mouths of those who observe Lucy Snowe, who is described as sour and cantankerous in terms identical to those used by certain Belgian critics of Charlotte Brontë herself.[62]

Egalitarianism is not the only feature of Belgian life lauded by both Lucy and Crimsworth. They express approval, too, of the Belgian knack of living economically. The low cost of living in Brussels was one of the main reasons why Charlotte, along with so many of her cash-strapped compatriots, headed there rather than to more glamorous but expensive capitals such as Paris. Charlotte's novels contain references to her preoccupation with getting and saving money, and Crimsworth tells us that in Belgium you could live on less than half the income required in England, as the sensible Belgians did not waste money on needless show. Whereas the English were 'abject slaves to ... the desire to keep up a certain appearance ... I have seen a degree of sense in the modest arrangement of one homely Belgian household that might put to shame the elegance, the superfluities, the luxuries, the strained refinements of a hundred genteel English mansions.'[63]

The preference for an economical lifestyle was widely recognised as a Belgian characteristic. In the words of a historian of the period, a major difference between Belgium and France was that in the former the emphasis was on 'être' (being), in the latter on 'paraître' (appearing).[64] 'René Gange', the author of the article *Une Anglaise à Bruxelles* already referred to, points out that 'This is precisely why so many English families settle in this *flat* and *insipid* land. Miss Brontë, it seems to us that in this respect all the intellectual and moral advantages are on the side of the modest Belgians. The good sense in which we excel should not be despised.'

Charlotte's denigrating remarks about Belgians are the product of ignorance, concludes René Gange. 'Belgium is full of English men and women who undoubtedly don't share her opinions, and like being here so much they even leave their bones here.'[65] It is true enough that few commentators would appear to have endorsed Charlotte's view that the Belgians' principles were 'rotten to the core'. Indeed, the Abbé Pradt expressed the opposite view; for him, the Belgians were 'innately moral – you might say virtue is in their very blood'. He had nothing but praise for them as 'a good, frank, hospitable, hard-working, economical people, friends of order and regularity'.[66] Addison sums them up as a 'patient, well-meaning and good-humoured people, well-intentioned towards all'.[67] Even Lucy allows her Labassecourien pupils to be good-natured, describing them as 'inert, but kind-natured, neutral of evil, undistinguished for good'.[68]

... and sensuality: 'Eat, drink, and live'

Charlotte's reactions to her host country were by no means all negative. *Villette* reflects not just the depression into which she gradually sank at the Pensionnat but also the heightening of perception resulting from immersion in a culture where everything was different. Like the sauce accompanying Lucy's first meal in Villette, which contains both sugar and vinegar, the foreign culture afforded a mixture of sensations both sweet and sour and at any rate stimulating in their novelty: 'odd ... but pleasant' is Lucy's verdict on her first supper.[69] Not least of the stimulations offered was that of the senses. Despite Lucy Snowe's disapproval of what she sees as the Catholic church's encouragement to its followers to 'eat, drink, and live',[70] leaving the care of their souls to their confessors, Charlotte was fully alive to the pleasures of the Continental *art de vivre*. She liked the clothes, noting the simple elegance of Continental fashions compared with the showy but ill-fitting garments of British visitors. She liked the food. The simplest fare pleased her. Belgian readers note her fondness for *pistolets*, still ubiquitous in the Belgian capital today. These were bread rolls with a gash in them; the name is believed to be derived from a coin called a 'pistolet' rather than from that word's usual meaning of 'pistol'. Paulina De Bassompierre in *Villette* puns on the word when she butters a roll for her father and tells him 'There ... are your "pistolets" charged'.[71] Charlotte knew nothing of the *tables d'hôte* in the hotels that lodged her better-off compatriots, groaning under the weight of twenty different dishes, like that of the Hôtel de Suède where Thackeray put up in the early 1840s. He claimed to have tried practically every dish on the table without suffering from indigestion as he would undoubtedly have done in England.

> 1, Green pea-soup; 2, boiled salmon; 3, mussels; 4, crimped skate; 5, roast-meat; 6, patties; 7, melons; 8, carp, stewed with mushrooms and onions; 9, roast-turkey; 10, cauliflower and butter; 11, fillets of venison

piques, with asafoetida sauce; 12, stewed calf's-ear; 13, roast-veal; 14, roast-lamb; 15, stewed cherries; 16, rice-pudding; 17, Gruyere cheese, and about twenty-four cakes of different kinds. Except 5, 13, and 14, I give you my word I ate of all written down here, with three rolls of bread and a score of potatoes. What is the meaning of it? How is the stomach of man to be brought to desire and to receive all this quantity? Do not gastronomists complain of heaviness in London after eating a couple of mutton-chops? ... But look at the difference here: after dinner here one is as light as a gossamer.[72]

(The Belgians are traditionally so fond of their food that, so the story goes, during the fighting in the Revolution hostilities were suspended in the lunch hour.) Unlike Thackeray, Lucy Snowe is in no danger of indigestion. She is content with coffee and buttered rolls. In the last pages of *Villette* she and M. Paul pledge their love for each other over hot chocolate and *pistolets*.

Summing up Belgian bourgeois life at this period, Carlo Bronne stresses the importance of the pleasures of dress and the table, pointing out that these were catered for by many of the commodities traditionally manufactured in Brussels – cloth, lace, pastries.[73]

In *Charlotte Brontë's Secret Love*, Jolien Janzing paints a picture of a *bon vivant*, epicurean Brussels that assails the senses and contrasts with the austere and Spartan way of life in Haworth. There is much emphasis in the novel on sensory pleasures: eating, drinking, fine clothes – and sexual pleasure. Belgian women are 'plump and white' like fat geese. The most voluptuous of all is the full-lipped Arcadie Claret, Leopold I's mistress, whose liaison with the married king parallels and counterpoints Charlotte's brief flirtation with the married Heger. Even Mme Heger, perpetually pregnant, is presented as voluptuous, a 'corset of conventions' necessary to 'keep her passions in check'.[74] As for Belgian men, they are 'womanisers', even if not quite such masters of the arts of seduction as the Parisians or Italians. In contrast, English women are lacking in voluptuousness, Charlotte being a prime example of this deficiency, and English men 'have no opera in the blood': 'The Londoner proposes to his chosen one – after three walks accompanied by an old aunt – in the same sober tone in which he bids for a healthy mare at the market.'[75]

In Janzing's novel, Charlotte is seduced not just by Heger but by the pleasures of Continental life. On return to Haworth, she finds it 'backward' and lacking in aesthetic taste, and misses Continental food. Scenes of the carnival festivities, to which she is taken by her tutor, are used to reinforce the hedonistic depiction of Brussels. When Heger took the real-life Charlotte to see the carnival celebrations she was dismissive of them, but in Janzing's novel her reflection is 'how great the temptation is to abandon her resistance and let herself be carried away by sensual pleasure'.[76] Heger encourages her not to resist, calling her a 'Calvinist' when she declines to drink beer with him during their outing.

Charlotte does, however, accept Heger's advances to her, availing herself of a feature of Continental life that is hinted at in *The Professor* and *Villette*: moral laxity in sexual matters. In *The Professor*, Pelet, the French director of the school where Crimsworth teaches, boasts of affairs with married women. This laxity in questions of marriage is extended to Pelet's Belgian fiancée Zoraïde Reuter, who, Crimsworth believes, would be more than willing to enter into an extra-marital affair with Crimsworth after her marriage to his employer. The pupils at her school are presented as sensual and sexually precocious. In Janzing's novel, too, the kind of moral laxity traditionally associated with France is applied to Belgium. The Catholic Constantin Heger is not just flirtatious with his wife's pupils but ready to embark on a full-blown affair with Charlotte. Charlotte, for her part, is willing enough to abandon English Puritanism and melt in his arms – though she becomes indignant when he is not prepared to leave his wife for her and merely offers her a clandestine affair.

Janzing, Dutch-born and herself a Protestant, was reared in the Catholic Flanders. The view of Belgium in her novel chimes in with Charlotte's perception of the Catholic Labassecouriens, 'fat, ruddy, hale', as being concerned only with the things of the flesh.[77]

Pistols and *pistolets*

In an article published in 1956,[78] Marie Gevers, a leading Belgian writer of her generation, introduces some reflections on the Brontës into an account of a trip to what was then the Belgian Congo for a tour lecturing on the poet Émile Verhaeren, a founder of the Symbolist school and an important figure in Belgian literature. Verhaeren was born in 1855, and Gevers' lecture tour was in 1955 to mark the centenary of his birth. Gevers was aware that 1955 was also the centenary of the death of Charlotte Brontë. She was an admirer of the Brontës who had been deeply moved by the accounts she had read of their childhood, and her memoir includes some musings about the very different worlds in which the English writer and the Belgian one had grown up. Her observations highlight some of the differences between the two cultures as seen through Belgian eyes.

Gevers begins with a picture of the Brontës' childhood drawn from her reading. It was a bleak one. 'The Brontës' motherless childhood was one of strict and rigid Puritan inflexibility. For their father, virtue signified violence and hardness. He ripped up his wife's dress because he judged it too frivolous. His puny children were deprived of meat, fish, butter and eggs, in order to teach them to despise the things of this earth. In the mornings they were woken not by a mother's kiss but by the pistol shots fired by their father – his favourite pastime.' (In contrast, in Brussels Charlotte woke not to pistol shots but to the breakfast *pistolets*, the oddly-named Belgian bread rolls of which she was so fond.)

The children's intellectual nourishment, Gevers concludes, was as dry and arid as that provided for their bodies. It consisted of 'English politics – the debates of the Chamber of Lords – read in the papers by the Reverend Brontë. For heroes they were offered Wellington and Peel. For stories, the battles of Whigs and Tories. And as a pastime, they had walks on the desolate moors of *Wuthering Heights*.'

Gevers' impressions were not dissimilar to those of many English-speaking Brontëites before the emergence of new biographies that gave a more balanced and less joyless view of the Brontës' upbringing. These impressions were based on exaggerated stories of Patrick's eccentricities relayed in the first edition of Mrs Gaskell's life, which were repudiated by him and omitted in a subsequent edition: tales of his insistence on a vegetarian diet, with his children being reared chiefly on potatoes (in fact Patrick denied ever prescribing a meat-free diet for his family), his cutting up his wife's silk gown, burning the children's boots because he considered them too brightly coloured, and sawing up chairs and firing pistols out of the back door to work off rages. It is true that since the Luddite riots of his younger days Patrick had slept with a loaded pistol by his side, but his morning shots were fired to discharge the weapon, a wise precaution in a house full of children.

There could have been no greater contrast than that between Charlotte's life and Emile Verhaeren's, juxtaposed in Gevers' imagination by the coincidence that Charlotte died in the year Verhaeren was born. Verhaeren's childhood, passed in a village on the banks of the river Scheldt in East Flanders, was an affluent one in the heart of an affectionate family, a comfortable bourgeois existence punctuated by the christenings and communions, marriages and funerals that brought the family together around tables laden with succulent dishes. His first volume of verse, *Les Flamandes* (The Flemish Women), paints a picture of Flemish life as one of plenty. His poems celebrate the farms in the fertile countryside around his birthplace, their kitchen rafters and tables groaning with hams, black puddings, fowls; the drinking and gorging on feast days; the well-rounded contours of rosy-cheeked milkmaids who might have walked straight out of Rubens paintings.

Against this background of good living and good eating, it is not surprising that well-fed Belgian readers dwelt with horrified fascination on accounts of the Brontës' childhood. The material deprivations of their life, in particular the vegetarian regime supposedly imposed by their father, made them objects of particular pity, as did the absence of what was perceived as normal family life: in place of cheerful family meals round the table, the morose father eating apart in his study, leaving his children to dine alone on their frugal fare of potatoes and rice pudding. Their privations were seen in the context of English Protestantism, with Patrick the epitome of a stern, repressed Puritan, bringing up his children without any manifestations of affection and denying them the most innocent of pleasures, such as toys and picture books. Very different in Gevers' view was the Catholic faith in which she and Verhaeren were reared, 'imbued with the tenderness of devotion to the Virgin': a gentle and joyous religion.

Like Verhaeren, Gevers had been brought up in a well-off and loving family. She had had a happy marriage and was the mother of three children. The compassion she felt for Charlotte was for the privations of her adult life as well as her childhood. What awaited Charlotte in Brussels, she said, was 'a hopeless love, trampled by the indifference and egoism of the man who inspired it, Constantin Heger'. Gevers' viewed Charlotte's marriage at the age of 38 as a melancholy one, a mere marriage of convenience. 'Charlotte did not even have what she begged for from Heger, the crumbs from the rich man's table.'

Exceedingly misanthropic and sour

Thus, one aspect of Charlotte's legacy in Belgium is fascination in her life story, particularly in the contrasts it offers with typical Belgian life experiences; knowledge of that story has coloured Belgian readers' responses to her views on their country.

These responses are wide-ranging. By some readers Charlotte is seen as vindictive and spiteful. A guide to famous Britons with links to Brussels states that at the time of their stay in the city 'Charlotte and Emily were already well on the way to becoming old maids', that 'they hated the country and the people' and that Charlotte used the cover of fictitious names in order to give vent to her pent-up feelings and disapproval of Catholic Belgium.[79] There is perhaps some justification for the guide's unflattering description of the sisters as spinsters, at least where Charlotte was concerned; at twenty-seven, her age by the time she left Brussels, she was on the shelf by the standards of her time, and felt herself to be so. The implication is, of course, that she was frustrated with her lot and that her bitterness against Belgium grew in part out of this. Her own remark that she became 'exceedingly misanthropic and sour' in Brussels would seem to support this.

Marysa Demoor believes that Charlotte 'projected her frustrations on all Belgians.'[80] For the writer of the hostile article *Une Anglaise à Bruxelles*, one thing that explains Charlotte's attitude to Belgium is her unenviable position as assistant mistress in a Brussels boarding school. The writer points out, however, that Charlotte would in all likelihood have been treated far worse at a school in the more snobbish France or England.[81]

In the opinion of many Belgians, Charlotte's portrayal of their country in her novels was born out of motives of revenge for her disappointment in love. In the view of the author of an article in *L'Indépendance Belge* in 1926, the explanation for the 'malice' that made *Villette* and *The Professor* so offensive to Belgians was to be found in Charlotte's letters to Heger published a decade earlier, which revealed the highly 'morbid' nature of her passion for him. Her novels were driven by the fury of a woman scorned.[82] The view of *Villette* as a novel of revenge was also taken by the writer Lucien Christophe in his 1939 article *Le roman bruxellois de Charlotte Brontë*. The 'Labassecouriens', he tells his readers, can do nothing right. If Charlotte's story requires a priest of noble appearance, he has to be French, since all Belgian priests have an inferior physiognomy. Christophe admits that some of Charlotte's observations on Belgians are pertinent, but, he says, 'they are inspired too much by malignity and resentment' – resentment both at Heger's lack of response to her appeals and what she regarded as her unfair treatment by Madame. 'One can't help suspecting that if the Hegers had been just a little more open-hearted towards her, Belgium would never have become "Labassecour", Ostend "Boue-Marine" or Brussels "Villette"'[83] – just as it is supposed that if Baudelaire had found an appreciative audience

for his lectures in Belgium and made some money out of them, he would never have spewed out the hundred or so pages of vitriol published posthumously as *Pauvre Belgique*.

Charlotte's early twentieth-century French biographer the Abbé Dimnet had his own theory about her attitude to the Belgians. It was his opinion that, although unwilling to admit it even to herself, Charlotte made a mistake in choosing Brussels as her destination, and that her uneasy consciousness of her error was the cause of her ill humour during her time in Belgium. Since the French Revolution, it had been common for English girls seeking a Continental finishing school to opt for Belgium or Switzerland rather than France, but in Charlotte's case, Dimnet was convinced that she would have been much happier in Paris. 'Even during those periods when Englishmen have been the most resolutely set against whatever did not correspond to their own ideas and customs, they have never resisted the charm of Paris.' Puritanical and narrow as Charlotte was in her attitudes to foreignness, she would have been charmed by the French capital, and 'when one is charmed, one is near to being persuaded.' France, Dimnet said, was a great nation, superior in its qualities of mind and in its arts. Charlotte knew this, and in France she would have felt it. In Belgium she found that she had to be content with second best, a counterfeit. Whenever she praised some feature of Continental life, he said, as often as not it turned out to be French rather than Belgian, for example the skill of Continental dressmakers. He concluded, 'It seems to me extremely probable that her judgement of what she called continental manners and even of Catholicism would have been very different had she lived in France'.[84] This is debatable, since Charlotte was a sardonic observer wherever she was. She had a keen appreciation of the French language and literature but the French characters in her novels are not objects of admiration. Adèle, Jane Eyre's French pupil, is coquettish and frivolous, M. Pelet in *The Professor* arrogant and cynical, a Parisian colleague of Lucy's cold and unprincipled and Rosine, the French portress, fickle and vain.

For Charlotte, one reason for disapproval of Belgians was simply that they were not English. 'Belgium is not England, and its ways are not our ways,' muses Crimsworth in *The Professor*.[85] Had this comment been made in a spirit of acceptance, had Charlotte tolerated or even relished foreign ways, both *The Professor* and *Villette* would have been very different books, but her attitude was almost invariably critical and judgemental. From the moment Charlotte set foot in Ostend, says Dimnet, she displayed the arrogance of the typical English 'petite bourgeoisie' abroad. The traveller abroad, said the French writer Texier, in an account of his travels in Belgium in the 1850s, should make his observations in a spirit of good humour and benevolence. He should shake off his national prejudices at the border with the dust of his shoes.[86] Thackeray, who admits in an account of a trip to Belgium to having his own 'handsome share' of the 'national conceit that every Englishman possesses', mocks many things Belgian, but does not do so ill-naturedly, stopping himself in full flow on the 'bad taste' of the fantastical carvings on pulpits in Belgian churches with the caution to himself, 'But let us not be too supercilious and ready to sneer'.[87]

Charlotte's share of English conceit was exacerbated by her general tendency to find fault in a spirit of petty criticism that her biographer Ernest Dimnet regarded as unworthy of her. One has only to compare her impressions of the Pensionnat Heger with those of another former pupil, the American Janet Harper, to perceive in what a different spirit Charlotte might have made her observations. The good-natured Harper observed nothing but sweetness and light at the school.[88] One reason for Charlotte's much darker vision, of course, is that her writer's eye delved so deep and so mercilessly into the psyche of those she scrutinised.

For Delinka Dominkovits, the author of a university dissertation at the Université Libre de Bruxelles entitled *Charlotte Brontë and Brussels*, Charlotte, in common with many foreigners, made no effort to understand Belgium. She came to the country totally unprepared for what she would find. 'In her haste to come to Brussels, Charlotte perhaps forgot to find out more about Belgium and Belgian customs. She just wanted to learn French and see galleries and churches. She seemed unaware of what living among foreigners implied.'[89]

In the view of some Belgian commentators, Charlotte simply uses Belgium as a foil to set off the virtues of Britishness. Marysa Demoor, in her book on British perceptions of Belgium, points out that in this Charlotte was not alone. She was one of a series of British writers who, Demoor believes, present a negative view of Belgium in which 'the Belgians stand for everything that a good Briton is not'. She cites Conrad (*Heart of Darkness*) and Ouida (*A Dog of Flanders*) as two of the other writers who propagate this negative perception. Although Charlotte was not the first to do so, Demoor holds her particularly responsible for influencing generations of Britons against Belgium because her works are read by so many British schoolchildren.[90] British schoolchildren, however, are more likely to read

Jane Eyre, which has nothing to say about Belgium, than *Villette* or *The Professor* or even *Shirley*, in which the character of Hortense Moore gives Charlotte the opportunity to poke fun at some Belgian traits.

For Elisabeth Bekers, too, writing about Charlotte Brontë and *Villette* in *Écrire Bruxelles/Brussel Schrijven*, Charlotte uses Brussels as a means of demonstrating the superiority of the Protestant way of life. She is less interested in painting a picture of the Belgian way of life than in affirming the soundness of British and Protestant values, as exemplified by characters such as Lucy and Graham Bretton, as opposed to Catholic European ones – unlike Thackeray, who in *Vanity Fair* uses the Brussels setting chiefly in order to satirise British society.[91]

For both Demoor and Bekers, Belgium is used by Charlotte to confirm her British identity. The assertion of national identity in confrontation with a foreign culture was voiced in its crudest form by a French writer, Baudelaire ('If you go to Belgium you'll be less severe about your own country. You'll thank God He made you French and not Belgian'),[92] while in the words of a British one, the poet Samuel Rogers, 'The more we become acquainted with the institutions of other countries, the more highly must we value our own.'

The author of a university dissertation entitled *Love versus xenophobia in the works of Charlotte Brontë*, Tina Noens, refers to the confrontation between Continental and British values in Charlotte's novels as a sort of re-enactment of the Battle of Waterloo. Lucy, in the classrooms of the Pensionnat, finds herself defending England and its heroes against France and Napoleon.[93] Waterloo, a scene of victory for the Brontës' hero Wellington, was key to the British sense of national identity and could be seen as the culmination of a centuries-old struggle between French and English values, a culmination that took place on Belgian soil. No Briton in Belgium in 1842 could forget it for long.

Tina Noens explores the 'uneasy balance' in Charlotte's novels between xenophobia and the attraction of the foreign. In common with other Britons who crossed the Channel, Lucy Snowe and Crimsworth would not have left England for Belgium had they not felt the lure of the Continent in the first place – even if, once there, they adhere strongly to their Englishness and display colonial attitudes. An example is Crimsworth's disparaging attitude towards the Flemish, even if he affirms his moral superiority in this respect to the Frenchman Pelet, who treats his Flemish employees like an underclass. Both Lucy's and Crimsworth's sense of national identity is reinforced by their stay in a foreign country. It is true that they both fall in love with foreigners, but in the case of Francis Henri, the foreigner is half-English, an Anglophile who is happy to allow Crimsworth to anglicise her even further before they return to England.[94]

With M. Paul the case is different; both he and Lucy retain their own national characteristics and have to learn to respect each other's. Charlotte was strongly attracted by the 'foreignness' of M. Paul and his real-life originator Heger, although in fact the traits that Lucy finds most appealing in M. Paul are precisely those that distinguish him from the average 'Labassecourien', such as his passionate nature, accounted for by his 'Spanish blood'. Despite mutual attraction the two do not marry and live happily ever after, and in the opinion of some Belgian readers the cultural differences between them played a part in the author's decision not to allow their union.

In discussing Charlotte's xenophobia, some Belgian commentators point out that Lucy comes to realise that xenophobic feelings are not a one-way street, since 'these clowns of Labassecour secretly hate England'. M. Paul, for one, attacks Britons in general and British women in particular, lambasting not just their insolence and pride but their physical appearance (their thin arms and slovenly dress).[95] In fact the woman who becomes Lucy's antagonist, Mme Beck, has a much higher opinion of English women in general than M. Paul does, and employs English nursery governesses for her children:

> She had a respect for 'Angleterre'; and as to 'les Anglaises', she would have the women of no other country about her own children, if she could help it ... she would talk to me ... about England and Englishwomen, and the reasons for what she was pleased to term their superior intelligence, and more real and reliable probity.[96]

Mme Beck's Anglophilia was widespread in Belgium at the time. Charlotte and Emily do appear to have encountered anti-English sentiment among the pupils of the Pensionnat Heger, but one suspects that their own standoffishness had something to do with this.

Whatever she may have said ...

By no means all Belgians reject Charlotte's picture of their country and its inhabitants outright. Some remark on the shrewdness of her observations,

Jacques De Decker describing her as an observer who was 'a little ingenuous, but no fool'.[97] Lucien Christophe, while deploring the spirit in which her observations are made, acknowledges that 'The pictures of Belgian manners sketched by Charlotte Brontë's acerbic pen reveal littlenesses and ridiculous sides to Belgian life that still ring true today. She seized on traits that are permanent ones, and we can still learn from some of her caustic reflections.'[98]

The Brontëite journalist Louis Quiévreux went even further. In 1957 he told his Belgian readers about a BBC TV adaptation of *Villette*, to be seen by British viewers in six weekly instalments starting on 14 July. Belgians could feel proud, he said, that, unusually, the British were going to watch a drama about Brussels. Should the Belgians feel offended by any aspects of the novel? Not in Quiévreux's view. 'The producers of this adaptation of *Villette* have tactfully omitted certain passages about the inhabitants of "Labassecour", such as the "stupidity and vulgarity" of "the natives" or the secret hatred of England felt by "the clowns of Labassecour" … The British don't want our feelings to be hurt.' These precautions were unnecessary, said Quiévreux. 'They needn't worry. We Belgians do not feel hurt. Charlotte Brontë said some pertinent things about us. And if we take umbrage at what she said, what are we to think of Baudelaire and Voltaire, who saw in Belgium only what was ridiculous and base?'[99]

It is not surprising that Belgians are able to be forbearing about Charlotte's remarks in light of the fact that they have forgiven Baudelaire's far more savage attacks. 'Belgium doesn't bear a grudge against him,' in the opinion of the editors of *Pauvre Belgique*.[100] 'We don't bear him any resentment', says the nineteenth-century Belgian writer and politician, Edmond Picard, in an essay on 'the Belgian soul'. In a comment similar to Quiévreux's on Charlotte, he expresses the view there was some foundation for certain of Baudelaire's attacks on Belgium – at any rate, the Belgium of his time.[101]

A charitable explanation of Charlotte's attitudes sometimes advanced by Belgian readers is that she was not in a healthy state of mind during much of her time in the country. For the

▲ Charles Baudelaire (1821–1867).

author of the dissertation *Charlotte Brontë and Brussels*, Charlotte's tendency to the 'hypochondria' (melancholy or depression) of which her characters William Crimsworth and Lucy Snowe are also victims made her see reality as much darker than it was. While she was writing *Villette*, her sombre recollection of Belgium as a place where she had been unhappy made her remember it as an oppressive nightmare in which Belgians seemed hardly human.[102]

This is reminiscent of Baudelaire's mental state while in Belgium. In 1932 the female writer of a column for women readers in the daily newspaper *La Nation Belge* marked the publication of the first complete French translation of *Villette* with an article titled 'Miss Baudelaire'. In it, she compares Charlotte's treatment of Belgians in the novel with the French poet's *Amoenitates Belgicae* (Belgian Pleasures), a collection of satirical poems similar in subject and spirit to his *Pauvre Belgique*. The columnist (who had a childhood recollection of an elderly Louise Heger visiting her school) attributes Charlotte's own attacks to her frustrated love for Heger. She does not appear to feel any ill-will against Charlotte. Rather, she feels compassion for what she suffered in Brussels – the same compassion that she feels for Baudelaire. 'Poor Charlotte, initiated under our sky into the torments of hopeless love, sad Baudelaire, alone and penniless in Brussels, a prey to the torments of the malady that was soon to kill him, kindly Belgium smiles indulgently at your fury. She remembers simply that you were great and that you were, in our country, unhappy.'[103]

Louis Quiévreux, too, coupled Charlotte's name with Baudelaire's, in an article penned after a visit to the Hôtel du Grand Miroir at 28 rue de la Montagne where the French poet spent his two years in Brussels. The building was about to be demolished and it was a last opportunity to walk in Baudelaire's footsteps in the spot where he had suffered and scrawled his acrimonious notes for *Pauvre Belgique*. Recalling Baudelaire's tribulations in Brussels, Quiévreux recounts that the poet's friend Félix Nadar organised a flight in a hot air balloon from Brussels and invited Baudelaire to join the 'aeronauts'. Baudelaire accepted eagerly. It was one means of escaping, if only briefly, from the city he had come to hate but in which his own inertia kept him trapped month after month. The flight took place as planned from the Jardin Botanique, but at the last moment the balloon was found to be too heavy and Baudelaire had to be left behind. Even this rare treat was denied him.

Quiévreux thought of all this as he wandered along the dark, abandoned corridors of the Grand Miroir.

▲ The Hôtel du Grand Miroir where Baudelaire stayed from 1864 to 1866.

> I hardly thought of all the bad things Baudelaire wrote about us Belgians ... I thought only of his unspeakable sufferings, the sufferings of a soul in torment, caused by a physical ill, perhaps the most awful torment that hell can inflict on a human being. I saw him wandering, distraught, full of revulsion, in this city, so beautiful in my eyes, but where nothing spoke to his soul.
>
> Penniless, dreaming of a sudden fortune, he languished here, waiting – for what? Nothing here found grace in his eyes. Everything in Belgium left a taste of ashes in his mouth, as it did, some years earlier, for Charlotte Brontë.[104]

Many Belgians go further than simply forgiving Charlotte. There is satisfaction that she drew such inspiration from her time in Brussels, that her talent was nurtured in Belgium and that she fell in love with a Belgian, a satisfaction expressed in many guide books and newspaper articles. The author of the 'Miss Baudelaire' article considers that 'all Charlotte's mature literary work' was born of her love for Heger. Furthermore, she asserts that Emily's novel, too, sprang indirectly from the same Brussels source, and that Heathcliff's hopeless passion for Cathy must have been inspired by Emily's observance of what her sister suffered from her own hopeless love. In another article she goes still further, claiming that like Charlotte's heroes ('dark little ugly men whose strangeness and violence concealed their exceptional qualities'), Heathcliff too must have been inspired by Heger! 'We Belgians are entitled to feel some pride when we consider that, without the Brontës' stay in Brussels and its consequences, neither *Jane Eyre* nor *Wuthering Heights* – for Emily, like Charlotte, gave her hero many of the traits of the 'Black Swan' – would have enriched world literature.'[105]

Nearer our own time, this gratification in the inspiration that Charlotte drew from her time in Brussels is voiced in a 'Letter to Charlotte Brontë' by the Flemish novelist Kristien Hemmerechts, published in *De Standaard* in the year before the bicentenary of Charlotte's birth.

> Dear Charlotte,
>
> I often think of you. In one of the places where I teach, when I look out of the window I see St Gudule's Cathedral, and I think of your confession ... You were a staunch Protestant, you had a low opinion of Catholics and found them hypocritical and mendacious, and yet on 1 September 1843 you went to confession in the cathedral ... Many people have seen in this confession evidence of sin. They are convinced that you were confessing your forbidden love for Constantin Heger ... You came to Brussels to qualify yourself to open a school in England. ... Nothing came of these plans, but your time in Brussels was crucial for you, and we are proud of that, even though you were hard on our countrymen. You liked our *pistolets* but found our people cold, selfish, inferior, even animal. Ironically, though, you fell in love with one of those annoying Belgians ... Back home in England you transformed Constantin Heger into Edward Rochester, the hero of your masterly novel *Jane Eyre* ... The story flowed from your pen with a force and passion that shocked some readers and critics. ... But the novel became famous, so famous that the world will be commemorating your birth, 200 years ago on 21 April 1816.[106]

In another article, again referring to Charlotte's unflattering comments about the Flemish, Hemmerechts concludes, 'Today offence gives way to pride at this unflattering portrayal. Whatever she may have said, it is thrilling that the great English author wrote about "us".'[107]

---

1   *Revue Trimestrielle*, 1854, Vol. II, pp. 279–83.
2   François, *A Little Britain on the Continent.*
3   Roscoe, *Belgium: In a picturesque tour* (foreword).

4   *Revue Trimestrielle*, 1854, Vol. II, pp. 279–83.
5   Charlotte Brontë to Ellen Nussey in a letter dated July 1842. Smith, *The Letters of Charlotte Brontë*, Volume I, p. 289.
6   *Villette*, Chapter 38.
7   *The Professor*, Chapter 12.
8   *Ibid.*, Chapter 14.
9   Smith, *The Letters of Charlotte Brontë*, Volume I, p. 289.
10 *Villette*, Chapter 7.
11 *Le Soir*, 15 January 1890. The journalist was a woman who wrote under the name of René Gange.
12 *The Professor*, Chapter 7.
13 Christophe, 'Le roman bruxellois de Charlotte Brontë'.
14 *Villette*, Chapter 9.
15 *The Professor*, Chapter 12.
16 *Villette*, Chapter 9.
17 *Ibid.*, Chapter 21.
18 *The Professor*, Chapter 13.
19 *Ibid.*, Chapter 14.
20 *Ibid.*, Chapter 8.
21 De Vries, *Brussels: A cultural and literary history*, p. 93.
22 *La Nation Belge*, 15 September 1929.
23 Demoor, *The Fields of Flanders*, p. 66.
24 *Shirley*, Chapter 5.
25 Harper, Janet, 'Charlotte Brontë's Héger family and their school'. *Blackwood's Magazine*, Vol. 191, No 1158, April 1912, pp. 461–9. Reproduced in Ruijssenaars, *Charlotte Brontë's Promised Land*, pp. 87–92.
26 Source: Brian Bracken, researcher into the Heger family.
27 *The Professor*, Chapter 7.
28 J.R. Scott, *The Family guide to Brussels* (London: C Potter, 1871).
29 *Villette*, Chapter 34.
30 Geert Van Istendael, *Arm Brussel* (Amsterdam: Antwerp: Atlas, 1992), p. 66.
31 *Roe Head Journal*, 1836–37. Bonnell Collection, Brontë Parsonage Museum.
32 *The Professor*, Chapter 7.
33 Gautier, *Un Tour en Belgique*, p. 84.
34 *Villette*, Chapter 9.
35 *Ibid.*, Chapter 20.
36 Letter to Branwell Brontë, 1 May 1843. Smith, *The Letters of Charlotte Brontë*, Volume I, p. 317.
37 *Villette*, Chapter 8.
38 *Ibid.*, Chapter 20.
39 Hymans, *Bruxelles à travers les âges*, Volume III, p. 231.
40 De Pradt, *De la Belgique depuis 1789 jusqu'à 1794*, p. 12.
41 *Villette*, Chapter 27.
42 Bronne, *Léopold Ier et son temps*, p. 150.
43 *Ibid.*, p. 144.
44 Hippolyte Taine, *Philosophie de l'art, dans les Pays-Bas* (Paris: Baillière, 1869), p. 47.
45 *La Nation Belge*, 21 July 1946.
46 *Villette*, Chapter 41.
47 Addison, *Belgium as she is*, pp. 252–5.
48 *Villette*, Chapter 9.
49 Henne, *L'Étranger dans Bruxelles, ou Guide Historique*, p. 83.
50 Open sandwiches: slices of bread and butter or buttered rolls, often with a spread or topping.
51 Texier, *Voyage Pittoresque en Hollande et en Belgique*, p. 269.
52 Louis Blanc, *Lettres sur l'Angleterre* (Paris, 1865). Cited in Robert Gilsoul, *Les influences anglo-saxonnes sur les lettres françaises de Belgique 1850 à 1880* (Brussels: Palais des Académies, 1953), p. 101.
53 Gange, René, 'Une Anglaise à Bruxelles'. *Le Soir*, 15 January 1890.

54   *Villette*, Chapter 13.

55   Smithers, *Observations made during a residence in Brussels*, pp. 135–6.

56   *The Professor*, Chapter 12.

57   *Villette*, Chapter 29.

58   *The Professor*, Chapter 17.

59   *Ibid.*, Chapter 20.

60   Letter to Ellen Nussey, May 1842. Smith, *The Letters of Charlotte Brontë*, Volume II, pp. 284.

61   *La Dernière Heure*, 30 May 1939.

62   An article in *La Nation Belge* on 25 September 1932 describes Charlotte as being perceived during her stay at the Pensionnat as 'revêche', sour or crabbed. In Chapter 12 of *Villette* this same French word is used by Dr John in reference to Lucy.

63   *The Professor*, Chapter 21.

64   Hymans and Rousseau, *Le diable à Bruxelles*, p. 49.

65   *Le Soir*, 15 January 1890.

66   De Pradt, *De la Belgique depuis 1789 jusqu'à 1794*, p. 12.

67   Addison, *Belgium as she is*, p. 254.

68   *Villette*, Chapter 35.

69   *Ibid.*, Chapter 8.

70   *Ibid.*, Chapter 14.

71   *Ibid.*, Chapter 25.

72   Thackeray, *Little Travels and Roadside Sketches*.

73   Bronne, *Léopold Ier et son temps*, p. 160.

74   Janzing, Jolien, *Charlotte Brontë's Secret Love*, p. 91.

75   *Ibid.*, pp. 117–18.

76   *Ibid.*, p. 221.

77   *Villette*, Chapter 14.

78   Gevers, 'Les Brontë en Afrique' in *Revue Générale Belge*, 15 Septembre 1956. The episode is also related in Gevers' travel memoir *Plaisir des Parallèles*, pp. 88–103.

79   *Britse Sporen in Brussel*. Self-guided walk produced by Onthaal en Promotie Brussel.

80   Demoor, *The Fields of Flanders*, p. 63.

81   *Le Soir*, 15 January 1890.

82   *L'Indépendance Belge*, 11 January 1926.

83   *Le Soir*, 3 April 1939.

84   Dimnet, *The Brontë Sisters*, pp. 79–80.

85   *The Professor*, Chapter 8.

86   Texier, *Voyage Pittoresque en Hollande et en Belgique*, p. iv.

87   Thackeray, *Little Travels and Roadside Sketches*.

88   Janet Harper, 'Charlotte Brontë's Héger Family and their school', *Blackwood's Magazine*, Vol. 191, No. 1158, April 1912, pp. 461–9. Reprinted in Eric Ruijssenaars, *Charlotte Brontë's Promised Land*, pp. 87–92.

89   Dominkovits, *Charlotte Brontë and Brussels*.

90   Demoor, *The Fields of Flanders*, p. 69.

91   Acke and Bekers, *Écrire Bruxelles/Brussel Schrijven*, p. 130.

92   Baudelaire, *Pauvre Belgique*, p. 7.

93   *Villette*, Chapter 29.

94   Noens, *Love versus xenophobia in the works of Charlotte Brontë*. Noens is citing Anne Longmuir, '"Reader, Perhaps You Were Never in Belgium?": Negotiating British Identity in Charlotte Brontë's The Professor and Villette', in *Nineteenth-Century Literature* 64:2 (2009), pp. 163–88.

95   *Villette*, Chapter 29.

96   *Ibid.*, Chapter 8.

97   Jacques De Decker, 'Une anglaise et le continent: Charlotte Brontë à Bruxelles', *Le Soir*, 5 June 1991.

98   Christophe, 'Le roman bruxellois de Charlotte Brontë'.

99   *Le Soir*, 14 July 1957.

100 Baudelaire, *Pauvre Belgique*, pp. 207–8 (comment by the editors).

101 Edmond Picard, *L'âme belge* (1897). Reproduced in Aron, *La Belgique artistique et littéraire*, p. 96.

102 Dominkovits, *Charlotte Brontë and Brussels*.

103 *La Nation Belge*, 25 September 1932.

104 Published in Quiévreux, *Bruxelles, notre capitale*, pp. 91–2.

105 *La Nation Belge*, 15 September 1929. Charlotte called Heger the 'Black Swan' in a letter from Brussels to Branwell dated 1 May 1843.

106 *De Standaard*, 29 May 2015.

107 *Ibid.*, 25 April 2008.

CHAPTER FOUR

The Great Capital of the Great Kingdom of Labassecour: Brussels as 'Villette'

IN March 1939 *Time* Magazine reported on the curious case of Major General Sir Reginald Ford, who had recently been appointed Chief Divisional Food Officer for London and the Home Counties. What was odd about the 70-year-old Sir Reginald and his appointment was that he had accepted it only on condition that he could continue to live in Brussels, having made his home there in the comfortable suburb of Uccle. The granting of this request raised eyebrows in the press and the House of Commons, where it was debated heatedly. It had apparently been made with a view to the war that many were convinced was approaching; in peace-time the duties pertaining to the post were less onerous, but even so, there were questions about the suitability of an incumbent resident in Brussels. Sir Reginald shrugged off the criticisms, claiming that his presence was not required in his London office every day and that in any case, 'Heavens, man, I can get to London quicker than I could if I lived in Scotland ... I can hop on the 10 a.m. plane from Brussels and be in my office at 12.30 p.m.'[1]

Unlike some of the British and American journalists who reported on the appointment, a writer in *L'Indépendance Belge* expressed approval of a British citizen opting to commute between Brussels and London fifty years before the advent of the Eurostar made such a lifestyle choice less unusual. In a jocular letter addressed to Sir Reginald, the writer thanked him for the compliment he had paid Brussels and proposed that he be made an honorary citizen of the city. He rejoiced that Ford felt so happy in his cosy house in Uccle in a city where many of his compatriots had also made their home, concluding: 'You have avenged us against that brilliant but annoying Miss Brontë who humiliated our city by calling it 'Villette', in a book still sold widely today in which she said things about our citizens (with one exception) that still vex us. Now, thanks to you, everyone in England knows that today this 'Villette' is a clean, cheerful, hospitable town where you can live well – all the more so as it's cheap.'[2]

Whether or not they see Charlotte's choice of fictional name for Brussels as 'humiliating', Belgian readers of *Villette* often acknowledge the accuracy in many respects of her portrait of the city. 'Villette is the Brussels of the 1840s', states a 1957 guidebook.[3] In the words of the writer Charles Bernard, in an article in *La Nation Belge* marking the 1932 French translation of *Villette*, Charlotte's fictional city is recognisable as the Belgian capital by 'something undefinable but peculiar to the atmosphere of Brussels ... It is a sign of the author's genius that she eliminates everything that is local and specific so as to retain only the universal and extract the very essence of what is true and human in the absolute. While the novel necessarily belongs to its period, it goes well beyond being a study of the manners of that period.'[4] Other Belgian, readers, however, *have* found in *Villette* abundant examples of 'local and specific' elements of Brussels as well as of its essential atmosphere. For the author of an article in 1953, the centenary of the novel's publication, it is 'one of the books in which both the physical city and the soul of Brussels are most sensuously evoked'.[5]

Of course, the novel can be read without making any assocation with Brussels at all. While Belgian readers are intrigued by the view it gives of their capital, some have pointed out that the city Charlotte calls 'Villette' can equally be taken to denote a generic, unspecified town. Indeed, this can be seen as part of Charlotte's intention in giving it an anonymous name. Aside from her wish for anonymity and concealment for herself as the author, in view of the autobiographical nature of much in the novel, she appears not to have wished to tie Lucy's story to a specific place or time. For Elisabeth Bekers in *Écrire Bruxelles/Brussel Schrijven*, this intention is indicated by the generic name of 'Villette'. Although Charlotte based her fictional city on her impressions of the Belgian capital in the 1840s, and described in it actual Brussels places and events, the main focus of the novel, Bekers says, is Lucy's development rather than an examination of the mores of Brussels.[6]

A city described by a writer always becomes a city personal to that particular writer. Delinka Dominkovits's university dissertation on *Charlotte Brontë and Brussels*[7] points out that the realism of people and places in Charlotte's novels is a 'poetic realism'. Giving her city a fictional name is one indication that Villette is a transposition of Brusssels rather than a literal portrait and one way of making it personal to herself. Citing Charlotte's 'We only suffer reality to *suggest* – never to *dictate*',[8] Dominkovits points out that according to Charlotte's own account of her creative process, her fictional characters were often created from the 'germ' of a real person and then took on a life of their own in her imagination.[9] In the same way, Villette, while based on a real place, Brussels, is a city in which the real and the imaginary fuse to create a place personal to Charlotte Brontë. The name chosen, 'small town', is of course an *im*personal one (she is believed to have originally used the even more impersonal name of 'Choseville', echoing Ginevra Fanshawe's first reference to the city as 'chose', 'thing'; in one instance, in Chapter 27, this name slips through the editorial net). There is nothing impersonal, however, about Charlotte's evocation of the city in *Villette*.

Some of her impressions of it are sketchy and imprecise, providing tantalising glimpses of its streets on her rare outings when released from her duties in the Pensionnat. There is no mention of some of its most immediately recognisable landmarks; the monument to the fallen in the 1830 Revolution in Place des Martyrs is referred to but not the Hôtel de Ville, which struck Victor Hugo as 'the dazzling fantasy of a poet fallen out of the head of an architect',[10] or Grand Place, described by another French visitor as 'a chapter of Walter Scott in the middle of a novel by Balzac'[11]. Nor are there panoramic views of the city like those to be found in accounts left by visitors such as Gérard de Nerval. In his *Lorely: Souvenirs d'Allemagne*, Nerval has left a comprehensive picture of Brussels in Charlotte's time. In one passage he paints a panorama of the whole city: the Church of St Gudule on its height, behind it the soaring spire of the Hôtel de Ville and beyond that a confusion of stepped gables, belfries, towers, domes, on to the boulevards circling the city, the glasshouses of the Botanical Gardens glinting in the evening sunlight and the forest of masts on the canal.[12] Hugo sketches the cityscape in a poem about his time lodging in Grand Place. The square provided an imposing setting for the reveries of his time of exile, when he had leisure to dream and look around him. His Brussels is a city of 'high Flemish gables', 'old smoking rooftops' and, above them, 'the flight of the great drunken clouds'.[13]

Charlotte, who spent much of her time in Brussels in the classroom, had fewer glimpses of the open sky. Even her daily exercise was often taken behind the walls of that school garden, and Lucy Snowe spends a lot of time cloistered in the 'convent-like' Pensionnat deep in rue Fossette. The name is suggestive of a quiet enclave, buried away: 'fossé' means 'ditch' and 'fosse' is a pit. (In fact the literal meaning of 'Fossette' is 'dimple'.) It is clearly inspired by rue Isabelle, which was close to but removed from the fashion-

▲ Grand Place in 1843.

able Upper Town. Lucy can hear the life of Villette is going on around her but only its echoes reach her through the open windows of the classrooms – bells ringing from a nearby church, music from a band in the park only five minutes' walk away, carriages rumbling to balls or concerts. The city's streets are glimpsed in passing on Lucy's excursions outside the school, and are not described in detail. She crosses a brightly-lit square which we guess to be in the Upper Town, but she doesn't give it a name. She hurries on an errand across another square in the Lower Town, but all she tells us is that it is half-deserted and neglected, with overgrown paving stones.

The city often becomes not merely a backdrop to Lucy's adventures but a projection of her moods. Villette is a place where, like Charlotte in Brussels, Lucy is often depressed and solitary. It is the sense of her isolation in the city that makes its atmosphere so powerful in the scenes where she gets lost on the night of her first arrival, is driven by solitude to confess in a strange church or drifts alone amidst the crowds in the park at night in a scene startlingly modern in its near surrealism.

Villette is a place where Lucy is often unhappy. But it is also the place where she falls in love and develops emotionally. Louis Quiévreux wrote that *Villette* 'grew out of a love sorrow. It is full of Charlotte Brontë's tenderness, rancour, pain.'[14] She lived through a defining experience in Brussels and was both acutely happy and acutely miserable there. The glimpses of the city are illuminated by a disturbing and haunting light; without even naming Brussels as such, Charlotte Brontë places it more firmly in our imagination than any other novelist.

'An astonishing testimony'

While *Villette* is a city personal to Charlotte Brontë and in one sense a city of her imagination, for Belgian readers it is at the same time unmistakably Brussels. It is curious that it was a foreigner, an outsider who was often homesick in the capital, who has left one of the portraits of it of most interest to readers in Belgium. True, for many of them Charlotte's picture of Brussels and Brussels life is not a pleasant or good-natured one. 'Charlotte Brontë has drawn a cruel picture of our overly cosy, bourgeois life at that period', writes a journalist in 1940.[15] 'The view of Brussels in *Villette* is rather a bitter one,' according to *Le Soir* in 1982.[16] 'She mercilessly depicts the provincial Brussels of the time', in the words of a 2001 literary guide to Brussels.[17].

'She cuts to the quick with her knife of flint'.[18] Echoing the words of her biographer Dimnet, Belgian critics describe her impressions as acerbic, caustic, scathing. Nevertheless, they are so interested by them that they wish she had recorded more. 'What a pity,' lamented Louis Quiévreux in 1953, 'that instead of setting Charlotte and Emily to write essays on Peter the Hermit or the death of Moses, Heger did not ask them to write about what they saw in Brussels.'[19] The writer of an article in *Le Soir* in 1911 also regrets the fact that Charlotte didn't leave more impressions of the capital. At the time of the article, much of the city that she described had already disappeared; the Pensionnat and the Isabelle quarter had only just been razed.[20]

'This curious little book of Brussels memories,' writes a journalist in 1951, 'is all the more interesting given that there are so few chronicles of life in Brussels just after the Revolution.'[21] At that period, most of the novels in the city's bookshops were French: George Sand and Eugène Sue were read avidly, while Belgian novelists were virtually ignored even in their own country. Those writing in Charlotte's time were more interested in the glorious epochs of the country's past – generally when in revolt against foreign rule – than the more prosaic world of post-revolutionary Belgium. Charles de Coster, for example, who has been called the father of Belgian literature, was known for his sprawling epic *The Legend of Thyl Ulenspiegel*, a romance set during the sixteenth-century wars of independence against

Spanish rule. Celebrating Belgium's past was one way of forging the new country's sense of itself as a nation. But the 1840s were a lacklustre period in Belgian literature, whose flowering came later. The nineteenth-century Belgian novelists (many of them little read today) who did leave a picture of Brussels belong to the literary realism movement in the second half of the century. Historians, too, have somewhat overlooked Leopold I's reign, seen as dull and sandwiched between more dramatic epochs – the 1830 Revolution, and the urban and colonial expansion that took place in the reign of Leopold II (1865–1909).

Belgian readers of Charlotte's novels are plunged into mid-nineteenth-century Brussels by passages such as the following:

> I sought her on the Boulevards, in the Allée Verte, in the Park; I sought her in Ste. Gudule and St. Jacques; I sought her in the two Protestant chapels; I attended these latter at the German, French, and English services ...
>
> ... I had crossed the Place Royale and got into the Rue Royale, thence I had diverged into the rue de Louvain – an old and quiet street; I remember that feeling a little hungry and not desiring to go back and take my share of the 'goûter' now on the refectory-table at Pelet's, to wit, pistolets and water – I stepped into a baker's and refreshed myself on a couc? (it is a Flemish word, I don't know how to spell it), a Corinthe-anglice – a currant bun – and a cup of coffee, and then I strolled on towards the Porte de Louvain. Very soon I was out of the city and slowly mounting the hill, which ascends from the gate ...[22]

In the above passage the narrator of *The Professor*, William Crimsworth, having looked for Frances Henri all over Brussels, takes some refreshment on his way to the Protestant cemetery outside the city gates, where he finds her visiting her aunt's grave.

Perhaps the most fascinating aspect of *Villette* and *The Professor* for Belgian readers, writes Jacques de Decker in *Le Soir*, is 'the recording of forgotten details, such as the number of Protestant chapels in the centre of Brussels and the fact that services were in French, English and German – an example of how European Brussels was even then! And *couques aux raisins* were already being sold in rue de Louvain, just a stone's throw from the building where this newspaper is published.'[23]

▲ An artist's impression of the Protestant cemetery in Brussels.

For De Decker, '*Villette* is not very kind towards the capital of the young kingdom of Belgium, but for all that it remains an astonishing testimony of that capital[24] ... When we read *Villette* and *The Professor*, we take a keen pleasure in being able to visit the Belgium of a century and a half ago.'[25] A reviewer of Professor Gustave Charlier's *La Vie Bruxellois dans 'Villette'*, an essay which identifies the real events recreated by Charlotte in the novel, felt inspired to 're-read *Villette* in order to rediscover the true-to-life account of people, places, events observed in Brussels that, in the hands of the great novelist, take on an eternal value.'[26]

Petite grande ville

'Villette': 'little town'. Before we even open the book, Charlotte's use of the diminutive has conveyed the idea of the Belgian capital as small: a place to be considered possibly with mockery but possibly with affection too. There may be mockery in the sentence with which Lucy introduces us to the city's name for the first time, when she tells us that Villette is 'the great capital of the great kingdom of Labassecour',[27] but for the Flemish historian Sophie De Schaepdrijver, writing in 1990, the name is at once ironic and a term of endearment.[28]

Despite Charlotte's references to the mansions of the Haute Ville, betraying the provincial who had seen little of urban sights, the title of the novel suggests that she did not find Brussels to be the kind of great city she had dreamed of in Haworth when she first projected her European stay. It was not a capital such as London, which she had visited for the first time on her way to Belgium. In an early chapter of *Villette*, Lucy records the impact made on her by 'the spirit of this great London which I feel around me', starting with the mass of St Paul's Cathedral next to the inn where she puts up for the night, the 'mighty tone' of whose bell she hears tolling midnight.[29]

In contrast, the 'littleness' of the Belgian capital was the main impression recorded by Thackeray, who visited it around the same time as Charlotte:

> Early the next morning we walked through a number of streets in the place, and saw certain sights. The Park is very pretty, and all the buildings round about it have an air of neatness – almost of stateliness. The houses are tall, the streets spacious, and the roads extremely clean. In the Park is a little theatre, a cafe somewhat ruinous, a little palace for the king of this little kingdom, some smart public buildings (with S. P. Q. B. [*Senatus populus que bruxellinsis*] emblazoned on them, at which pompous inscription one cannot help laughing), and other rows of houses somewhat resembling a little Rue de Rivoli. Whether from my own natural greatness and magnanimity, or from that handsome share of national conceit that every Englishman possesses, my impressions of this city are certainly anything but respectful. It has an absurd kind of Lilliput look with it. There are soldiers, just as in Paris, better dressed, and doing a vast deal of drumming and bustle; and yet, somehow, far from being frightened at them, I feel inclined to laugh in their faces. There are little Ministers, who work at their little bureaux; and to read the journals, how fierce they are! A great thundering Times could hardly talk more big. One reads about the rascally Ministers, the miserable Opposition, the designs of tyrants, the eyes of Europe, &c., just as one would in real journals. The Moniteur of Ghent belabors the Independent of Brussels; the Independent falls foul of the Lynx; and really it is difficult not to suppose sometimes that these worthy people are in earnest. And yet how happy were they *sua si bona norint!*[30] Think what a comfort it would be to belong to a little state like this; not to

▴ The Belgian section of the Great Exhibition of 1851. In the centre is a plaster cast of the statue of Godfrey of Bouillon by Eugène Simonis, which was placed in Place Royale, Brussels, in 1848.

abuse their privilege, but philosophically to use it. If I were a Belgian, I would not care one single fig about politics. I would not read thundering leading-articles. I would not have an opinion. What's the use of an opinion here? Happy fellows! do not the French, the English, and the Prussians, spare them the trouble of thinking, and make all their opinions for them?[31]

Against this condescending stance of an Englishman towards the new country of Belgium can be set the impressions of a Belgian in London in the early 1850s. Lucien Jottrand was a writer and politican who recorded his time in the British capital in *Londres au Point de Vue Belge*, published in 1852. The previous year, his countrymen, along with other tourists from every corner of the globe, had flocked there to visit the Great Exhibition at the Crystal Palace, a symbol of the pride and self-confidence of a country at the height of its imperial ambitions; Charlotte was among the visitors. Belgium was represented at this huge exhibition together with its bigger European neighbours, and Jottrand recorded his gratification at this inclusion of his country, now celebrating just two decades of independence.

Comparing Belgium on the world stage to a shy young debutant at a ball, their gaucherie an object of ridicule to those around them, he argues that it is time for his country to cast off its timidity and become more self-confident. However, his pride that Belgium, small though it was, now existed as a sovereign state and counted for something in the world sits alongside a feeling of humility as he contemplates the sheer scale of the city hosting the exhibition, a city of over two million souls. Many of his impressions focus on that vast scale of London and the immensity of the spectacle it offered.

The contrast in size between the British metropolis and the Belgian capital, which at that time had a population of just 113,000, could not have been starker. Nor could the Belgian observer's modesty and readiness to admire what he saw across the Channel be more different from the supercilious tone so frequently adopted by a Thackeray or a Charlotte Brontë in Brussels.[32]

In the centuries when Belgium had been governed successively from Madrid, Vienna and Paris, Brussels had been little more than the chief city of an outlying province, and a decade or two of independence had not been enough for it to shake off its provincial character. For French visitors like Nerval, whose own capital numbered almost a million inhabitants, the provinciality was generally a negative feature. Brussels was 'at the same time a capital and a provincial town. It is Paris in its luxury and noise, but a big provincial town in the feeling of *ennui* you feel as soon as you enter.'[33] It was 'Parisian life in a narrow circle',[34] a 'petite grande ville.'

In a history of the city, the nineteenth-century writer Louis Hymans humorously relays an account, written in the 1840s, of the impressions of a Parisian visitor who finds himself alone in Brussels on a Sunday. The chronicler appears to have been a Belgian, viewing the capital critically as if through foreign eyes.[35] After morning mass at St Gudule, the French visitor follows the crowds to the park, where he is unimpressed by the spectacle of the Brussels bourgeoisie in their Sunday best. Once the strollers take themselves off to dinner, he calls on his few acquaintances in the city but finds that none of them are 'at home' to visitors, Sundays in Belgium being reserved for family gatherings (still true to this day!). Venturing out in the evening in search of diversion after a day of tedium, the Parisian finds that all those who were in the park earlier are now on the boulevards and the fashionable Allée Verte (the Champs Elysées of Brussels, leading to the village and royal palace of Laeken). The visitor rounds off the day's entertainment with an hour or two in one of the city's dark, noisy, smoke-filled hostelries, and goes to bed reflecting on the soporific nature of the amusements available in Brussels.

While admitting the Belgian capital's deficiencies with respect to Paris, Hymans defends 1840s Brussels from the charge of being soporific. On his second Sunday in the city, Hymans says, the French visitor will have a much better time. He will by now have acquired friends, who invite him to whist parties, *soirées dansantes*, or one of the *cercles* (clubs) where the city's male inhabitants whiled away their evenings (M. Pelet, Crimsworth's employer, belongs to several such clubs). Pointing out that the Belgian capital had 50 hotels, hundreds of inns and, with its theatres and museums, was by no means short of diversions, Hymans concludes that Sunday in Brussels in the 1840s was not much less amusing than in other capitals. Nevertheless, many observers' testimonies confirm that it retained something of the small-town atmosphere that Belgian readers detect in *Villette*.

In Charlotte Brontë's time the faubourgs had not yet swallowed up all the surrounding fields. In the summer of 1843 Charlotte, at a loose end in the deserted Pensionnat, often went walking in the countryside around Brussels, and in her time this countryside was never far away. William Crimsworth tells us that 'No inhabitant of Brussels need wander far to search

▲ The Allée Verte.

for solitude'; on his Sunday walk he finds himself, only a short walk from the Porte de Louvain, among fields spreading to the horizon.[36]

The countryside could even be found *within* the city gates. Many of the Belgian immigrants to the capital were peasants who retained their country habits and traditions in the heart of the city. Brussels was still a

▲ The Boulevard du Jardin Botanique.

▲ The Porte de Hal, the only one of the old fortified city gates still standing in Charlotte's time.

town of green spaces where laundry was spread out to dry, and of *étangs* (ponds) like the one near the Porte de Hal, lone survivor of the medieval city gates, where horses were taken to drink in the evening. These *étangs* dotted in and around Brussels, a town built on marshy terrain, can be found in its parks and squares to this day. They make appearances in *The Professor* and *Villette,* as when Crimsworth rescues a pupil from drowning on a rowing excursion.

The writer and politican Edmond Picard recalled the 1840s city of his youth as

'a provincial town that was only slowly getting used to its role as a new capital, still bound by the ring of the old ramparts where the toll gates now stood, a town of quiet streets and sleepy squares with grass growing between the paving stones, with a park that was no more than a big garden surrounded by a hedge. On the spot in Place Royale where Godfrey of Bouillon straddles his horse today grew a spindly young Tree of Liberty [planted when the country was annexed by the French Republic] protected by a wooden frame. On nights when the moon was full, the street lamps were not lit. In the bell tower of the Église de la Chapelle, a watchman kept a lookout for fire through the night and blew a horn each hour to prove that he hadn't fallen asleep...[37]

This is recognisable as the town that Lucy describes, for example on her excursion to the old Basse Ville to visit Mme Walravens, even to the grass in the deserted square where the old woman lives.

> It was quiet, grass grew between the broad grey flags, the houses were large and looked very old – behind them rose the appearance of trees, indicating gardens at the back. Antiquity brooded above this region, business was banished thence. Rich men had once possessed this quarter, and once grandeur had made her seat here.[38]

Not long after Charlotte departed it, this sleepy town was already being replaced by a modern, geometrically planned metropolis with streets meeting at right angles and spreading ever outward in an inexorable march of new faubourgs. The countryside was soon much further away, and even in her time the old-fashioned ways of the Lower Town were starting to disappear.

Later in the century, when Charlotte Brontë's Brussels had been replaced under Leopold II by a modern capital of wide, straight streets, people remembered with nostalgia the intricate tangle of narrow crooked ones described in *Villette*. Lucy tells us of becoming 'immeshed in a network of turns'.[39] Overhanging these streets were tumble-down lop-sided houses with projecting upper storeys. Particularly dilapidated were those backing onto the Senne, whose garden walls were lapped by its waters. The river flooded frequently, adding to the risk of typhoid and cholera. Commonly described as an open-air sewer, impossibly polluted by the printing works, breweries and dyeworks that lined its banks – the industries whose wheels it worked and whose waste it received – the Senne, while a source of disease, was also a placid, meandering river that formed an essential part of the life of the city and seemed to express its soul.

Baudelaire found no charm in this this provinciality. For him, Brussels was a sad, insipid town in which everyone looked half asleep ('only the dogs are alive', he said, while complaining of their incessant barking). He scrawled the words 'petite ville' in page after page of the notebooks in which he recorded his disgust and contempt at everything he witnessed.

'Petite ville,' he wrote, 'petits esprits, petits sentiments' ('little town, little minds, little sentiments').[40]

▲ The River Senne.

Alexandre Dumas could be as denigrating about Belgium as some of his compatriots. However, in the first impressions of Brussels that open his *Excursions sur les bords du Rhin* (1842) he paints an endearing picture. Belgian commentators have cast doubt on the veracity of many details in his account, but the sense conveyed of the small and modest scale of everything in the little capital was doubtless true enough. He relates how, on arriving at the Royal Palace with a letter of recommendation for King Leopold, he gained admittance to Leopold's private secretary and *éminence grise*, Jules Van Praet, 'more rapidly than I would have been admitted to the office of a second-rate banker in Paris.' Since Leopold, as was his wont, was not in Brussels but at his Laeken residence, Dumas made his way there and was at once admitted to see the monarch. (This might have had something to do with the fact that Dumas was friendly with one of Leopold's in-laws, a member of the French royal family, a detail he omits to mention.) After his interview with the King, Dumas returned to Brussels and went into a café to look at the newspapers. Reading that a woman whose body had been found in the canal at Laeken was rumoured to be a former mistress of the King who had been drowned on his orders, he turned to the man at the next table to express his surprise at the freedom of the Belgian press and found his neighbour to be none other than the King's secretary Van Praet, his host at the Palace earlier that morning, who was quietly eating a modest repast of two boiled eggs. Van Praet read the proffered article without batting an eyelid, merely remarking that journalists had to make a living. Then, as the King was at Laeken and his secretary did not appear to be overburdened with work, he offered to spend the rest of the day showing their French visitor the sights of the city.[41]

King Leopold's court was known for being somewhat low-key, particularly in the early years of his reign before he had won over the many members of the nobility and *haute bourgeoisie* who still supported the Dutch King William. Dumas' impressions chime in with Graham Bretton's lofty verdict in *Villette* on the court of the King of Labassecour as 'one of the compact little minor European courts, whose very formalities are little more imposing than familiarities, and whose gala grandeur is but homeliness in Sunday array.'[42]

Another writer who conveyed a sense of the small scale of everything Belgian as something charming was Robert Henry Addison. Addison, an Irish-born journalist and playwright who lived in Belgium for a time, took advantage of the flow of British tourists to the country in the wake of Waterloo to produce several guide books providing practical advice for Britons intending to settle there. Addison's Brussels is a gay, lively and inviting capital. His boundless enthusiasm paints the upper town (the lower he found 'dirty and irregular') as a delightful place full of English amenities.

The Flemish writer and Brontë admirer Leen Huet, who devotes several pages to Charlotte Brontë and *Villette* in her book *Mijn België*, writes about her discovery of Addison's Belgium after stumbling on his guide book, published at the time that Charlotte was in Brussels. Huet speculates that Charlotte might have had the book under her arm in her perambulations around the city. Huet's fascination in Addison's Belgium parallels that of Belgian readers of *Villette* and *The Professor*; like many Belgians, she welcomes the chance to see what she describes as her 'dull birthplace' illuminated by a new light when viewed through foreign eyes. In Addison's guide book, the light is a rosy one.

Huet is struck and touched by the newness of the little kingdom of Belgium as described by Addison only a decade after its creation. The impressions she gleans from him are reminiscent of Thackeray's 'Lilliputian' Brussels:

> Now, almost 160 years later, *Belgium As She Is* gives an impression of youthful innocence. In the same way as children play at houses, so the brand-new Belgians played the game of 'little country'. And they wanted an army, a colony, heirs to the throne; there were balls in the winter, boulevards with four rows of trees, trains, a spa, canals under construction – even a dentist who could stop the worst tooth decay with an amalgam of metals. Addison holds the nation up to the light as if it were a shiny new marble: for a moment, his readers are full of wonder at that clear, pristine surface, that fierce spiral of colour within.[43]

Contemporary impressions of Brussels thus confirm the aptness of Charlotte's name for the Belgian 'petite grande ville', a still small city with big ambitions for the future. Sophie De Schaepdrijver finds that Charlotte had a keen eye for the contradictions of 1840s Brussels, a brand-new capital that had retained deeply provincial habits,[44] while for Jacques De Decker, Charlotte's depiction of the capital bears witness to 'the ambivalent status of a city both modest and already destined to an international vocation'.[45]

A tale of two cities

Addison's enthusiasm was for the proud newness of the Haute Ville, the town of the affluent *rentiers*, and not for the commercial and predominantly working-class Basse Ville. The natural geographical division of Brussels into hill and valley, with the river Senne in the latter, split it picturesquely into two towns. Charlotte, in rue Isabelle, was housed in a genteel middle-class enclave on the hill linking these two different towns, a few minutes' walk both from the imposing buildings at the top and the teeming tenements of Dickensian squalor below. On leaving the Pensionnat, she generally headed up the hill towards the wide, well-lit streets of the Haute Ville, but sometimes she descended into the dark and sinister ones of the lower town, as does Lucy Snowe in *Villette*.

'Modern and brilliant on the outside, the capital of a people that is still young, Brussels encloses in its interior an ancient, solemn town', according to a Belgian guide to the city published in 1844.[46] For the American Brontëite Adeline Trafton, visiting in 1869, 'The old city of Brussels is crooked, and dull, and picturesque; but joined to it – like an old man with a gay young wife – is the beautiful Paris-like upper town, with its houses covered with white stucco'.[47] The Haute Ville with its healthy air was the home of ambassadors, dowagers walking spaniels and fashionable doctors. The lower town in the valley of the murky Senne housed not just the architectural treasures of the city's past but the cholera-ridden slums that were the shame of its present.

For the British politician and traveller Emerson Tennent, the ascent from the old town to the new was 'something like coming suddenly into the daylight from the dim scenery of a melodrama.'[48] Nerval had a similar impression: 'There are quarters plunged in abysses, others with snowy rooftops like the Alps'.[49] In the 'alpine' regions were rue Royale with its double row of gas candelabra (Brussels was the first town on the Continent to have gas lighting), and the Parisian-type shops of rue de la Madeleine and rue Montagne de la Cour, whose wares were displayed in large windows unlike the small leaded ones of the shops in the lower town. Down in the 'abyss', everything was dark.

In the view of the authors of a book on Belgian society published in 1851, the populations of the upper and lower towns belonged to two completely different worlds, two 'colonies' that existed in isolation from each other. These two colonies spoke different languages: French in the new town, a Flemish dialect of Dutch in the old. They kept different hours and wore different fashions. While the denizens of the Upper Town wore Parisian fashions, in the lower you could still see working-class women wearing the traditional *faille*, a black hooded shawl introduced during the period of Spanish rule, worn over the head and shoulders and falling down the front of the skirt like an apron.[50] The dress of the 'freshly and trimly attired foreign figures' Crimsworth sees hurrying to mass at the Church of St Jacques sur Coudenberg in the Haute Ville[51] is in contrast with that of

◀ A woman wearing the traditional Brussels 'faille'.

Mme Walravens' servant in the old town, who wears 'a very antique peasant costume, a cap … with long flaps of native lace, a petticoat and jacket of cloth, and sabots more like little boats than shoes'.[52]

The contrast between upper and lower towns forms part of the Brussels backdrop in *Villette*. Elisabeth Bekers writes that Lucy's initial positive impressions of the Upper Town with its 'buildings of palatial splendour'[53] are replaced by more sombre ones of the Basse Ville later in the novel, as when she wanders into the deserted square where old Mme Walravens lives. Bekers suggests that Lucy comes to see beneath the glamour that initially impresses her and perceive the neglect in some of the old quarters.[54] In the 1840s the old town was indeed neglected, with numerous public buildings in a state of disrepair. The dilapidated state of many of the capital's streets and buildings was as common a complaint then as it is today. Following independence, the city council was chronically short of funds. Until the outlying *faubourgs* started to be brought under the city administration in the 1850s, it was unable to raise enough money in taxes to fund the growing costs of Brussels as a capital. To add to its problems, much work was needed to repair the damage done in the fighting in the 1830 uprising. Another reason for the abandoned houses noted by Lucy in the Basse Ville was that the old families of Brussels had for generations been deserting their ancestral homes in the centre for houses in newer parts of town.

In *Villette* the play of new town versus old is used to reflect Lucy's state of mind. The city is often portrayed as the bright Haute Ville when she is upbeat – on her way to taste its pleasures with the Brettons, for example – and as a different, darker town, that of the Basse Ville, in moments of depression. In the upper town she is often in the company of her English friends; to the lower she mostly ventures alone, and has solitary encounters with *Bruxellois* and with Catholicism. In the 'grim' Basse Ville she experiences her darkest time of crisis, fainting in its streets after confessing to a Catholic priest. In a dusty bric-a-brac shop kept by an 'old Jew broker' she buys the bottle in which she buries Graham Bretton's letters and any hope of her love for him being returned. In an ancient house she learns the story of M. Paul's past, a story that shows him to be connected with a household in the Basse Ville.

The Old Town of Brussels provided Charlotte with a rich stock of Gothic elements that transformed it in her imagination into a place not just of mouldering buildings but of hunchbacked dwarfs and medieval interiors with 'arched passages' and 'mystic winding stairs'. Elisabeth Bekers points out that the Gothic elements incorporated by Charlotte were a staple feature of horror tales such as Mrs Radcliffe's, in which English Protestant heroines were the victims of abductions and macabre crimes in remote locations on the Catholic mainland. Lucy Snowe does not fall altogether within this tradition in that she is not abducted but goes to a Catholic country of her own free will, her story takes place in an urban setting rather than a haunted castle, and the novel, in many respects, belongs to the genre of realism rather than romance. As Bekers says, though, Charlotte's use of typically Gothic and Catholic leitmotifs, such as the ghostly nun who haunts the Pensionnat and the ever-watchful priest, is in a tradition of depicting foreignness and Catholicism in a sinister light. In the chapter entitled 'Malevola' in which we are first introduced to Mme Walravens, Belgian readers can view their capital metamorphosed into an eerie fairyland. ('Hoar enchantment here prevailed; a spell had opened for me elf-land – that cell-like room ... that arch and passage, and stair of stone, were all parts of a fairy tale.')[55]

One reference in *Villette* to the Basse Ville, however, is a realistic one. Lucy refers to her visits to the 'poor and crowded quarter of the city' accompanying 'Dr John' (Graham Bretton) on his errands of mercy. Charlotte would have caught glimpses of such quarters, for the slums were no more than a few steps away from the Haute Ville. Leading off the capital's most fashionable street, rue de la Madeleine, were dark, damp *impasses* (dead-end alleyways), hardly penetrated by sunlight, where thronged some of the town's poorest inhabitants, haggard and wan from lack of light and oxygen, their children tuberculous and scrofulous. The average life expectancy in the worst districts was 18, lower even than the average age of death (25) in the insalubrious Haworth in the same period. All the conditions were in place for the outbreaks of cholera that carried off hundreds of the city's inhabitants. Among the victims in 1842 was Martha Taylor, the sister of Charlotte's schoolfriend Mary, who died of the disease at her boarding school in the Koekelberg district.

Charlotte might have heard the city's social problems referred to by Heger, who, like Dr John, did something towards alleviating them. He is known to have done good works among the poor as a member of the Society of St Vincent de Paul. The Belgian section of this charitable organisation (the saint himself, St Vincent, is mentioned by Charlotte in *Villette*),[56] founded in France in 1833 to help Parisian slum dwellers, started up in the early 1840s. In *Charlotte Brontë's Secret Love*, Jolien Janzing highlights the horrendous conditions in the city's slums as the shameful underbelly of the hedonistic, pleasure-loving city which seduces Charlotte with its culture and good living. In Janzing's novel it is Heger who shows Charlotte the dismal alleys of this other Brussels when she accompanies him to his evening classes for working men.

Not everything was grim down in the Basse Ville, however. The city planners who razed much of it later in the century saw it in terms of its problems, but the lower town knew how to enjoy itself, in a manner aptly summarised by *Villette's* 'Eat, drink and live'. Every street had its unpretentious taverns with rows of oak tables under smoke-blackened joists. 'Brussels stopped eating only to drink,' in the words of the novelist Camille Lemmonier, who recorded his memories of the 1850s city of his childhood.[57] 'Nothing can be done in Belgium without smoking and drinking ...

◀ A Brussels
association
marching in
procession in
the late 19th
century.

The *faro* pumped in a single day would work a mill with several wheels,' in the opinion of Amédée Saint-Férreol, a French *proscrit* who was in Brussels in the same period.[58]

The city's inhabitants were devoted to tradition and to associations of all kinds, ranging from centuries-old guilds such as the Grand Serment des Arbalétriers (the Guild of Crossbowmen, which, as will be seen, had a close association with rue Isabelle) to a host of other societies. Each of them marched proudly with banners and ensigns to the rolling of drums on every possible occasion, celebrating kings, patron saints, anniversaries. On fête days not only was one of Brussels' tiniest inhabitants, Manneken Pis, dressed up for the occasion, but the city's largest citizens, the 'giants' of old legends, were paraded in its streets. There was a whole family of these giants, benevolently smiling figures whose nodding heads were on a level with the balconies decked with greenery. On fête days every street and square rang with military music and the placid city erupted into a bacchanalia.

'No other people love so much to enjoy themselves, and are amused by so little, as the Belgians,' wrote Saint-Férreol.[59] Verlaine, hearing the muted sounds of revelry in the streets from within the cell in the Petits-Carmes Prison where he spent the first weeks of his prison sentence, reflected that 'Brussels is the most good-naturedly cheerful, fun-loving town I know.'[60]

Although Lucy describes scenes of animation in the Haute Ville such as the fête in the park, her impressions of the Lower Town are of a sombre place rather than the jolly, sensual one evoked by Jolien Janzing in her description of the carnival celebrations in *Charlotte Brontë's Secret Love*. When Charlotte was taken to see the carnival by M. Heger, her comment in a letter was, 'The Carnival was nothing but masking and mummery ... It was animating to see the immense crowds and the general gaiety – but the masks were nothing.'[61] It is rather difficult to imagine her entering into the spirit of a Brussels fête day, and Lucy Snowe, in her encounters with Labassecouriens at the Pensionnat, does not appear to appreciate the rough, hearty good-nature that characterises Villette's inhabitants. In Charlotte's comment that it was animating to see the gaiety in the streets, however, perhaps there is a hint that part of her might have liked to join the dance.

In *Charlotte Brontë's Secret Love*, 'dissolute Brussels', with its relaxed Continental mores, is a place of desires and temptations where English inhibitions may be relaxed. It is also the scene of Charlotte's sexual awakening: 'It was here, in this mysterious city so far from home, that she would first become a real woman.'[62] In Janzing's novel it is Brussels, as well as Heger, that changes Charlotte into a different person from the virginal girl who leaves Haworth at the start of the novel. On frequent sallies into the centre, she is shown the sights, sounds and smells of a Brussels as pullulating with life as a scene by Brueghel. She ventures into the working-class parts of town around the canal, actually meets an inhabitant of the lower town, the Flemish workman Emile, and enters a tavern with him. The real Charlotte was fascinated by Brussels but never felt part of the life of the city, observing it as a detached and amused onlooker. The fictional Charlotte in the novel is pulled much closer into the life of the Brussels streets.

'A precise and diligently observed reality'

Charlotte's literary intention was not to give a detailed account of Brussels or make it immediately identifiable, and certain features of the city make no appearance in *Villette*. To take one example, she makes no mention of a custom that struck all visitors: the use of dog-drawn carts, used, in particular, by women and children selling milk. One animal employed for this purpose, a fictional dog called Patrasche, and his Flemish child owner Nello, were the heroes of the British writer Ouida's *A Dog of Flanders* (1872), a tale that has become so popular in Japan that a statue of the pair has been erected in Antwerp to please Japanese tourists. These working dogs were to be seen toiling in the streets in Charlotte's time and were still very much in evidence when Adeline Trafton, remembered today as the first literary pilgrim after Mrs Gaskell to write an account of a visit to the Pensionnat, visited Brussels in 1869 and dubbed it 'the paradise and purgatory of dogs':

> Scores of strings, with a poodle at one extremity and a woman at the other, may here be seen, with little rugs laid upon the ground for the pink-eyed puff-balls to rest upon. Truly Brussels is the paradise and purgatory of dogs. Anywhere upon the streets you may see great, hungry-eyed animals dragging little carts pushed by women; and it

◀ A Belgian dog cart, used to deliver milk.

is difficult to determine which is the most forlorn – the dog, the cart, or the woman. We never understood before what it was to 'work like a dog'.

Charlotte and Emily must have noticed the hard-worked dogs in the Lower Town as well as the spoiled pooches of the Upper. One can imagine Emily, in the tradition of generations of intrepid English female travellers who have rescued bullied donkeys and stray cats the world over, rushing to the defence of a working dog in the streets of Brussels. But none of Emily's impressions of the city were left to posterity, and Charlotte makes no reference to this curiosity of Belgian life. The only dog mentioned in *Villette* is the pampered school spaniel Sylvie, a favourite with M. Paul.

Other features of Brussels, however, are faithfully recorded in *Villette* and *The Professor*, providing many instances of the precision and minute observation of the Brussels setting pointed out by Gustave Charlier.[63] In contrast to the atmospheric, if vivid, sketchiness of some of the city scenes, we get the occasional precise snapshot of some detail of life in the capital in the 1840s. The carriage in which Lucy is being taken to a concert by the Brettons rolls through one of the city gates and the guards carry out a summary inspection. This tells us that in the Brontës' time the entrances to

▲ The toll gate at the Porte de Louvain.

the city were still guarded. The massive fortified gates of earlier centuries had gone, replaced by modern ones, but because a toll (not abolished until 1860) was still exacted for goods entering the city, there were toll booths manned by guards who searched incoming vehicles – or in some cases, if Charlotte is to be believed, made a 'pretence of inspection'.

The novels record the city's weather patterns: its overcast sky, the days when 'a clammy fog from the marshes crept grey' round the town,[64] the freezing cold of winter, and the summer heatwaves punctuated by thunder storms like the one that overtakes Crimsworth and Frances on their way home from visiting the cemetery, and the one that traps Lucy in Mme Walravens' house while she waits for its fury to abate.

Charlotte also records the black stoves that were used in Belgium to heat the rooms, instead of open fires as in England. Both Lucy and Crimsworth refer to these ubiquitous contraptions, generally a 'dismal-looking'[65] black, though Mlle Reuter's parlour boasts a more genteel green porcelain one. While acknowledging the effectiveness of these ugly stoves, Crimsworth welcomes the more familiar and cheerful sight, for an Englishman, of a wood fire burning in Francis Henri's lodgings. The British traveller Henry Smithers disliked these Belgian stoves:

> The mode of warming the rooms is very disagreeable; the chimneys are closed, and wood is principally burnt in iron stoves, which project into the room, and a long iron pipe goes up the chimney; after a company has been some time in a room thus heated, and the door closed, it becomes quite suffocating and unwholesome.[66]

Like William Crimsworth, the French *proscrit* Amédée Saint-Férreol missed the wood fires of his home country, which might have afforded him and his fellow exiles in the 1850s some consolation for the rigours of the Brussels climate. He complained of the use of coal in their stead:

> The sun is pallid, the climate humid; the winters are long, the heat short-lived but stifling, the changes in temperature sudden and frequent; moreover, not only is one deprived of the generous wine that cheers and warms the blood, but coal, covering everything in thick soot and dense smoke, replaces the bright, crackling wood fires beside which, poker in hand and feet on the fender, one builds such wonderful castles in the air.[67]

Lucy Snowe becomes reconciled to the stoves at Mme Beck's, which she comes to see as 'dark comforters' when she is despondent and suffering from the 'severity of a continental winter'. She is often to be found huddled by their warmth.

> I remember the black stoves pleased me little when I first came; but now I began to associate with them a sense of comfort, and liked them, as in England, we like a fireside.[68]

Another feature of life in Brussels is noted by the observant Lucy on her first arrival in the city by coach on a cold, wet evening in early March.

> We passed through a gate where soldiers were stationed – so much I could see by lamplight; then, having left behind us the miry Chaussée, we rattled over a pavement of strangely rough and flinty surface.[69]

The street paving of Brussels was often commented on critically by foreign visitors. Its paving stones seem to have been particularly inhospitable, and this, added to the uneven terrain, made progress up and down its steep streets difficult for both man and beast. For Gérard de Nerval, one distinctly provincial aspect of the capital was its 'detestable little irregular paving stones, like nail heads'. He claimed that it was like walking on eggshells; you risked twisting your ankle at every step. When it rained, the gaps between the stones put your ankles at risk of getting soaked as well as sprained: 'The street becomes a sort of archipelago, with each cobblestone like a lilliputian islet'.[70] He attributed the unusually high number of lame people in the capital to this cause. An added hazard was the Brussels housewives' mania for scrubbing the pavements and washing down the streets even when it was raining.

The hard paving made for noisy traffic. Although rue Fossette itself, like its real-life originator, rue Isabelle, is 'well-paved' and quiet, from within the Pensionnat Lucy can hear 'the ceaseless roll of wheels on the tormented pavement' of the streets around.[71]

Beyond the city, the paved chaussées were so hard on carriage wheels that a guide book advised travellers to drive on the unpaved ground at the side.[72] The Belgian roads were a subject of complaint by Byron when one of his carriages broke down between Bruges and Ghent en route to Italy in

1816. A century later, the country's roads were still poor according to Octave Mirbeau, who reported that all four of his car tyres burst after he journeyed from Paris to Brussels in one of the first motor cars.

The pavements for pedestrians, inadequate or lacking in Charlotte's time, are still a subject of complaint today, residents and tourists alike objecting not just to fouling by the city's dogs but to loose paving stones hazardous to ankles. On rainy days it can feel as if the risk of finding yourself ankle-deep in a puddle is as high as in the time of Gérard de Nerval, warily negotiating the paving stones of Brussels in the 1840s with his Parisian boots. 'People here wear very stout shoes,' he observed.

Lastly, a notable feature of nineteenth-century Brussels, and one that some visitors also found objectionable, was a device that facilitated the spying habits recorded in *Villette*.

Charlotte was not the only foreign observer to perceive Brussels as a city of spies. For the French visitors Nerval and Baudelaire, it was a town in which everyone seemed to be constantly watching everyone else. Baudelaire wrote of the Belgians' obsessive curiosity about their neighbours. Nerval noted that while many women appeared to spend the day closeted indoors – possibly a relic of Spanish customs – the fact that they appeared little at their windows and balconies did not prevent them from knowing everything that was going on in the street, thanks to hinged mirrors attached to the window casements that allowed them to see without being seen.[73] These were often remarked on by visitors. Adeline Trafton tells us that there was

> 'a little mirror outside of every window, placed at an angle of forty-five degrees, so that Madame, sitting within, can see all that passes upon the street, herself unseen.'[74]

Théophile Gautier tells us that these concentric mirrors were placed outside in such a way that the image caught in them was reflected in another mirror placed on a table inside.[75]

Frances Trollope noted these devices on houses all over Belgium. 'By means of mirrors placed on the outside of the drawing-room windows, those who sit within are enabled to see all that passes without; and yet never be guilty of the indecorum of appearing at the window.'

However, by her own account the decorum of the watchers within did not always prevent them from being seen by those without:

As these machines are arranged with hinges, which admit every variety of position, they are not infrequently so placed as to present to the passer-by, the reflection of a pretty face, while the person to whom it belongs is safely esconced within. The first time I saw one of these contrivances, my attention was drawn to it by the vision of a young bright-looking countenance, peeping at me from amidst a profusion of ringlets; and as it was surrounded by a square frame, I thought, at the first glance, that it was a picture, hung out of the window to show that portraits, done in the same style, were to be seen within. A few steps ... showed me who the artist was.[76]

In fact these mirrors, which were common in the Netherlands as well as Belgium, served a practical purpose. With their aid, Madame or Mademoiselle, occupied on an upper floor, could see at a glance who was at the door and instruct the servant accordingly. Visitors to the city, however, took them to be an indication of the predilection for spying so often noted by Baudelaire as well as by Charlotte Brontë. For the French poet, the mirrors at the windows were a sign of some of the worst of the Brussels characteristics he enumerated: *ennui*, stupid curiosity, laziness. The capital's 'esprit de petite ville', small-town mentality, he claimed, made it a place of gossip and scandal-mongering where 'universal and reciprocal distrust' reigned.[77] People 'listened at doors, made holes in doors'.[78]

In *Villette* this aspect of life is so all-pervading that scores of academic papers have discussed the theme of spying and surveillance in the novel. Examples of how Mme Beck employs these tactics to control the girls and teachers under her watch, not only spying herself but employing her under-lings to do it for her, are so numerous that they fill pages. Lucy tells us that Madame, shod in her 'shoes of silence', would 'glide ghost-like through the house, watching and spying everywhere, peering through every keyhole, listening behind every door'.[79] M. Paul, too, spies on Lucy and others without scruples. In common with other Protestant critics of perceived Catholic or 'Jesuitical' behaviour, Charlotte regarded such habits as a feature of life in a Catholic country. 'We were under the surveillance of a sleepless eye: Rome watched jealously ... through that mystic lattice,' claims Lucy, referring to the opening in a confessional.[80]

In page after page, Charlotte conveys this atmosphere of secrecy and distrust without any specific references to mirrors attached to windows.

But there are in fact two references in the novel to just such contrivances. The first is when M. Paul informs Lucy that he uses a mirror as an aid when watching the Pensionnat garden from his room in the adjoining boys' school, a room he has rented expressly for the purpose of observing 'female human nature', as he puts it.[81]

And an earlier chapter would seem to indicate that Charlotte was aware of the window mirrors on Brussels houses. In Chapter 10, Lucy is sitting in the same room as Dr John, who has come to the Pensionnat to tend one of Mme Beck's children and is waiting for Madame to receive him. Lucy, ostensibly hard at work at her sewing, is in reality observing the handsome young doctor, to whom she is already becoming attracted (the Protestant Lucy, shadow-like and unobserved in her corner, does as much surreptitious watching of others as any of the Catholic characters she criticises – as did Charlotte herself). Suddenly Dr John, becoming aware of her gaze, asks her why she is observing him. What is it that has made him realise that her eyes are upon him?

> I saw that his notice was arrested, and that it had caught my movement in a clear little oval mirror fixed in the side of the window recess – by the aid of which reflector Madame often secretly spied persons walking in the garden below.

Were there any such mirrors in the casement windows of the Pensionnat Heger? We do not know, but Charlotte must surely have seen them at the windows of other houses in Brussels. They were known as *espions*, spies. For Edmond Texier, who perceived Brussels as a city where people were as curious about their neighbours as in the small towns in the south of France – where, incidentally, the equivalent of the Belgian *espions* were the spyholes in front doors – the window mirrors for seeing what was going on in the street were yet another sign of the Belgian capital's provinciality.[82]

It is just one of many details in *Villette* that bear out Gustave Charlier's remark that the novel unfolds against 'a backdrop of a precise and diligently observed reality'.[83]

The reference in *Villette* to the *espions* at windows is one of the images caught in the mirror that Charlotte Brontë held up to the Brussels of her time. The little mirrors on the outside of houses in fact remained a common sight well into the twentieth century, but the provincial city reflected in

Villette, to the fascination of Charlotte's Belgian readers, was soon to vanish for ever.

1   *Time*, 6 March 1939.
2   *L'Indépendance Belge*, 25 February 1939.
3   Biebuyck, *Bruxelles: ville en forme de cœur*.
4   *La Nation Belge*, 22 August 1932.
5   *Le Soir*, 22 July 1953.
6   Acke and Bekers, *Écrire Bruxelles/Brussel Schrijven*, p. 132. Bekers is quoting from Kate E. Brown, 'Catastrophe and the City. Charlotte Brontë as Urban Novelist', in *Nineteenth-Century Literature* 57, 3, 2002, p. 368.
7   Dominkovits, *Charlotte Brontë and Brussels*.
8   Letter to Ellen Nussey, Smith, *The Letters of Charlotte Brontë*, Volume II, p. 285.
9   Letter to George Smith, 6 December 1852. Smith, *The Letters of Charlotte Brontë*, Volume III, p. 88.
10 Letter to his wife Adèle, 17 August 1837.
11 Emile Montégut, *Les Pays-Bas: impressions de voyage et d'art* (Paris: Germer Baillière, 1869), p. 59.
12 Nerval, *Oeuvres*, p. 812.
13 In the poem *À Jules Janin* (1854).
14 Quiévreux, 'Bruxelles, les Brontës et la famille Héger'.
15 *La Meuse*, 5 February 1940.
16 *Le Soir*, 19 February 1982.
17 Joël Goffin, *Sur les pas des écrivains à Bruxelles* (Brussels: Éditions de l'Octogone, 2001).
18 Dimnet, *The Brontë Sisters*, p. 83.
19 Quiévreux, 'Bruxelles, les Brontës et la famille Héger'.
20 *Le Soir*, 6 April 1911
21 Jacques Debu-Bridel in *L'Eventail*, 30 November 1951.
22 *The Professor*, Chapter 19.
23 De Decker, 'Une Anglaise et le continent: Charlotte Brontë à Bruxelles', *Le Soir*, 5 June 1991.
24 De Decker, *Le Soir*, 26 January 1999.
25 De Decker, 'Une Anglaise et le continent: Charlotte Brontë à Bruxelles', *Le Soir*, 5 June 1991.
26 *La Nation Belge*, 13 July 1947.
27 *Villette*, Chapter 6.
28 De Schaepdrijver, *Elites for the Capital? Foreign Migration to mid-nineteenth-century Brussels*, p. 9.
29 *Villette*, Chapters 5–6.
30 'Did they but know it'.
31 Thackeray, 'Little Travels and Roadside Sketches'.
32 Jottrand, *Londres au point de vue belge*, pp. 6–8.
33 Nerval, *Œuvres*, p. 904.
34 *Ibid.*, p. 813.
35 Hymans, *Bruxelles à travers les âges*, p. 135.
36 *The Professor*, Chapter 19.
37 Edmond Picard, *Confiteor* (Brussels: Veuve Ferd. Larcier, 1901).
38 *Villette*, Chapter 34.
39 *Ibid.*, Chapter 15. In *Brussels in Winter* (1938), W.H. Auden writes of 'streets tangled like old string'.
40 Baudelaire, *Pauvre Belgique*, p. 197.
41 Dumas, *Excursions sur les bords du Rhin*, pp. 3–8.
42 *Villette*, Chapter 20.
43 Huet, *Mijn België*, p. 14.
44 Comment made in correspondence with the author.
45 Introduction to De Vries, *Brussels: A cultural and literary history*, pp. ix–x.

46 Baron, *La Belgique Monumentale, Historique et Pittoresque*, p. 145.

47 Trafton, *An American Girl Abroad*, Chapter 9, 'A Visit to Brussels'.

48 Tennent, *Belgium in 1840*, pp. 193–4.

49 Nerval, *Oeuvres*, p. 812.

50 Lesbroussart, *Types et caractères belges contemporains*, p. 185.

51 *The Professor*, Chapter 19.

52 *Villette*, Chapter 34.

53 *Ibid.*, Chapter 12.

54 Acke and Bekers, *Écrire Bruxelles/Brussel Schrijven*, p. 131.

55 *Villette*, Chapter 34 'Malevola'.

56 In Chapter 36. Referring to the 'honeyed voice' of the Catholic tract left by M. Paul in Lucy's desk, Lucy tells us that 'St. Vincent de Paul, gathering his orphans about him, never spoke more sweetly'.

57 Lemonnier, *La Vie Belge*, p. 48.

58 Saint-Férreol, *Les proscrits français en Belgique ou la Belgique contemporaine vue à travers l'exil*, p. 112.

59 *Ibid.*, p. 179.

60 Paul Verlaine, *Mes prisons* (Paris: L. Vanier, 1893), p. 32.

61 Letter to Ellen Nussey, 6 March 1843. Smith, *The Letters of Charlotte Brontë*, Volume I, p. 311.

62 Janzing, *Charlotte Brontë's Secret Love*, p. 63.

63 Charlier, *La vie bruxelloise dans 'Villette'*, pp. 101–2.

64 *Villette*, Chapter 36.

65 *The Professor*, Chapter 7.

66 Smithers, *Observations made during a residence in Brussels*, pp. 148–9.

67 Saint-Férreol, *Les proscrits français en Belgique*, p. 91.

68 *Villette*, Chapter 21.

69 *Ibid.*, Chapter 7.

70 Nerval, *Oeuvres*, p. 905.

71 *Villette*, Chapter 14.

72 *A handbook for travellers on the Continent: Being a guide through Holland, Belgium, Prussia and Northern Germany and along the Rhine, from Holland to Switzerland* (London: John Murray, 1850), p. 81.

73 Nerval, *Œuvres*, p. 911.

74 Trafton, *An American Girl Abroad*.

75 Gautier, *Un Tour en Belgique*, p. 71.

76 Trollope, *Belgium and Western Germany in 1833*, p. 36.

77 Charlier, *Passage: Essais*, p. 135.

78 Baudelaire, *Pauvre Belgique*, p. 55.

79 *Villette*, Chapter 8.

80 *Ibid.*, Chapter 36.

81 *Ibid.*, Chapter 31.

82 Texier, *Voyage Pittoresque en Hollande et en Belgique*, p. 256.

83 Charlier, *La vie bruxelloise dans 'Villette'*, p. 91.

CHAPTER FIVE

'What women to live with!':
Charlotte and the Art Exhibition

A N aspect of *Villette* particularly interesting for readers in Belgium are the glimpses it provides of the cultural life of Brussels. Elisabeth Bekers points out that, as Thackeray had done in *Vanity Fair* a few years earlier, Charlotte portrays Brussels as a lively and pleasure-loving city, whose culture impresses even the coolly critical Lucy Snowe (Charlotte's original surname for her was 'Frost').[1] It may have been no more than a 'villete' compared with London, whose museums Charlotte had visited on her way to Belgium, but her time in the Belgian capital was her first experience of urban life.

Gustave Charlier's article *La vie bruxelloise dans 'Villette'*, first published in 1933 in the year after the publication of the first complete French translation of *Villette*, did much to bring the novel to the attention of Belgian readers. Charlier pointed out that while a lot had been written about the importance for Charlotte of the Pensionnat and of Constantin Heger, relatively little had been said about the places and events beyond rue Isabelle that she describes in the novel. Charlotte and Emily were not always immured in the Pensionnat and they did taste some of the culture of the Belgian capital. Charlier carried out detailed research on three events attended by Lucy Snowe in order to ascertain whether they corresponded to events actually attended by Charlotte. These are the art exhibition that features in Chapter 19 ('The Cleopatra'), the concert attended by the royal family in Chapter 20 ('The Concert') and the nocturnal fête in the park to commemorate the Belgian revolution, described in Chapters 38 and 39.

To these three, Charlier added a fourth. He assumed that the account in Chapter 23 of a performance by the actress 'Vashti' corresponded to one of twelve performances in Brussels by the French actress Elisa Félix (known by her stage name of 'Rachel') in July and August 1842, which Charlotte could have seen. Rachel's visit to Brussels was a highlight in the city's cultural calendar, and Lucy Snowe's account of the profound impression made on her by 'Vashti's performance is often cited by Belgian readers. It has frequently been assumed that the description amalgamates a performance of Rachel's that Charlotte saw in Brussels with two performances she is known to have attended years later in London, in June 1851. Sadly, it seems certain that Charlotte did not in fact see Rachel in Brussels and that her description is based solely on the London performances she witnessed,[2] though while in Brussels she would have been aware of the excitement surrounding the actress's visit.

Charlier highlights the freshness of Charlotte's impressions. 'She had never before lived in a city. And she was in a foreign country for the first time. Her eyes were opening to sights new to her and, for her, almost exotic. She lost no detail of this novel spectacle.' Despite Lucy's refusal to be impressed by some of the cultural life of Labassecour, at other times we can see in her Charlotte the neophyte, naïvely dazzled by the glamour of the Haute Ville. For Belgian readers, Charlotte is thus at the same time an observer who laid bare the provinciality of mid-nineteenth-century Brussels and a provincial herself, an unsophisticated visitor from a rural backwater experiencing urban life for the first time.

Charlier was struck not just by the immediacy of Charlotte's impressions of events but by her almost total recall of them ten years later when writing the novel. It was not only the Pensionnat whose every detail was engraved indelibly in her memory. The same was true of things she saw only once – a concert, a play. He checked Lucy's accounts against those in newspapers of the time. He found that her description in Chapter 20 of a concert in a splendid hall, attended by the royal family, was corroborated by press reports, as was that of the concert in the park. He was also able to identify the two paintings that Lucy describes in unflattering terms when she visits a gallery in Villette, and to compare her reactions with those of contemporary Belgian art critics.

A reviewer of Charlier's essay wondered whether Charlotte might have kept Brussels newspaper reports of the events she describes and used them to refresh her memory when writing her novel.[3] It is an intriguing thought, but it seems more likely that, as Charlier supposed, the events she re-creates so precisely in *Villette* were engraved in her memory.

What women to live with!

Charlotte went to Brussels with her imagination fired by letters from her friend Mary Taylor describing the city's sights. She longed, in particular, to visit its art museums. She had always loved drawing, copying engravings and painting. As a schoolgirl she had impressed her companions with her knowledge of great artists. She had spent hours poring over prints of famous paintings, but the first time she had an opportunity to see some of the originals was when she finally spent some hours in London art galleries on her way to Belgium. She must also have spent some spare hours in the museums and galleries of Brussels. And yet how typical it is of Lucy Snowe that rather than enthusing about the Flemish masters, she expresses nothing but contempt for most of what she sees in Villette's galleries. Always the independent-minded rebel against convention, she finds herself unable to admire the works of art 'it was considered orthodox to admire' and finally gives up the struggle to appreciate them, no longer afraid to admit that 'ninety-nine out of a hundred' of the pictures she sees, including many so-called masterpieces, leave her cold. The one percent for which she has praise are those that seem to her to be true to nature. But rather than dwelling on those worthy of her admiration, in the chapter 'The Cleopatra' she instead picks out two that she finds particularly laughable specimens of contemporary Belgian art. Lucy's first salvo of mockery is discharged from her seat on a bench 'duly set for the accommodation of worshipping connoisseurs' before the picture that 'seemed to consider itself the queen of the collection'. Her description, a sample of Charlotte in her most heavily sarcastic vein, has often been quoted.

> It represented a woman, considerably larger, I thought, than the life. I calculated that this lady, put into a scale of magnitude suitable for the reception of a commodity of bulk, would infallibly turn from fourteen to sixteen stone. She was, indeed, extremely well fed: very much butcher's meat – to say nothing of bread, vegetables, and liquids – must she have consumed to attain that breadth and height, that wealth of muscle, that affluence of flesh. She lay half-reclined on a couch: why, it would be difficult to say; broad daylight blazed round her; she appeared in hearty health, strong enough to do the work of two plain cooks; she could not plead a weak spine; she ought to have been standing, or at least sitting bolt upright. She had no business to lounge away the noon on a sofa. She ought likewise to have worn decent garments; a gown covering her properly, which was not the case: out of abundance of material – seven-and-twenty yards, I should say, of drapery – she managed to make inefficient raiment. Then, for

▲ 'The Cleopatra'. Lithograph by Louis Ghémar of Une Almée by Edouard De Biefve.

the wretched untidiness surrounding her, there could be no excuse. Pots and pans – perhaps I ought to say vases and goblets – were rolled here and there on the foreground; a perfect rubbish of flowers was mixed amongst them, and an absurd and disorderly mass of curtain upholstery smothered the couch and cumbered the floor. On referring to the catalogue, I found that this notable production bore the name 'Cleopatra'.[4]

Leaving aside certain details added or exaggerated by Charlotte, the picture in question has been identified by Gustave Charlier and others as Édouard De Bièfve's *Une Almée* (an 'Almeh' was an Egyptian dancing girl), which was exhibited at the Salon de Bruxelles, a triennial art exhibition held in the capital in August–October 1842. The venue for the exhibition was the fine arts museum located in the former palace of Charles of Lorraine, on the Place du Musée, which also housed a public library and natural history museum. The Place du Musée was also where the Protestant chapel was located.

In singling out this painting for mockery among her memories of the exhibits at the 1842 Salon, Charlotte had alighted by chance or design on a work by one of the painters most esteemed by the Belgian regime. The 33-year-old Édouard De Bièfve, a painter in the Romantic historical style, had been hailed as a rising star and had triumphed the previous year with

▲ The 1830 *Salon de Bruxelles.*

what was to be his best-known picture, the huge *Compromise of the Dutch Nobles in 1566,* depicting a key moment in the Revolt of the Spanish Netherlands. Typical of the vogue for history paintings, it had been commissioned by the Belgian government ten years after the Revolution as part of its promotion of works of art and literature celebrating sixteenth-century Low Countries heroes, seen as the forerunners of the patriots who had finally secured the country's freedom from foreign rule in 1830.

What did Belgian visitors to the Salon make of De Bièfve's Eastern dancing girl, christened 'Cleopatra' by Lucy Snowe? Lucy takes issue with M. Paul's objection to an unmarried young lady like herself contemplating such a supposedly indecent painting, and some Belgian readers see his prudishness as an example of the narrow-minded provinciality of the Catholic Brussels of the time. Charlier points out that M. Paul's reaction is not surprising given that De Bièfve's painting was perceived as overly suggestive by some Belgian commentators. Artistically, it failed to make a stir and was very far from receiving the acclaim accorded to De Bièfve's Dutch nobles of the previous year; Lucy Snowe's lack of enthusiasm was echoed by many reviewers. As Charlotte's (admittedly exaggerated) description would suggest, the indolently reclining female figure was felt to be suggestive of the

94

inmate of a harem rather than a graceful dancer. Her features were criticised as vulgar and neither the subject nor its execution deemed worthy of de Bièfve's talent.

In the succeeding years, in fact, De Bièfve failed to live up to the promise of 1841. His subsequent production was mediocre; his next major commission, a work entitled *Rubens establishes peace between Spain and England*, was a spectacular flop.

Lucy Snowe is enjoined by M. Paul to turn her attention away from the scantily-clad Cleopatra to what he considers a more elevating work, a series of paintings entitled *The Life of a Woman*. Charlier identifies this as Fanny Geefs' *La Vie d'une Femme*, consisting of three paintings, Piety, Love, and Sorrow. The first shows a young girl leaving a church, the second a mother with her baby, and the third a young widow grieving at her husband's tomb. The set of paintings described by Lucy consists of four paintings rather than three, but in most other respects her description corresponds to Geef's pictures.

> They were ... a set of four, denominated in the catalogue 'La vie d'une femme.' They were painted in rather a remarkable style – flat, dead, pale, and formal. The first represented a 'Jeune Fille', coming out of a church-door, a missal in her hand, her dress very prim, her eyes cast down, her mouth pursed up – the image of a most villainous little precocious she-hypocrite. The second, a 'Mariée', with a long white veil, kneeling at a prie-dieu in her chamber, holding her hands plastered together, finger to finger, and showing the whites of her eyes in a most exasperating manner. The third, a 'Jeune Mère', hanging disconsolate over a clayey and puffy baby with a face like an unwholesome full moon. The fourth, a 'Veuve', being a black woman, holding by the hand a black little girl, and the twain studiously surveying an elegant French monument, set up in a corner of some Père la Chaise. All these four 'Anges' were grim and grey as burglars, and cold and vapid as ghosts. What women to live with! insincere, ill-humoured, bloodless, brainless nonentities! As bad in their way as the indolent gipsy-giantess, the Cleopatra, in hers.

The title alone indicates that Charlotte would have had Geefs' triptych in mind for the set of paintings Lucy sees. Used by Charlotte as a pretext for an attack on a concept of womanhood she despised, they were also an example of what she saw as the mediocrity and sentimentalism of a particular school of painting in her host country.

The triptych was admired by some critics. The newspaper *L'Emancipation* described it as 'full of delicate poetry'.[5] *La Revue Belge* rhapsodised about what it called a 'delightful painting'.

> This painting has been a success with the public, for every heart understands what the heart has so well conceived and art has so well expressed. Piety: a graceful young girl coming out of a church, her face radiant with youth, beauty and goodness. Love: a young mother with a newborn baby on her knee; no longer soft youthfulness, but a woman who has become a wife and mother and whose joys have already been mingled with some anxieties. Maternal love, that enduring passion, the only one to which women can give themselves unrestrainedly, the love for the child she has felt moving in her womb, shines in the beautiful eyes turned in gratitude towards heaven and the white forehead where we can already see some trace of life's trials. Sorrow: the young widow with her child mourning at her husband's tomb: pale, thinner, faded, ravaged, far from the tranquillity that piety gave her, from the great joy that love inspired in her, she is now experiencing the poignant realities of death, which has struck down the man she called husband. This is Geefs' concept of the life of a woman, and in expressing these thoughts she has captured the intimate fibres of the heart and made them vibrate profoundly; everything in this painting is simple, pure, sincerely felt and perfect, and the amiable woman who is always occupied by thoughts poetical and tender is revealed in it in her entirety.[6]

Among the critics, however, there were plenty of dissident voices. In his essay on *Villette*, Gustave Charlier points out that 'the bad taste of the inhabitants of "Labassecour" was not as universal as the disdainful Lucy seemed to believe'. The writer Victor Joly's opinion of Fanny Geefs' triptych coincided in many points with Charlotte's own. For him, Geefs' figures, 'misunderstood souls wandering on this sad earth', bore the stamp of a sentimentality that was the deplorable result of the literature of the period. They had 'nothing of humanity apart from their form', seeming to be 'nourished by moonbeams'. Generally depicted in drooping postures with their eyes turned heavenwards, they made him long for the sun-bronzed skin tones of

◀ Fanny Geefs: self-portrait (1841).

Titian's robust and ardent figures. Geefs', he complained, were nothing but 'pale carnations of meringue hues, moonlight figures, all vapour and mist'.[7]

These two contrasting reactions by contemporary Belgian critics bear out the opinion of Geefs' fellow artist Antoine Wiertz (of whom more shortly), expressed in an article on the exhibition, that on questions of art and good taste no two opinions were alike.[8] The following year *La Vie d'une Femme*, which became one of Geefs' best-known paintings, won a gold medal at the Salon de Paris.

Whatever Charlotte thought of the painting and its vision of woman's destiny, Fanny Geefs née Corr might have been someone to interest her. Fanny Corr's own life story seems to have borne little resemblance to that of the woman depicted in her triptych. She was what Charlotte longed to be: a creative artist earning her living by exercising her craft. Charlotte herself had at one time had thoughts of becoming an illustrator. Fanny had trained at a young age in a special Brussels *atelier* for women painters. Born in 1807, the daughter of Irish immigrants, she was, unusually for a woman at that period, a professional painter who, moreover, tackled large canvases on historical and religious subjects as well as traditionally more 'feminine' subjects such as women and children. She had made a name for herself at a young age and was commissioned to paint portraits of Leopold I's Queen, Louise.

It will be remembered that the heroine of Anne Brontë's *The Tenant of Wildfell Hall*, Helen Graham, earns her living as a painter after leaving her abusive husband. Together with writing, it was one of the few professions accessible for middle-class women at the time apart from teaching. It is worth remembering, too, another distinguished Belgian woman artist. Louise Heger, Charlotte's favourite among the Heger children, only four years old when she left Brussels, became a landscape painter. She was a generation younger than Fanny Geefs, but achieved success as an artist at a period when it was still unusual for women to enter the field as professionals. Louise, an eccentric character who smoked cigars like George Sand, had a studio at the bottom of the Pensionnat garden.

Charlotte might have been interested to know – and conceivably did know – that Fanny was the wife of Guillaume Geefs, one of the most reputed sculptors in Brussels and the creator of one of its most celebrated statues, that of the French diplomat General Belliard. Charlotte would have seen this statue every day, since it was at the top of a set of steps leading down from rue Royale to rue Isabelle and the Pensionnat. Guillaume Geefs was also responsible for the monument to the fallen in the 1830 uprising in the Place des Martyrs. A certain Mrs Wemyss Dalrymple, author of a Brussels guide book published in 1839, recorded visiting the Geefs' studio. Referring to the great artistic tradition of the Low Countries, Mrs Wemyss Dalrymple considered that painting and sculpture were thriving in Belgium post-Independence and reported that the Geefs were leading lights in these two arts: 'The same roof contains the sculptor and the painter, as the fair partner of Mr Geefs, well known as the accomplished Miss Corr ... has established herself as an artist. A stranger ... is certain of an affable reception from this gifted couple.'[9]

Bruxelles capitale, Paris province

A more familiar name today than either De Bièfve or Geefs was another rising star in the Brussels art world who also exhibited in the 1842 Salon and is still remembered, though possibly not in the way he would have liked. This was the 36-year-old painter Antoine Wiertz. Charlotte makes no mention of any painting that can be attributed to him. Her literary purposes were served by her memories of the two pictures Lucy describes: two very different destinies of woman, providing an opportunity for a lively debate with her colleague

M. Paul in which their cultural and religious differences come into play, one of the many clashes in the novel between British Protestantism and Continental Catholicism. But Charlotte would have seen Wiertz's work at the Salon, and might well have heard about him while in Brussels.

Antoine Wiertz was of the same generation as De Bièfve and the Geefs; all four were born between 1806 and 1808, representing the rising generation of the new Belgian state. In one of her essays for M. Heger, *Letter from a poor painter to a great lord*, Charlotte voices her own ambition and her conviction of her genius in the person of a young painter. Like her imaginary artist, Wiertz had never had the least doubt of his own genius, and at the time of the 1842 Salon there were many in Belgium willing to take him at his own estimation. He was even proclaimed the 'new Rubens'. A painter of vast canvases, chiefly on religious subjects such as *The Fall of the Rebellious Angels*, exhibited the previous year, his taste was for the monumental. His work had many elements of Romanticism, though his models included Rubens and Michaelangelo. In his article on the 1842 Salon he rejoiced that he and his contemporaries were reacting against what he regarded as the errors of the previous century and returning to the principles of the Old Masters, by which he wanted the art of his own time to be judged. He trusted that his generation of artists, among whom he cited De Bièfve as one of the best, would found a school of painting in Belgium to rival that of the great Flemish masters.

Like the young artist in Charlotte's essay, Wiertz had experienced the struggles and disappointments of an apprentice painter. His work had not been appreciated in Paris, where he had studied. His self-confidence and what many saw as his conceit appeared to be undiminished by this and had won him enemies, but there was praise for the two main works exhibited by him in the 1842 Salon. One of these was the monumental *Revolt of Hell against Heaven*. It was too large for the exhibition hall and was housed in the Temple des Augustins, a church used for exhibitions. The *Revue Belge* saw 'faults but also many beauties' in this depiction of a titanic struggle, massive bodies twisting and turning in all directions as the angels hurl their adversaries, the demons, into the gulf: 'This great poetry transports us.'[10]

The other main work of Wiertz's in the Salon was hung in the exhibition hall and could well have been seen by Charlotte. This was *The Martyrdom of St. Denis*, which displayed the excesses and lurid Romanticism of an artist whose work strove for the sublime but all too often veered instead into the realm of the ridiculous. In this painting, Wiertz's decapitated saint has seized

◀ Antoine Wiertz:
*Revolt of Hell against
Heaven* (1841).

▶ Antoine Wiertz:
Martyrdom of St Denis
(1842).

his own severed head in both hands and is offering it to his executioners, who recoil in horror.

It is amusing to picture Charlotte doing likewise, and to imagine what she might have said about this picture. Like Wiertz she was a Romantic; she had no objection to the grandiose in art. The Brontës were admirers of the works of John Martin, prints of some of whose paintings hung in the Parsonage (incidentally, one of Martin's main patrons was Leopold I of Belgium). Martin painted apocalyptic scenes of biblical subjects, influenced by the work of Milton and reflecting the current taste for the 'sublime'. Large weather events – floods, storm – with small figures dwarfed by vast, rugged landscapes were featured in canvases such as *The Destruction of Sodom and Gomorrah*, or *Joshua Commanding the Sun to Stand Still upon Gibeon*. But in the flesh-filled paintings of Antoine Wiertz, oozing a preoccupation with suffering and torture, Charlotte would probably have seen the excesses of Romanticism and would certainly have seen what she perceived as Catholic morbidity. She loathed the 'lecture pieuse' that was an evening ritual at the Pensionnat, when the inmates were read stories of martyred saints, described by her in Chapter 13 of *Villette* as 'nightmares of oppression, privation, and agony'. If she did see any of Wiertz's paintings while in Brussels, we can imagine the recollection darkening her own nightmares in her times of depression in the city.

In 1850 Wiertz asked the Belgian government to build him a huge *atelier* for his colossal canvases, in return pledging to donate all his largest works to the state. His request was granted, and after his death in 1865 the *atelier*, located in the Leopold quarter, became a state museum. By this time the number of his admirers had dwindled. Adeline Trafton visited the museum in 1869.

> After leaving the church [St Gudule] we wandered among and through the picture galleries in the old palaces of the city, – galleries of modern Belgian art ... where were numberless flat old Flemish pictures, and dead Christs, livid, ghastly, horrible to look upon. The best of Flemish art is not in Brussels. Among the galleries of modern paintings, that of the odd artist, recently deceased, Wiertz, certainly deserves mention. It contains materials for a fortune to an enterprising Yankee. The subjects of the pictures are allegorical, parabolical, and diabolical, the scenes being laid in heaven, hell, and mid-air. In one, Napoleon I is represented surrounded by the flames of hell, folding his arms in the Napoleonic attitude, while his soldiers crowd

around him to hold up maimed limbs and ghastly wounds with a denunciatory and angry air. Widows and orphans thrust themselves before his face with anathematizing countenances. In fact, the situation is decidedly unpleasant for the hero, and one longs for a bucket of cold water. Many of the pictures were behind screens, and to be seen through peep-holes – one of them a ghastly thing, of coffins broken open and their risen occupants emerging in shrouds. Upon the walls around the room were painted half-open doors and windows with pretty girls peeping out; close down to the floor, a dog kennel, from which its savage occupant was ready to spring; just above him, from a latticed window, an old *concierge* leaned out to ask our business. Even in the pictures hanging upon the walls was something of this trickery. In one the foot and hand of a giant were painted out upon the frame, so that he seemed to be just stepping out from his place; and I am half inclined to think that many of the people walking about the room were originally framed upon the wall.[11]

Wiertz's paintings had elements of the surrealism that was be so important in Belgian art in the twentieth century. The museum remains open to this day, and many visitors record the nightmarish effect on them of his gigantic canvases. The American novelist John Dos Passos, who lived in Brussels as a child in the last years of the nineteenth century, recalled how his childhood terrors were fed by visits with his mother to the Musée Wiertz, 'full of huge red paintings, the work of a mad painter.'[12]

Today the museum finds itself in the European quarter of Brussels, an anomaly among the buildings of the European Union institutions. And yet in one way it is an oddly appropriate site for it, since long before the European Union existed, Wiertz dreamed of a Brussels that would be the capital of Europe. In a pamphlet written in 1840 entitled *Bruxelles capitale, Paris province*, he outlined his ambition for Brussels (already growing rapidly) to expand to a capital of 4 million inhabitants, four times the size of Paris, which had a million at the time and would thus be relegated, said Wiertz, to the status of a provincial city in comparison. Wiertz hated the French capital for its scant enthusiasm for his work. This turning of the tables on Paris, of which Brussels was so often seen as a mere satellite, did not come about; today, with over two million inhabitants, Paris is twice the size of Brussels. But with the Belgian capital now the heart of the EU, Wiertz's dream can in one sense be said to have been realised.

Today the little-visited Wiertz museum, regarded as a curiosity, is something of an embarrassment to the Belgian state, seemingly saddled with it for evermore. The grandiose ambitions of this artist who viewed himself as a colossus in a small country were not realised for himself any more than for his capital. Carlo Bronne cites Wiertz's works as an example of the mediocrity of the art of the period and remarks on the lack of aesthetic taste in mid-nineteenth-century Belgium, thereby vindicating Charlotte Brontë's opinion (as voiced by Lucy Snowe) of much of what she saw in the 1842 Brussels art exhibition.[13]

The Brussels depicted by Charlotte as 'Villette' was very far from being the capital of which Wiertz dreamed. In Carlo Bronne's opinion, the caustic spirit in which she observed its culture was often justified, since the aspirations and ambitions of 'a young nation still searching for itself' outstripped its actual achievements. Writing of Charlotte's account of the works she saw at the Salon de Bruxelles, Bronne refers to the 'flat and conformist' painting popular at the time.[14]

Gustave Charlier expressed eloquently his view that Charlotte Brontë was not just a highly Romantic novelist but at the same time an accurate recorder of life in 1840s Brussels.

> Where people were concerned, she may have distorted their traits. She sometimes did it to the point of caricature, prompted by her prejudices, her biases, her mood and her secret passion. But the things she described remained as they had survived in her tenacious memory, scarcely altered by slight inaccuracies. They give the novel a setting and precision so exact, place it in the framework of a truth so minutely observed, that a singularly romantic fiction takes on, as we read, the disquieting note of a lived reality.[15]

1 Acke and Bekers, *Écrire Bruxelles/Brussel Schrijven*, p. 130.

2 During a visit to London, Charlotte told her friend Amelia Taylor in a letter of 7 June 1851 that she was to see Rachel perform that night: 'I wonder whether she will fulfil … expectation – as yet it has not been my lot to set eyes on any serious acting for which I cared a fig.' In a subsequent letter of 11 June she reports to the same correspondent, 'I have seen Rachel – her acting was something apart from any other acting it has come in my way to witness – her soul was in it – and a strange soul she has … it is my hope

to see her again.' This would seem to indicate that it was the first time Charlotte had seen the actress and, therefore, that she had not seen her in Brussels in 1842. Smith, *The Letters of Charlotte Brontë*, Volume II, pp. 633–5.

3   *Le Soir*, 12 July 1947.

4   *Villette*, Chapter 19.

5   *L'Emancipation*, 8 September 1842.

6   *Revue belge*, Vol. 22, September–December 1842, pp. 130–31.

7   *Le Globe*, 8 September 1842. Cited in Charlier, *La vie bruxelloise dans 'Villette'*, p. 80.

8   Wiertz, *Salon de 1842*.

9   Wemyss Dalrymple, *The Economist's New Brussels Guide*, p. 62.

10 *Revue belge*, Vol. 22, September–December 1842.

11 Trafton, *An American Girl Abroad*.

12 Dos Passos, John, *Fragments d'une enfance bruxelloise*, 1966.

13 Bronne, *Léopold Ier et son temps*, pp. 150–51.

14 Bronne, *Belles étrangères en Belgique*, p. 145.

15 Charlier, *La vie bruxelloise dans 'Villette'*, pp. 101–2.

CHAPTER SIX

King of the Farmyard:
Charlotte and the 'King of Labassecour'

A ND now all was prepared: but one compartment of the hall
waited to be filled – a compartment covered with crimson, like
the grand staircase and doors, furnished with stuffed and cushioned
benches, ranged on each side of two red regal chairs, placed solemnly
under a canopy.

A signal was given, the doors rolled back, the assembly stood up,
the orchestra burst out, and, to the welcome of a choral burst, enter
the King, the Queen, the Court of Labassecour.

Till then, I had never set eyes on living king or queen; it may consequently be conjectured how I strained my powers of vision to take in
these specimens of European royalty. By whomsoever majesty is
beheld for the first time, there will always be experienced a vague
surprise bordering on disappointment, that the same does not appear
seated, en permanence, on a throne, bonneted with a crown, and
furnished, as to the hand, with a sceptre. Looking out for a king and
queen, and seeing only a middle-aged soldier and a rather young lady,
I felt half cheated, half pleased.

Well do I recall that King – a man of fifty, a little bowed, a little grey:
there was no face in all that assembly which resembled his. I had never
read, never been told anything of his nature or his habits; and at first
the strong hieroglyphics graven as with iron stylet on his brow, round
his eyes, beside his mouth, puzzled and baffled instinct. Ere long,
however, if I did not *know*, at least I *felt*, the meaning of those characters written without hand. There sat a silent sufferer – a nervous,
melancholy man. Those eyes had looked on the visits of a certain
ghost – had long waited the comings and goings of that strangest
spectre, Hypochondria. Perhaps he saw her now on that stage, over
against him, amidst all that brilliant throng. Hypochondria has that
wont, to rise in the midst of thousands – dark as Doom, pale as

Malady, and well-nigh strong as Death. Her comrade and victim thinks to be happy one moment – 'Not so,' says she; 'I come.' And she freezes the blood in his heart, and beclouds the light in his eye.

Some might say it was the foreign crown pressing the King's brows which bent them to that peculiar and painful fold; some might quote the effects of early bereavement. Something there might be of both these; but these as embittered by that darkest foe of humanity – constitutional melancholy. The Queen, his wife, knew this: it seemed to me, the reflection of her husband's grief lay, a subduing shadow, on her own benignant face. A mild, thoughtful, graceful woman that princess seemed; not beautiful, not at all like the women of solid charms and marble feelings described a page or two since. Hers was a somewhat slender shape; her features, though distinguished enough, were too suggestive of reigning dynasties and royal lines to give unqualified pleasure. The expression clothing that profile was agreeable in the present instance; but you could not avoid connecting it with remembered effigies, where similar lines appeared, under phase ignoble; feeble, or sensual, or cunning, as the case might be. The Queen's eye, however, was her own; and pity, goodness, sweet sympathy, blessed it with divinest light. She moved no sovereign, but a lady – kind, loving, elegant. Her little son, the Prince of Labassecour, and young Duc de Dindonneau, accompanied her: he leaned on his mother's knee; and, ever and anon, in the course of that evening, I saw her observant of the monarch at her side, conscious of his beclouded abstraction, and desirous to rouse him from it by drawing his attention to their son. She often bent her head to listen to the boy's remarks, and would then smilingly repeat them to his sire. The moody King started, listened, smiled, but invariably relapsed as soon as his good angel ceased speaking. Full mournful and significant was that spectacle! Not the less so because, both for the aristocracy and the honest bourgeoisie of Labassecour, its peculiarity seemed to be wholly invisible: I could not discover that one soul present was either struck or touched.[1]

Among Charlotte's accounts in *Villette* of events she attended in Brussels, her description of King Leopold I, under the guise of the King of Labassecour, is of particular interest to Belgian readers. She saw him at a concert in the new Salle de la Grande Harmonie at the top of rue de la Madeleine, on the site of today's Place de l'Albertine. Inaugurated in 1842, during the Brontës' stay, the hall was the creation of Cluysenaar, the rising young architect who designed the Galeries St Hubert a few years later.

Belgium was a country of music lovers. 'Belgium excels in the arts that speak to the senses: music and painting', in the words of Amédée Saint-Férreol.[2] Every village had its musicians, every town its choral societies and orchestras. Music was everywhere in the streets of Brussels, accompanying every fête and every fair. Although Lucy's report of most of the performances she hears in the Salle de la Grande Harmonie is as sardonic as her account of the art exhibition, in the chapter about the fête in the park the music whose strains reach her ears from the kiosque speaks powerfully to her senses as she wanders through the crowd in search of the source of the irresistible sound.

The concert at which Lucy sees the King has been identified by Gustave Charlier as one Charlotte must have attended on 10 December 1843. It was organised by the Société de la Grande Harmonie, described by her as the 'principal musical society' of Villette, a charitable association that had been organising concerts, balls and gala evenings since its foundation in the early years of the century and counted many city worthies among its members. The association is mentioned by name in *The Professor*, when Crimsworth tells us that his employer Pelet has gone out to 'pass the evening at the Salle of the Grande Harmonie or some other club of which he was a member'.[3] It was the rendezvous of the Brussels bourgeoisie and its balls attracted 'the finest specimens of our fresh and opulent bourgeois beauty'.[4]

The beauty of Belgian women was commented on by Gérard de Nerval, who like Charlotte had occasion to observe them in a theatre. At a theatrical production in Flanders he found himself, like Charlotte in the Salle de la Grande Harmonie, as absorbed in contemplation of the audience as of the spectacle on stage: 'The audience is itself a spectacle. The women are framed in the boxes like portraits. There are charming ones among them, most of them blonde, of a dazzling freshness that speaks of quiet nights and long days of repose, their pink lips like flowers, their glowing rosy cheeks like autumn fruits.'[5] The French writer Théophile Gautier also waxed enthusiastic over the charms of Belgian women. His primary motive in visiting Belgium in 1843 was to see living models of the women he admired in Rubens' paintings, with their beautiful bodies 'full of health, mountains of pink flesh from which fell torrents of golden hair'.[6]

Charlotte acknowledged the physical charms of the Labassecouriennes as exemplified in *Villette* by M. Paul's god-daughter and ward, Justine Marie, whom Lucy initially jealously supposes to be his fiancée:

A girl of Villette stands there – a girl fresh from her pensionnat. She is very comely, with the beauty indigenous to this country; she looks well-nourished, fair, and fat of flesh. Her cheeks are round, her eyes good; her hair is abundant ... good-humoured, buxom, and blooming, she looks, at all points, the bourgeoise belle.[7]

However, Charlotte, painfully conscious of her own childlike and undersized figure, tended to be deprecating about buxom women, seeming often to estimate the capacity of their brains in inverse proportion to the volume of their bodies. When Hunsden expresses a preference for well-developed female forms, Crimsworth, defending Frances's slight physique, challenges his friend to 'kindle life in the tallest, fattest, most boneless, fullest-blooded of Rubens' painted women'.[8]

Her observation of the Labassecouriennes in the concert hall is similarly unflattering. Their features are 'regular but round, straight but stolid; and for their depth of ... passionless peace, a polar snow-field could alone offer a type'.

Her description of the hall itself was much more enthusiastic. It was 'that of a marvelling neophyte', says Gustave Charlier in his article *La vie bruxelloise dans 'Villette'*. 'No place of public entertainment had it ever been my lot to enter yet,' Lucy Snowe tells us, and at the time of her stay in Brussels Charlotte had hardly seen more of such places than her heroine. Her description of Cluysenaar's hall is that of a young woman who had never set eyes on anything comparable, but by all accounts the hall was indeed impressive and the concert on 10 December 1843 a particularly grand one. 3,000 people were crammed into the room that night; the carriages, Quiévreux tells us, stretched all the way down rue de la Madeleine.[9]

We alighted under a portico where there was a great bustle and a great crowd, but I do not distinctly remember further details, until I found myself mounting a majestic staircase wide and easy of ascent, deeply and softly carpeted with crimson, leading up to great doors closed solemnly, and whose panels were also crimson-clothed. I hardly noticed by what magic these doors were made to roll back – Dr. John managed these points; roll back they did, however, and within was disclosed a hall – grand, wide, and high, whose sweeping circular walls, and domed hollow ceiling, seemed to me all dead gold (thus with nice art was it stained), relieved by cornicing, fluting, and

▲ La Salle de la Grande Harmonie.

garlandry, either bright, like gold burnished, or snow-white, like alabaster, or white and gold mingled in wreaths of gilded leaves and spotless lilies: wherever drapery hung, wherever carpets were spread, or cushions placed, the sole colour employed was deep crimson. Pendant from the dome, flamed a mass that dazzled me – a mass, I thought, of rock-crystal, sparkling with facets, streaming with drops, ablaze with stars, and gorgeously tinged with dews of gems dissolved, or fragments of rainbows shivered. It was only the chandelier, reader, but for me it seemed the work of eastern genii: I almost looked to see if a huge, dark, cloudy hand – that of the Slave of the Lamp – were not hovering in the lustrous and perfumed atmosphere of the cupola, guarding its wondrous treasure.

Charlier testifies to the accuracy of her memories of the evening's programme. Checking them against newspaper reports, he found that the details she gives correspond to the concert of 10 December, down to the lottery for the benefit of the poor that ended the proceedings, at which the numbers are drawn by 'two little girls, of five and six years old', and Lucy – aptly, given her encounters in Villette with cigar-smoking men – wins a cigar case. (No event in Belgium, where many workers were paid starvation wages, was complete without a lottery or collection for one of the numerous char- ities in aid of the poor.) Enthusiastic though she is about the venue, Lucy records the efforts of the solo singers with her usual refusal to be impressed by what pleases the crowd, and has unreserved praise only for the 'hearty exertions' and 'rousing choruses' of several provincial choral societies composed of 'genuine, barrel-shaped, native Labassecouriens'. The reviews in the papers endorsed her view of the choral singing as the best part of the evening's entertainment.

At the concert in the park, too, it is the sound of a choir that arrests Lucy's attention. Accounts by visitors to Belgium bear witness to to the national passion for singing. Taine reported that every mining community had its choral society and that it was common to hear workmen singing well and in chorus over their work or when returning home after the day's labour.[10]

For Belgian readers, the most historically interesting aspect of Charlotte's account of the concert is not her description of the hall or of the performers but the glimpse she gives them of Leopold I, first King of the Belgians. Charlier observes with amusement that the young Englishwoman seems to have been much more absorbed in observing the occupants of the royal box than in attending to what was happening on the stage.

She had only this one opportunity to observe the King, barring the moment a few months earlier, on 18 September, when she saw the royal carriage flash by in rue Royale when Queen Victoria was in town, and caught a brief sight of the stout little English Queen, accompanied by her consort, chatting vivaciously to King Leopold and Queen Louise seated opposite. Yet her description of the King fascinates Belgians commentators, Charlier, for one, calling it 'singularly suggestive'.

What kind of man was King Leopold and how accurate was Charlotte's interpretation of his facial expression and demeanour?

She was not the only observer to comment on Leopold's melancholy expression. His face, or at any rate his public face, was described as an impas- sive mask, cold, sad, severe and distant. By 1843, when he was 53, it was lined and thin-lipped. In youth his good looks had turned female heads. On a visit to London when a young lieutenant-general fighting Napoleon, Prince Leopold of Saxe-Coburg had certainly made an impact on Princess

Charlotte Brontë by George Richmond, 1850.

The Coudenberg Palace in the 17th century, by Jan Brueghel the Younger.

Panoramic view of Brussels c. 1850 by Paul Lauters, showing the Park with the royal palace at the south end (on the left) and the parliament building opposite it at the north end (on the right). The spire of the Town Hall can be seen in the distance left of centre and the twin towers of St Gudule to the right. Rue Royale skirts the far (west) side of the park. The steps leading down to rue Isabelle from rue Royale were opposite the avenue that crosses the park left of centre.

Mme Reuters (on left). Fat, rubicund and jolly, she epitomises William Crimsworth's idea of a 'Belgian old woman'. Illustration for *The Professor* by Edmund Dulac, Dent, London, 1922.

Rosine (on left), the French portress at Mme Beck's, described as 'airy, fickle, dressy, vain, and mercenary'. Illustration for *Villette* by Edmund Dulac, Dent, London, 1922.

La Vie d'une Femme by Fanny Geefs, 1842.

Arcadie Claret (1826–1897), mistress of Leopold I of Belgium (1790–1865) for the last 20 years of his life.

Lucy has a sighting of the ghostly nun in the Pensionnat garden. Illustration for *Villette* by Edmund Dulac, Dent, London, 1922.

Rue Isabelle and the gateway to the Jardin des Arbalétriers, the exercise ground of the guild of crossbowmen. The Pensionnat Heger occupied the site in the 19th century.

The Brussels Ommegang in 1615 by Antoine Sallaert.

The grave of Constantin and Zoë Heger in the Watermael-Boitsfort municipal cemetery.

The Heger family by
Ange François (1847).

The Park and the Palais
de la Nation (parliament
building), by William
Brown.

▲ Leopold I of Belgium, Louise Marie of Orléans and their children, c. 1848.

Charlotte of Wales, daughter of the gross Prince Regent ('Prinny', the future George IV). As the sole legitimate grandchild of the mad George III and thus well in line for the throne, Charlotte in turn was an attractive match for the ambitious Leopold. Vivacious and headstrong, she persuaded her father to agree to the marriage after breaking off her engagement with William, Prince of Orange, the suitor of his choice. Leopold and Charlotte married in 1816. Despite their differences in temperament – while she identified with the passionate Marianne in *Sense and Sensibility*, Leopold, mature and sober for his years, was the personification of sense – the couple were deeply in love.

In later years, Leopold remembered the months of his marriage to Charlotte, particularly after they moved to Claremont House in Surrey, as a paradise lost. They both revelled in the freedom of life in the country amid the rolling grounds of Claremont. With a comfortable income and the prospect of a future as the consort of the Queen of England, Leopold's greatest ambitions seemed set to be realised. Charlotte was soon expecting a child, and the royal pregnancy was followed with interest up and down the country. Neither Leopold's hopes nor the country's were to be realised, however: Charlotte died after giving birth to a stillborn child, only eighteen months into the marriage. Leopold was inconsolable. He had lost the woman with whom he had found happiness as well as the role he had looked forward to. An Anglophile, he felt as English as he did German, and on his deathbed – after 35 years as King of the Belgians and over twenty as the husband of a French princess – dreamed of being buried by Charlotte's side at Windsor.

By 1831, when he accepted the invitation to be monarch of the new state of Belgium – having just turned down the throne of Greece because of that country's political instability – the sadness that Charlotte Brontë observed on his features had become his habitual expression. He accepted the throne of the new little kingdom without great enthusiasm, but hoped it would fulfil his wish for a role on the European stage worthy of his considerable political and diplomatic skills. When he sailed from Dover to take up his new position, he showed unusual emotion as the white cliffs receded from sight. He was leaving a country he knew and loved to embark on a risky venture in one unknown to him. As was Charlotte Brontë when she made the crossing a decade later, albeit under rather different circumstances. She and Leopold were alike, at any rate, in discovering that Belgians could be rather unruly and difficult to manage. At this stage in the new nation's history, its future as a viable country remained in doubt and its inexperienced politicians were viewed in many quarters as little better than a pack of revolutionaries.

By the time Charlotte saw Leopold in the Salle de la Grande Harmonie, he had been pilot of the kingdom she called 'Labassecour' for 12 years and had steered it dexterously through some choppy waters. For years after the revolution, the Dutch did not renounce their hopes of regaining the country, while the Belgians had no experience of self-government. Moreover, in the first years of Leopold's reign the outcome of the Revolution was by no means accepted by all Belgians; there was enough support for King William among Leopold's new subjects to make things difficult for him. But by 1843 the stability and viability of the new country were assured. Leopold had taken a keen interest in industrial developments in Britain, and he promoted the industrialisation of Belgium and the building of a railway network to compensate for the loss of river transport after the separation from the Netherlands. On her return to Belgium at the start of her second year, Charlotte was able to make the journey to Brussels on the recently-opened railway line from Ostend.

▲ The Royal Palace of Laeken.

By 1843, Leopold had many reasons to be satisfied with his achievements. He also had the relief of knowing that his dynasty as well as the country he ruled was established on a firm footing. In 1832 he had married Louise Marie of Orléans, the daughter of Louis Philippe I of France. Their first son had died, but a second, the future Leopold II, was born in 1835. It was this boy, the Duke of Brabant, nicknamed by Charlotte the 'Duc de Dindonneau' ('turkey chick'), who accompanied his parents to the concert at which she saw the royal family. The royal couple had two other children, Philippe (born in 1837) and Charlotte (1840), who was her father's favourite.

Both Belgium and its royal family were prospering, and Leopold's popularity was high. So why did he look so sad? He did not carry the burden of responsibility lightly, and described himself as the Atlas holding up his little kingdom. However, there seems something almost wilfully Byronic in the melancholy that had accompanied him since the death of his first wife and that Charlotte was so quick to spot. One of his ministers, deploring the unsociability that drove him to escape whenever he could to his country retreat, the remote Tour du Rocher in the Ardennes in southern Belgium, complained that the King was a man who appeared to have everything, yet was – or believed himself to be – unhappy. He might be said to be a sufferer

▲ The Château d'Ardenne, Leopold I's retreat in the Ardennes in southern Belgium. On the left is the Tour du Rocher, a tower built by Leopold where he often stayed when hunting.

from spleen. At the palace of Laeken outside Brussels, which he chose as his residence because its grounds, landscaped in the English style, reminded him of Claremont, he went for long walks, while in the hills around his Ardennes estate he hunted until exhausted.

His biographers have pointed out that cool and calculating as Leopold was as a statesman, he had a romantic side under his phlegmatic mask.[11] He often regretted turning down the Greek crown offered to him just before that of Belgium, and on his deathbed wrote: 'Belgium is no more than prose. It is Greece that would have satisfied the poetic aspirations of my soul.'[12] On his deathbed, too, Leopold asked a pianist to play him music by Wagner, a favourite composer of his.

Romantic heroes – like the ones in Charlotte Brontë's youthful fiction – have a tendency to suffer from *ennui* as well as melancholy. By the time Charlotte saw him, Leopold had achieved the mission he had set himself when he accepted the Belgian throne. He had known nothing about the country when he made his 'Joyeuse Entrée' into Brussels in 1831; now, after years of micro-managing its affairs –the members of the Belgian parliament soon found that Leopold intended to involve himself very closely indeed in the day-to-day running of the country – he felt that he knew Belgium and its ways very thoroughly. Well enough, in fact, to be starting to feel bored with it.

'A man too big for his surroundings' is how one Belgian reader of *Villette* sums up King Leopold I as depicted by Charlotte.[13] He found his small kingdom a restricted arena for the skills he knew he possessed, and couldn't forget the much grander dreams and aspirations that had fired him when he was married to his first wife. One way of compensating for the limited sphere Belgium offered was to try to expand his influence in the wider arena of European affairs and keep a close eye on the balance of power on the Continent, a balance to which the neutrality of his own country, small as it was, was key. It gave him a pretext to escape from Brussels whenever he found it stifling, which, to judge from his frequent journeys to other European courts, must often have been the case. Ties could be forged with the other European powers by extending the influence of the Coburg dynasty, notably by matchmaking. His sister had married George IV's brother, the Duke of Kent, and it was their child Victoria who became Queen. Leopold had been a mentor and second father to Victoria. He had even found a husband for her in his nephew, Prince Albert of Saxe-Coburg. Another outlet when he found Belgium too constricting was to dream of a Belgian empire or at any rate colony – an ambition to be realised not by him but by his son, who as Leopold II became the founder and notoriously ruthless exploiter of the Belgian Congo.

Charlotte had quickly recognised in the Belgian monarch a fellow-sufferer from the 'hypochondria' or depression to which she herself was prone and from which she suffered acutely while in Brussels – the malady that drove her to the confessional. She was right in her intuitive conviction that he was a victim to melancholy and nightmare. Had she known more about his character – Lucy claims to have known nothing about the King before scrutinising him in the concert hall – she might have found further points of affinity with this essentially solitary soul, whose face, she said, resembled no other in the hall. Quite apart from the aura of kingliness that would inevitably set him apart in her eyes, she concluded from her perusal of his features that he was not like the Belgians any more than she was. This was hardly surprising, since like her he was a foreigner in Belgium. Like her, too, he was a Protestant in a Catholic country. As a Lutheran, he was driven by the Protestant work ethic and sense of duty that Charlotte contrasted favourably with the indolence and hedonism she perceived in her Belgian pupils. His faith was non-negotiable: his response when enjoined by his daughter-in-law, on his deathbed, to convert to Catholicism so that he could be buried next to Queen Louise was a decided 'Nein'. In a country characterised by its love of good living, guided by the Catholic creed that Charlotte summed up as 'eat, drink, and live', the King was an ascetic who in his latter years liked to dine on an unvarying menu of lamb chops accompanied by boiled potatoes and served in silence.

What of Queen Louise, in whose face Charlotte read the 'subduing shadow' of her husband's melancholy and whom she describes as being, like him, very different in looks and temperament from her Belgian subjects?

Like Leopold, Louise of Orléans was a foreigner. Life in Belgium was for her a life of exile, as a Frenchwoman who never ceased to miss Paris and the family she had left behind in marrying Leopold. On her first evening in Belgium as a newly-wed she cried so much that Leopold was reduced to tears as well, out of sympathy.

Thus, like Charlotte, the Queen was homesick in Brussels. She had been married against her will, at the age of 19, to a man 22 years older than her who was not in love with her. She came to admire her husband's qualities, just as he came to respect and admire hers – in fact she came to be almost morbidly devoted to him – but she was not happy at Laeken as she had been at the French court, and the highlight of her day was the arrival of letters from Paris. Like Charlotte in letters home about her Belgian pupils, Louise recorded her impressions of her subjects in letters to her family and friends which reveal an unexpectedly sharp wit and powers of observation under a timid and docile exterior. Defending herself when told off by her father for being over-critical of her Belgian subjects, she wrote, 'Even if I told the Belgians that Brussels is a hundred times more brilliant than Paris, that I love Belgium more than France, that all Belgian women are pretty, that everyone here has superb teeth, that the discussions in parliament are interesting and more sensible (which isn't saying much) that in the French parliament, etc., etc., they wouldn't believe me and would thank me even less for my lack of sincerity than they do for my silence.'[14] Despite such remarks, she recognised the Belgians' worth. Her first impression of her new subjects, along the route of the royal procession when she entered Belgium as a new bride, was of their good nature. In turn, she won their affection in spite of her timidity and reclusiveness.

In her observation of the royal couple, Charlotte picked up on the fact that neither seemed happy, and that in her efforts to rouse her husband from his abstraction by talking of their child the Queen could not succeed more than momentarily. If he showed little interest in his son it is not surprising, given that the future Leopold II, who was difficult and unmanageable as a child, always claimed that his father never cared for him. Leopold was a distant father, except perhaps to his favourite child, his daughter Charlotte. But the Queen had deeper reasons than this for unhappiness in her marriage. Despite her husband's fine qualities and quasi-paternal affection for her, he had never loved her as he had his first wife. 'All I want is to be your friend, your only friend', she wrote to him in 1849, acknowledging that 'I'm not what I would have liked to be, I'm no longer young and don't have any of the talents or charms that could have made things pleasant for you ... This impossibility of doing something for you has been the thorn in my happiness.'[15] Acutely conscious of her own shortcomings, she added that if she was not entirely happy she blamed herself alone and not him. Like Charlotte Brontë's letters to Constantin Heger, Louise's words to her husband were a cry of pain, an acknowledgement that she knew she loved more than she was loved.

There were reasons for her unhappiness that she did not touch on and for which she *could* have reproached Leopold had she chosen to do so. All his life he was susceptible to the charms of pretty young women. There were many other women in his life and Louise could not have been unaware of this. Around the time that Charlotte saw him at the concert, Leopold met a woman who was to be very important to him in his last two decades. She was pretty and she was very young indeed – just 18 years old to his 53. Her name was Arcadie Claret, and it was not long before she was installed in rue Royale as his mistress. She bore him two sons, the first in 1849. Leopold was deeply in love and Arcadie's journal entries speak of a passion that was mutual despite the 36-year age difference. After Louise's death in 1850, Arcadie was moved to a château near the King's palace at Laeken and remained devoted to him until his death in 1865, nursing him in his last years.

Arcadie Claret was disapproved of by the public. However, she could offer the King the sensuality he craved and did not find in his wife (Louise admitted that her worsening health prevented her from 'fulfilling her duties as a wife')[16] and the beauty and youth that Louise was acutely aware she lacked. Although the Queen was only in her thirties at the start of Leopold's liaison with Arcadie, her health, not improved by five pregnancies, was always delicate – she was to die of pulmonary disease in 1850 at the same age as Charlotte Brontë, 38 – and she considered herself well past her youth. Moreover, Arcadie was an accomplished pianist who could play the music Leopold loved; at the time of his marriage to Louise he had regretted, in a letter to his niece Victoria, that his new wife was not fonder of music. And her lively, cheerful personality was what the ageing King needed to rouse him from his melancholy.

Louise was not lively or cheerful, a deficiency of which she was doubt-less aware. When Charlotte spoke of the 'reflection of her husband's grief' on her face, it might have been truer to say that the Queen herself was a victim of depression as much as her husband. In her eighteen years in Belgium she never recaptured the happiness of her Parisian childhood. Charlotte guessed something of the tragedy of a king who had everything and yet was not happy. Did she also glimpse something of the tragedy of a queen unable to be the companion to her husband that she longed to be?

An item in the satirical journal *Méphistophélès* in 1846 gives an irrev-erent view of Leopold, his marriage and his ménage with Arcadie. Given that Charlotte hit on the name of 'Duc de Dindonneau', 'Duke Turkey Chick' for Leopold's son and dubbed Leopold himself the King of Labassecour (the 'farmyard' or 'poultry yard'), it is intriguing to find a farmyard and turkey theme in this satire, a fable that refers covertly to the King and his adulterous relations with Arcadie. The fable, *La Gardeuse de Dindons* (The Turkey Keeper) may have been suggested by the Grimm brothers' *The Little Goose Girl*. In the German fairy tale, a princess sent to marry a prince is forced by her maid-in-waiting to change places with her, the maid posing as the princess and becoming the prince's affianced bride while the real princess has to guard geese.

> A great personage who lives in a princely abode in the outskirts of Brussels (when he is not rolling in a post chaise along all the highways of the Continent) happening to be walking one day by chance, or rather out of *ennui*, in the vicinity of the farmyard [*la basse-cour*], spied a young girl who was feeding the poultry. The grand personage approached her and, having been able to appreciate the freshness and abundance of her charms with the aid of his lorgnette, engaged her in conversation. What took place between them is not known, but some time later the great personage's wife, passing by the turkey-keeper's cottage, was not a little astonished to hear the sound of a piano issuing from it ... Curious to know the meaning of this, she entered and found, seated at a superb piano, a young girl, attired in velvet and silk, with jewels on every finger! The great lady, who knew what her illustrious husband was capable of, guessed perfectly well

▲ *La gardeuse de Dindons*. Cartoon depicting Leopold I and his mistress Arcadie Claret.

the reason for this metamorphosis in the turkey-keeper's dwelling. As a prudent and well-brought-up person, however, she withdrew without saying anything.

Nevertheless, she informed her husband of her displeasure at this unseemly arrangement, observing that it was quite enough to have harems prepared for him, in the manner of post houses, in every corner of Europe where he deigned to take his august person, without having to appropriate turkey keepers from his own farmyard to boot....[17]

Gardeuse de dindons was a term that could refer to a pretty peasant girl, while one connotation of *dindon*, turkey-cock, here implicitly used to refer to Leopold, was a pompous know-all. In an accompanying cartoon, Leopold, brandishing a net, is depicted in pursuit of the young turkey-herd in the farmyard near his palace at Laeken. As the King attempts to catch the girl, a priest tries to stop him by hanging on to his coat tails.

The cartoon in question gave rise to a court case against *Méphistophélès*. The journal was acquitted, but as a result of the case a new law was passed making it illegal to insult the person of the King and his family. It is highly unlikely that Charlotte knew about the satirical piece, but her own references to turkeys and farmyards are a curious coincidence.

Leopold died fifteen years after Louise with the name 'Charlotte' on his lips. It is not known whether he was thinking of his first wife or of his daughter, who was in Mexico with her husband, the Austrian Archduke Ferdinand-Maxmilian, recently crowned Emperor of that country. Maxmilian's acceptance of the Mexican crown was an ill-fated venture that was to end in tragedy. He was executed only three years later; Charlotte ended up insane.

In Jolien Janzing's novel *Charlotte Brontë's Secret Love*, the theme of Leopold and Arcadie's relationship is intertwined with that of Charlotte's growing feelings for Constantin Heger. The two are presented as contrasting stories of forbidden, adulterous love with, of course, very different outcomes.

One verdict on the accuracy of Charlotte Brontë's portrait of Leopold is that of his biographer Carlo Bronne. Summing up the paradox of the King's situation and state of mind in 1843, the year in which Charlotte observed him, Bronne remarks that 'The more he succeeded in all his endeavours, the more demanding he became; the more his people supported him, the more distant he became; the more his family grew, the more solitary he appeared.'

Yet, Bronne goes on to say, nobody perceived this paradoxical bitterness 'except for the simple daughter of a Yorkshire pastor staying at the Pensionnat Heger, who saw the King for the first time at a concert of the Grande Harmonie'.[18] He then cites Charlotte's description of the King in full. His estimation of Charlotte's perspicacity is borne out by other commentators. The writer Charles d'Ydewalle, in an article about Leopold I's reign, states that 'the best portrait of Leopold is Charlotte Brontë's in *Villette*'.[19]

Charlotte's perceptiveness is astonishing if, like Lucy, she knew little or nothing about the King's character and her conclusions were based solely on her observation of him on this one occasion. In fact Lucy's claim cannot be fully applicable to Charlotte, who had heard at least something about the Belgian King and his entourage. In a letter to Emily a couple of months earlier, recounting how Queen Victoria's visit had enlivened Leopold's court, she described that court as being as sombre and gloomy 'as a conventicle'.[20] Given that the King's 'bereavement' is mentioned in her description of him in *Villette*, she must also have known of his previous marriage to her namesake.

However, Bronne's comment that only Charlotte's eyes pierced beyond the mask of the King's face to his soul is a remarkable testament to her powers of perception and an indication of why her Belgian readers find her observations so absorbing. Her impressions as a visitor new to Brussels, and indeed to city life and public scenes, were fresh and vivid. Her accounts have an honesty and emotional involvement that make them compelling, while the disguise of fictional names gave her the confidence and security to speak with complete freedom of what she saw. Under the absurd name of the 'King of Labassecour', King of the Farmyard, she bequeathed to the Belgians a rare and intimate glimpse of their first monarch.

1   All citations from *Villette* in this chapter are from Chapter 20, 'The Concert'.
2   Saint-Férreol, *Les proscrits français en Belgique*, p. 117.
3   *The Professor*, Chapter 8.
4   Newspaper article of 1890s quoted in Quiévreux, *Bruxelles, notre capitale*, p. 61.
5   Nerval, *Œuvres*, p. 927.
6   Gautier, *Un tour en Belgique*, p. 3.
7   *Villette*, Chapter 39.
8   *The Professor*, Chapter 24.
9   Quiévreux, *Bruxelles, notre capitale*, p. 61
10 Hippolyte Taine, *Philosophie de l'art, dans les Pays-Bas* (Paris: Baillière, 1869), p. 46.
11 For example Patrick Roegiers, *La spectaculaire histoire des rois des Belges* (Paris: Editions Perrin, 2007), p. 30.
12 Bronne, *Léopold Ier et son temps*, p. 188.
13 In an article in *Nieuws van den Dag*, 14 June 1950.
14 Bronne, *Léopold Ier et son temps*, p. 99.
15 *Ibid*, p. 228.
16 Defrance, *Léopold Ier et le clan Cobourg*, p. 231.
17 *Méphistophélès*, 22 October 1846. Mentioned in Gita Deneckere, *Leopold I. De eerste koning van Europa* (De Bezige Bij, Antwerp, 2011), pp. 335–6.
18 Bronne, *Léopold Ier et son temps*, p. 147.
19 *La Nation Belge*, 21 July 1946.
20 Letter to Emily, 1 October 1843. Smith, *The Letters of Charlotte Brontë*, Volume I, p. 331.

CHAPTER SEVEN

'Brussels' Revenge' or 'The Mysterious Destiny of the Brontës': The Destruction of Charlotte Brontë's Brussels

Grave of a broken heart

THE Salle de la Grande Harmonie is one of many buildings associated with the Brontës that is no longer standing today. For almost a century after Charlotte attended the concert at which she saw Leopold I, it continued to host balls and concerts for the bourgeoisie and nobility of Brussels. But just before the Second World War it was demolished, a victim, like so many other buildings, of the projects of the Brussels city planners. Louis Quiévreux, writing after the War, tells the story.

It was in 1937. The *Jonction Nord-Midi* [the rail link connecting the North and South train stations] was winning its most deplorable victories. Like Goering but with more precision, it carried out its work of devastation. Nothing escaped its fury: street after street fell before it. Under its blows, beauty perished and ugliness, clad in concrete, iron and grey, prepared its depressing entry.[1] On a spring day, 25 May, the last pillars of the Salle de la Grande Harmonie came crashing down.

The ballroom crumbled amid the din and a cloud of dust. A ghost emerged from the ruins: that of Charlotte Brontë, who on 10 December 1843 attended a concert given by the Société de la Grande Harmonie[2]

This was not the only occasion on which Quiévreux, indefatigable chronicler of the destruction of many of Brussels' historical streets and buildings in the twentieth century, imagined the ghost of Charlotte Brontë, as the pickaxes fell or the bulldozers moved in, rising from the ruins of a place associated with her.

He was not the only *Bruxellois* to have visions of Charlotte's ghost. She is often described as having 'left her heart' in Brussels; in *The Secret of Charlotte Brontë*, Frederika Macdonald tells us that Charlotte left 'her broken heart buried'[3] in the grave of her hopeless love, and a romantic imagination readily imagines the site of that grave as being the garden of the Pensionnat Heger. Mme Heger discouraged any talk of Charlotte among the pupils, and as seen in an earlier chapter, Macdonald did not hear her name mentioned during her two years at the school. However, Zoë Heger's ban does not appear to have been entirely successful. She was not able to prevent ghostly visitations by the Englishwoman, or at any rate rumours of such visitations. In his childhood memoir, the poet Iwan Gilkin relates something he heard from his sister, who was a pupil at the Pensionnat in the late 1870s.

> Initiates knew that a famous English novelist, Charlotte Brontë, had formerly been an assistant mistress at the Pensionnat Heger-Parent, that her heart had beaten for the handsome young Heger and that she had put him into an autobiographical novel. The little *pensionnaires* repeated the legend to each other in whispers; better still, it was claimed that on fine summer evenings the ghost of the young Englishwoman sometimes appeared in the garden among the flowering bushes. Did it come to breathe the perfumes of the past and relive the idyll interrupted by Destiny and Duty? It was of these things that the young demoiselles talked in low voices, for it was forbidden to speak about them. The boldest of them, when they went to the church of St Jacques sur Coudenberg close to the school, tried to pick out the confessional where the poor Englishwoman, staunch Protestant though she was, overcome by the torment of her heart, had prostrated herself at the feet of a Catholic priest. In the little world of the Pensionnat Heger, this adventure, which had thrilled so many readers the world over, still earned old M. Heger a sentimental and respectful admiration.[4]

The *demoiselles*, or perhaps Gilkin's memory, had mistaken the church — it was in the Gothic St Gudule, not the neo-classical St Jacques sur Coudenberg in Place Royale, that Charlotte had confessed to the priest. However, the passage shows that her name was kept alive at the Pensionnat even if Madame shuddered to hear it, and the whispered tale must also have been relayed by the *pensionnaires* in many Brussels households.

▲ Artist's impression of the Pensionnat garden (1858).

Given that Lucy Snowe is startled in the garden of the fictional Pensionnat by apparitions of the ghost of a nun, according to legend 'buried alive for some sin'[5] – a forbidden love, perhaps – it seems fitting that years after Charlotte's death, the garden of the Pensionnat Heger should have been rumoured to be haunted by the ghost of the English author herself, visiting the site of her own forbidden love. Perhaps it was by an old pear tree like 'Methuselah' in *Villette*, at whose foot Lucy Snowe sees the spectral nun after burying her letters from Graham Bretton, that Charlotte's own ghost, according to the story, appeared on summer evenings.

Some thirty years after Gilkin's sister heard the story, the Pensionnat and the streets surrounding it were demolished. There would be no more teenage girls in rue Isabelle to pass on the legend of sightings of Charlotte, and nothing of the school remained for her to grace with her ghostly presence. Dead writers leave more than their ghosts, however. In the words of the author of a Brussels guide book (*Bruxelles: Ville en forme de Coeur*), the illustrious figures – 'glorious or dolorous' – who have passed through a city become a part of it. Brussels, he says, is partly made up of what those celebrated foreigners have 'left of their love or glory'. Or of their pain. He enjoins the visitor to the city to remember that he or she treads in the steps of Baudelaire, walks in streets along which Dumas' *fiacre*[6] drove, sits on a bench on a spot where Charlotte Brontë passed, goes through a doorway entered by Hugo, goes into a café where Verlaine and Rimbaud sat.[7]

Most of the taverns and cafés where the French writers drank and talked, such as the Prince of Wales in rue Villa Hermosa or the Café des Mille Colonnes in Place de la Monnaie, have gone, but you can still have a meal or a beer in the streets round Grand Place that they frequented. But Charlotte Brontë did not spend time in hostelries in the old town centre, and virtually all the places in which she did spend time have disappeared – not just the Pensionnat, but practically every site associated with her, including the school where her friends the Taylors studied and even the cemetery where Martha Taylor was buried.

> Vanished, rue Isabelle, one of the most beautiful streets of old Brussels. Disappeared, the château de Koekelberg school. *Fini*, the Protestant cemetery in St Josse. Razed, the Salle de la Grande Harmonie where Charlotte attended a concert … So where can we find her shade? Not at the Monnaie Theatre, which burned down thirteen years after she may have seen the actress Rachel there. Not in the Quartier de la Putterie [on the site of the present Central Station]

◀ The fire that destroyed the Théâtre de la Monnaie in 1855.

which she would have crossed … Perhaps a wandering of her soul lingers on in the Park where she was thrilled by the Chinese lanterns at a night-time fête.[8]

'The breeding ground of a great novel'

Rue Isabelle disappeared over a century ago, and 'would hardly be heard of today had it not been the breeding-ground of a great novel, *Villette*', in the opinion of André De Vries, author of *Brussels: A cultural and literary history*.[9] While his remark shows the importance of Charlotte's stay in the street in keeping its memory alive in guide books, rue Isabelle in fact had an interesting history in its own right long pre-dating the Brontës, and a special charm felt by all who visited it.

By the nineteenth century it had become a quaint backwater, a 'provincial corner in the midst of the city'.[10] Lying nine metres lower than the Haute Ville and the park, it was accessed from rue Royale by a dramatically long staircase, known as the Passage de la Bibliothèque. These steps led down from a small square behind the statue of General Augustin Daniel Belliard, the French ambassador to Belgium following the 1830 uprising, who played an important part in the negotiations that led to the country's independence. The view of the city from the top of the steps looking out over the spire of the Hôtel de Ville in Grand Place was one of the most impressive in Brussels.

In previous centuries, the Quartier Isabelle had been anything but a sleepy backwater. It was adjacent to the ducal palace of Coudenberg, and in the middle ages, under the rule of the Dukes of Brabant and of Burgundy, had housed the mansions of the court nobility. Rue Isabelle, however, dated from the seventeenth century. It was built in 1625, during the period of Spanish dominion, by the Archduchess Isabella, daughter of Philip II of Spain. The governorship of the Archdukes Albert and Isabella is remembered fondly as a rare period of peace and prosperity in the city's turbulent history when its proud tradition of pomp and ceremony was revived. The devout Isabella wanted a direct route from the palace to the church of St Gudule, hitherto accessible only by a steep and circuitous one. Rue Isabelle was built as a private road for use by her and her courtiers for that purpose.

The new street, which skirted the old ramparts along a stretch of the former city walls, passed through the *Jardin des Arbalétriers*, the exercise ground or garden of the Grand Serment des Arbalétriers. This ancient guild of crossbowmen had been key to the city's defence in the middle ages and in later

▲ Little houses in rue Isabelle, built by the Archduchess Isabella for her archers and halberdiers.

centuries, as a kind of police force and guard of honour, still retained many privileges. (Archery has long been officially the national sport of Belgium.) The crossbowmen were particularly dear to Isabella's heart. She enjoyed huge popularity with them after her success as a markswoman when she brought down the target at the Guild's annual competition in 1615 and was crowned 'King' of the Grand Serment for that year. When part of the Guild's exercise ground had to be expropriated for her street, the transaction was conducted amicably; in exchange for the land expropriated, Isabella built a mansion, the 'Domus Isabellae', for the guild's festivities and a row of around thirty little houses to house the archers and halberdiers who formed the yeomen of the guard.

After the seventeenth century, the nobles moved out of the quarter to pastures new and the street declined in importance. In 1731 the Coudenberg palace was destroyed by fire, and towards the end of the century the new Place Royale and royal quarter were built on and around the site. With the construction of rue Royale, rue Isabelle was no longer needed as a route to the cathedral. The Quartier Isabelle became a quiet area, 'secluded', like Villette's rue Fossette, 'in the built-up core of a capital'.[11] Moreover, the street along which Isabella and her court had processed in all their solemn splendour suffered the ignominy of becoming a mere cul-de-sac; when Place

Royale was built, at a much higher level than the Coudenberg palace, the end of rue Isabelle that had led to the Coudenberg was buried under the new development.

Due to its retired nature, the district was an ideal setting for the girls' boarding school started by Zoë Parent in 1830 in a large house built at the turn of the century, with a spacious garden on the site of the Jardin des Arbalétriers. In the years before she opened her Pensionnat, there had been a secondary school on the same site.

If the Upper Town was that of government and the Lower that of commerce, this intermediate area on the slope between the two could be called the quarter of learning and education. As a former aristocratic district it contained large properties with gardens, some of which provided premises for the schools that were established there in the nineteenth century. One site used for educational premises was the former Hospice Terarken. This was a complex of buildings, close to the Pensionnat, on the corner of rue Terarken and rue des Douze Apôtres, the two streets that formed a triangle with rue Isabelle. Early in the century the few old women left in the hospice

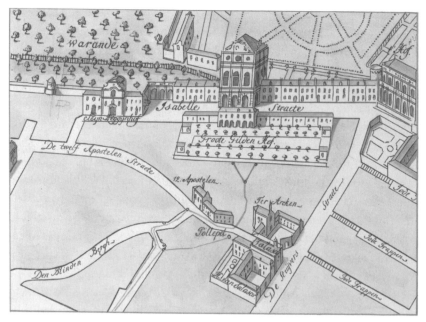

▲ Map showing rue Isabelle, the Domus Isabellae and the Jardin des Arbalétriers, c. 1750. It shows the triangle of streets formed by rue Isabelle, rue des 12 Apôtres and rue Terarken. It also shows the Hospice Terarken on rue Terarken, where the Athénée Royal moved in 1838, and the Salazar Chapel on rue des Sols.

▲ The Palais Granvelle in rue des Sols, which housed the Université Libre de Bruxelles from 1842 to 1928.

were transferred to the Béguinage. In 1839 the Athénée Royal, the state boys' school where Constantin Heger taught, moved to new buildings constructed on the Hospice land. Heger had married Zoë Parent in 1836. His main workplace was now literally a stone's throw away from home, just on the other side of the wall that divided the two establishments.

In 1842, the year the Brontës arrived, an important event took place in the Isabelle quarter that caused one historian to dub it the 'Quartier Latin' of Brussels.[12] The Université Libre de Bruxelles, the capital's first university, founded in 1834 shortly after Independence, was installed in the historical Palais Granvelle on rue des Sols. This arcaded Italian Renaissance palace built in the sixteenth century by Cardinal Granvelle, an unpopular minister of Philip II, housed the university until 1928, when it moved to the Solbosch campus. Heger's son Paul taught there and became its Vice-Chancellor in his latter years. His name was given to the main street in the new campus, Avenue Paul Héger.

For a time, the neighbourhood also contained the royal library, which was moved to the 'Domus Isabellae' after the old palace burned down. When the Domus was demolished in its turn at the end of the nineteenth century it was its function as a library that gave the name of Passage de la Bibliothèque to the staircase built on the site.

▲ Panoramic view of rue Isabelle showing the Pensionnat on the left and the Cathedral in the background.

After Charlotte's death, Elizabeth Gaskell was one of the first literary 'pilgrims' to descend this stone staircase, the foot of which was directly opposite the main entrance of the Pensionnat. In her *Life of Charlotte Brontë* she describes rue Isabelle as a place in a time warp: 'From the splendour of today in the Rue Royale, if you turn aside, near the statue of the General Belliard, you look down four flights of broad stone steps upon the Rue d'Isabelle. The chimneys of the houses in it are below your feet The Rue d'Isabelle looks as though it had been untouched by the innovations of the builder for centuries; and yet any one might drop a stone into it from the back windows of the grand modern hotels in the Rue Royale, built and furnished in the newest Parisian fashion.'[13] Mrs Gaskell's novelist's imagination was captured by the quaint, old-fashioned appearance given to the street by Isabella's cottage-like houses, which she compared to almshouses in an English village and a Brussels historian to the dwellings in Belgian béguinages. But the Pensionnat was a nineteenth-century building and many houses in the street, now occupied by middle-class tradesmen and professional people, had been modernised since the time of Isabella.

In the succeeding years, Elizabeth Gaskell was followed down those four flights of steps by Brontë enthusiasts from Britain and America. Their records of these pilgrimages are accounts of stepping into a secret and enchanted world, the most poignant visits being those made just before the school's demolition in 1910. Modern Brontë fans looking for traces of the two writers in today's Brussels, however, are likely to be soon disappointed. On the site of the Pensionnat Heger and its romantic garden stand two massive modern buildings: the Art-Deco Palais des Beaux-Arts ('Bozar') housing one of the city's main concert halls, and a bank building. Brontëites armed with a detailed guide book can succeed in tracking down a couple of truncated vestiges of the old streets that the Brontës walked along. These include a section of rue Terarken behind Bozar. Apart from these, the Quartier Isabelle, which lay close to today's Mont des Arts and Central Station, disappeared at the turn of the twentieth century.

It was the railway, the pride and joy of the new Belgian state and its King in the Brontës' time (the railway line that opened between Brussels and Mechelen in 1835 was the first on the Continent) that led to the destruction not just of the Quartier Isabelle but of many other historical districts in the capital.

The railway project that turned huge swathes of the city into a building site throughout the first half of the twentieth century was the *Jonction Nord-Midi*. The Belgian capital has always been a hub of international traffic, and

▲ The Pensionnat shortly before it was demolished, c. 1910.

the inconvenience of the lack of a fast transport link between the North and South stations was already apparent in the nineteenth century. Brussels, a city of trams, did not have a metro until the 1960s, a century later than London and over half a century after Paris. A rail link was therefore decided on to connect the two stations, though there were decades of debate about whether to take it round the periphery of the city or drive it through its heart. Once the latter route was determined on, the Isabelle quarter with its picturesquely-named streets was doomed. The plans were approved in 1903. The tunnel for the underground section of the link was excavated from the surface, and the devastation this caused, greatly prolonged due to the suspension of the work during the two World Wars, lasted forty years and led to the demolition of 1,600 buildings and the eviction of 12,000 *Bruxellois*. It was destruction on a larger scale even than the major public works project of the late nineteenth century – the covering over of the river Senne between 1867 and 1871.

The plans for the *Jonction Nord-Midi* included the construction of the Central Station close to the site of the Pensionnat, between the Cathedral and Place Royale. It was designed by Victor Horta, the architect who was also responsible for 'Bozar'. The area around the new station was completely redeveloped, and the fate of the Isabelle quarter was sealed by the building of a new road, rue Ravenstein. Ascending from the lower town to the upper in a curve to reduce the gradient, it replaced the steep rue Montagne de la Cour, the glamorous shopping street the Brontës had known. The dramatic difference in levels between the two parts of town had always posed a problem for traffic. Gérard de Nerval marvelled that the capital of 'the flattest country in the world' should be cursed with so many hills and have so many street names containing the word 'montagne'.[14] In Charlotte's time, visitors to the city noted the difficulty experienced by horses in pulling their conveyances up the hill. In his guide to Belgium, Addison advised English visitors taking up residence in Brussels to hire horses locally rather than bringing their own: 'The precipitous paved hills shake them sadly and often strain their loins'.[15] Some of the old thoroughfares seem to have been almost as steep as Main Street in Haworth, on whose cobblestones Mrs Gaskell, in the opening chapter of her *Life of Charlotte Brontë*, describes the horses' hooves slipping as they struggled to gain a grip on their ascent to the Parsonage at the top of the hill.

Rue Ravenstein was one of the pet projects of Leopold II, as was the 'Mont des Arts' just along from the Pensionnat site. Like rue Ravenstein,

▲ Victor Horta's Palais des Beaux-Arts ('Bozar') on the site of the Pensionnat, completed in 1928.

this was a scheme for linking the upper and lower towns: a cascade of steps, gardens and waterfalls tumbling down the hill. Finished just in time for the 1910 World Fair, it had a makeover to a much more severe look in the 1950s with the construction of the forbidding building that now houses the Royal Library.

By 1910, when the Pensionnat was demolished, most of the Isabelle quarter had gone. Leopold II died in 1909, too late to see the completion of the Mont des Arts. Horta's Palais des Beaux-Arts, built on the site of the Pensionnat in the 1920s, had its origin in another project of Leopold's, who had dreamed of an even larger complex for the arts, sciences and literature. The steps that lead down today from rue Royale, replacing the old Passage de la Bibliothèque, were also built in the 1920s.

'The mysterious destiny of the Brontës'

The titles of numerous books and websites convey the nostalgia of histori-cally-minded *Bruxellois* for a vanished or lost Brussels, a *Bruxelles disparu* or *Bruxelles perdu* that fell victim to relentless urban development from the second half of the nineteenth century. Time after time, more conservative solutions such as cleaning up insalubrious 'slum' areas rather than razing them were discarded in favour of large-scale destruction and insensitive rebuilding, which continues to be the favoured option of the city planners today. Post-war, a new word was coined for this: 'Bruxellisation'.

In the 1890s, the Dutch-Belgian artist Jacques Carabain recorded the areas due for demolition to make way for the Jonction in a series of around 60 watercolours. These were commissioned by the Brussels Bourgmestre Charles Buls, who in opposition to Leopold's schemes had proposed more modest plans that would preserve as far as possible the character of the old quarters. Thwarted in his endeavours by the King and his entourage, Buls resigned in protest in 1899. Carabain's pictorial records of this Brussels soon to be *disparu*, a Brussels already doomed when he painted it, are bathed in the mellow, melancholy light of anticipatory nostalgia. Among the streets he preserved in paint are the narrow curve of rue Isabelle with the Porte des Arbalétriers (the old gateway to the former Jardin des Arbalétriers), and the neighbouring rue Terarken housing the Hôtel Ravenstein, a turreted Burgundian manor house.

The aching nostalgia for the streets and buildings immortalised by Carabain in watercolour has been expressed by many in writing. Victor Tahon of the Royal Archaeological Society of Brussels, in his history of rue Isabelle, *La Rue Isabelle et Le Jardin des Arbalétriers* (1912), written at the time of the demolition of the Isabelle quarter, described 'this poor old quarter, condemned and resigned' as 'an unfortunate victim of these new times': 'The age-old buildings, witnesses of so many humble joys, of so many sorrows small and great, will soon be no more than a heap of rubble.[16]

Tahon's history is an elegy for the secluded corner of Brussels whose memory is today in part perpetuated by its link with Charlotte and Emily Brontë. Tahon does not mention the Brontës, but he does speak of the Pensionnat, thanks to which, he says, the sleepy street that rue Isabelle had become by the end of the eighteenth century was not completely forgotten in the nineteenth. The ghosts that Tahon visualised when writing his book were not those of Charlotte and Emily but, rather, of the archers of the Guild of the Crossbowmen and the Archduchess Isabella and her courtiers. His history of the street shows that Charlotte Brontë was fortunate in her choice of school in more ways than one: it is hard to imagine a more picturesque or historically rich location or one more calculated to fire a novelist's imagination. Tahon's foreword, a funeral dirge for a much-loved piece of one city's heritage, is a poignant comment on the sacrifices demanded in the name of progress in towns the world over.

Have you ever lingered, in the evening. in old abandoned and deserted streets, doomed to an imminent death?

Have you savoured the charm of their seclusion, the enchantment of their calm, melancholy atmosphere?

Have you ever thought, when leaving them, that soon, in a few days, these old streets will be no more and that your eyes will never, ever again see these familiar scenes?

On one of those warm evenings of last April, I walked for the last time round the silent twists and turns of the Isabelle quarter.

I wandered for a long time along its steep, winding, narrow streets, badly paved, poorly lit, with their old-fashioned, picturesque gabled houses. A quaint, peaceful enclave, a provincial corner vegetating quietly on its hill, far from the bustle and noise of the big boulevards whose lights criss-cross the busy, ultra-modern Lower Town.

Marché-au-Bois, Montagne-des-Aveugles, rue des Douze Apôtres, rue du Parchemin, rue des Sols, rue de la Cuiller-à-Pot, rue Terarken, rue Isabelle, streets and lanes with old Brussels names, born long ago, you have grown up, you have lived and now you are going to end. How many things you have seen, how many generations have walked in you!

You are going to end and in your place will spring up new, unknown avenues, lined with big new houses in composite styles devoid of national character. You are going to end and in a few months a whole new quarter will rise in your place, so different from yours which emerged so slowly out of the old Brussels sand!

But that's the way of things. Everything changes!

The expanding city wants wide, straight arteries, rapid means of communication. The city, which has become a great capital, wants spacious, symmetrical houses, well-aired and well lit, equipped with all modern conveniences. It wants monumental buildings to house its banks, symbols of the country's industry and commerce.

C'est la vie. We have to submit to it![17]

The walk related in the passage was Tahon's last visit to the Quartier Isabelle. As the sun sank behind the Hôtel de Ville, he slowly climbed the steps up to the Belliard statue, leaned on the balustrade of the little square at the top and said his final goodbye to the quarter below 'as he would have done to an old and much-loved person'. That was in April 1909. By December of that year most of it had gone.

▲ Rue Terarken and the Hôtel Ravenstein.

In 1953 *Le Soir* ran a series commemorating the history of the *Quartier* in drawings with captions, cartoon style. With the completion of the Central Station in 1952, most of the last remaining remnants of the old quarter had now disappeared. Charlotte and Emily's stay there is included as an important part of its venerable history, 'the last ray of the street's splendour'. In a picture illustrating its demise, the sinister silhouette of a workman raises a pickaxe while behind him the ghosts of Charlotte and Emily join that of the Archduchess Isabella. The ghost of the street's creator is illustrious company for the shades of two ungracious English visitors who inhabited it so briefly. The series ends with a description of the new neighbourhood that rose from the ruins of the old: the sweep of the new rue Ravenstein, mounted arrogantly high above the level of the modest streets it replaced; the bulk of Bozar and of the mastodon-like bank building, crushing beneath them any traces of the classrooms and garden of the Pensionnat.[18]

In an article published around the same time, Louis Quiévreux recounts going one evening in search of his two favourite Brussels ghosts. He found himself on the site of the Pensionnat, having been to see the 1948 film of *Hamlet* in the cinema at Bozar. Emerging at dusk, he decided to go for a stroll in the area and make a note of any places still standing from the Brontës' time. He scribbled them down on his programme for *Hamlet*. The list was soon finished. This was before the completion of the Central Station, and parts of the surrounding area were still in various stages of demolition or marked for demolition. Quiévreux wandered down into what was left of rue des Sols, the continuation of rue Terarken. Still standing in that street –

◀ The destruction of the Isabelle quarter. The ghosts of Charlotte and Emily (centre) join that of the Archduchess Isabelle (on the right) as a workman raises his pickaxe.

though not for much longer – was a landmark of old Brussels: the Chapelle Salazar, dating from the fifteenth century, close to the site of the old university building, which had already disappeared.

In medieval times there had been a Jewish community in the Quartier Isabelle, and this chapel had been built on the site of a synagogue after the Jews were accused of desecrating some hosts and driven from the quarter. The Brontës would sometimes have walked down the 'escaliers juifs' whose name recalled that period, the steps leading down from a series of small streets connecting rue Terarken with rue Montagne de la Cour. As he contemplated the chapel, Quiévreux 'seemed to see two frail silhouettes': Emily and Charlotte Brontë, to whom all the buildings that distinguished the neighbourhood must have been familiar sights. 'But let's leave this desolate spot', Quiévreux wrote, 'and go down into the lights of the town . . . Brussels, obeying the mysterious destiny of the Brontës, has effaced their traces'. The chapel disappeared in 1955, and today only a stump of rue des Sols

◄ The Salazar chapel near the Pensionnat Heger.

remains, cut off by a car park. Quiévreux ends his article with some words from the film he had just seen: 'The rest is silence.'[19]

'An hour of joy'

At the time the Pensionnat was destroyed, its Brontë link does not appear to have been of interest to the Brussels authorities and nobody of influence in Belgium seems to have suggested preserving the school as a shrine to the two British writers. Despite press articles by British and American visitors who viewed the school before it disappeared, there was little protest from the English-speaking world either and no concerted campaign, not even by the Brontë Society, to save the Pensionnat for posterity.

Belgian interest in the school as a literary link came when it was too late to save it, with the steady growth in popularity of the Brontës throughout the twentieth century. The Brussels historian and archivist Guillaume des Marez devoted a paragraph to the Brontë sisters in his history of the Isabelle quarter *Le Quartier Isabelle et Terarken* (1927). Like many writers on the Belgian side of the Channel and not a few on the other side, he paints a bleak picture of their Yorkshire life. Haworth is described as a sad village of 'sullen' and 'scowling' houses, all the siblings as so sickly that their father's financial resources were exhausted in tending them, and Patrick and Branwell as already moribund when the sisters returned to Yorkshire from Brussels. Des Marez refers to their time at the Pensionnat as one of the few bright moments in their dreary lives. 'Now that there is more and more interest in their works, I thought it of interest to recall the memory of these poor but noble girls, who came to taste an hour of joy in the peaceful Pensionnat of rue Isabelle.'[20]

This view of Charlotte's time in Brussels was rather different from that of British biographers, most of whom perceived it as troubled and downright unhappy. For her biographer Wemyss Reid, writing in 1877, what pleasures she had experienced at the Pensionnat had been dark and guilty ones: 'She had tasted strange joys, and drunk deep of waters the very bitterness of which seemed to endear them to her'[21]. But Des Marez was not the only Belgian commentator to imagine Charlotte's and Emily's stay in rue Isabelle as the one happy time in a life of otherwise unremitting gloom. Louis Quiévreux, too, contrasted the 'gloomy parsonage' with the 'cheerful Rue Isabelle.'[22]

Belgians seem to have taken a particularly dim view of life in Haworth. Maurice Maeterlinck, in some passages on Emily Brontë in his essay *Wisdom*

▲ *La Vie des Soeurs Brontë*, series in *Le Soir*, 1957. Charlotte and Emily, in the Pensionnat garden, keep their distance.

▲ *La Vie des Soeurs Brontë: La Passion de Charlotte*. Charlotte takes leave of Heger.

and Destiny, describes life at the parsonage in the 'dark, desolate, solitary, miserable and sterile little village of Haworth'. There can never, he says, have been a childhood and youth so 'friendless, monotonous and dreary' as that of Emily and her siblings. They spent their lives 'gravely watching the monotonous flight of the hours', a monotony broken only, according to Maeterlinck, by their father's 'appearing each evening in the rectory parlour to read aloud the appallingly dreary debates of the House of Commons'.[23]

Des Marez's reference in 1927 to rue Isabelle's link with the Brontës shows that a remark made the previous year by a British resident of Brussels and Brontë enthusiast, Edgar de Knevett, that 'Belgians have no great interest in (quite intelligibly), and perhaps no great love for, Charlotte Brontë' was not entirely true.[24] But in any case, whatever lack of interest there was in the Brontës in earlier years was more than compensated for in the mid-twentieth century by Louis Quiévreux (born 1902), the writer and journalist whose name recurs so frequently in connection with theirs. Charlotte and Emily had in him a fervent advocate. As is the case with so many Anglophone Brontëites, there was something obsessive in this Belgian *Brontiste's* passion for the two sisters.

Quiévreux, who often wrote under his literary pseudonym of 'Pierre Novalier', is remembered as a chronicler of Brussels' past. In an introduction to a guide book on the capital he recalls the moment in his youth when he first became fully aware of his passionate love for his native city.

He was standing before a panoramic painting by the Flemish artist Antoine Sallaert of a procession in Brussels in the time of the Archdukes Isabella and Albert. Small figures, representing every echelon of seventeenth-century Brussels life, wind their way past houses with stepped gables. This depiction of a whole epoch, in all its rituals, 'revealed my passion to me and awoke in me a burning curiosity to know everything about my city'. It made him, he said, a tireless *flâneur* threading its streets, turned him into an obsessive porer-over of yellowed maps in the silent dead of night, 'tracing with a fingertip the route of streets gone for ever, murmuring their lost names'.[25]

Quiévreux's love for his city and its history meant that he was often angry. The 1950s saw some of the capital's most ruthless destruction and redevelopment. In article after article, he chronicled the history of doomed streets and railed against what he called the 'official vandalism' of the urban planners who were severing the city's few remaining links with its past. Some of his most evocative passages were about the Isabelle quarter. And whenever he mentioned the Isabelle quarter, he referred to what for him was its most striking association: Charlotte and Emily Brontë's stay at the Pensionnat Heger.

Quiévreux was an Anglophile who wrote books on British institutions and literature. He had been an English teacher and had worked as a correspondent for British newspapers during the German occupation in the Second World War. As a regular contributor on Brussels life and history for *Le Soir* and other newspapers, he did more than any other Belgian to promote interest in the city's Brontë link. The 1950s afforded many opportunities to do so, since the decade saw not just the disappearance of some of the last buildings of the Isabelle quarter but the centenary of the publication of *Villette* (in 1953) and of Charlotte Brontë's death (in 1955). But Quiévreux took any and every opportunity to bring the Brontë sisters to the attention of his readers. An article on the *coup de grâce* dealt to the Isabelle quarter by the demolition of the Salazar Chapel, soon after the opening of the Central Station, was entitled *La fin dernière du Quartier Isabelle aux souvenirs des Sœurs Brontë* ('The final end of the Isabelle quarter with its memories of the Brontë sisters').[26]

As a connoisseur of Brussels history, Quiévreux was able to offer glimpses of the Brussels of the Brontës, a Brussels about which he knew much more than any Brontë scholar. In an article entitled *Bruxelles, les Brontës et la famille Héger*, he filled in his readers on some of the personalities in the Brussels cultural scene in 1842–43.[27] Adolphe Sax was inventing the saxophone. The sculptor Eugène Simonis was working on the statue of Godfrey de Bouillon that stands today in Place Royale in place of the Tree of Liberty of the Brontës' time. Another sculptor, Guillaume Geefs, known for the Belliard statue, had just finished his monument for the tomb in Laeken cemetery of the Spanish soprano Maria Malibran, a hugely popular Brussels celebrity who died in 1836 at the age of only 28. Charlotte might have seen her tomb on a jaunt to Laeken.

Releasing his fancy to roam at will in the streets where the Brontës had trodden, Quiévreux conjures up Brussels celebrities then alive whom the sisters might have passed in the streets around the Pensionnat and with whom – had they not, as he says, been 'shy, unsociable Protestants who did not frequent any Brussels circles' – they might even have engaged in conversation. They might have passed by Charles de Coster, who became one of the major Belgian novelists. He was only sixteen at the time, but, muses Quiévreux, 'Might he and Charlotte have seen each other in the street? If they had known what they were to become, how they would have spoken to each other! What friends they would have become!'

Unexpected connections

If Quiévreux amused himself imagining encounters the Brontës might have had in the city's streets, other writers, as if to compensate for the disappearance of so many of the places where they trod, have been even more inventive in finding Brontë connections in Brussels. Although Grand Place, the jewel among the city's sights, is not mentioned by Charlotte either in her novels or her surviving letters, there is a legend in Brussels, cited confidently as fact in some guide books, that she returned to the capital in 1852 to write *Villette* in a building in the square.[28] In fact she never went back to Brussels after leaving it in 1844, but had she indeed made a return visit there to write *Villette in situ* she would have been most unlikely to stay in Grand Place down in the Basse Ville. Some guide books, undeterred by the fact that Emily and Anne had died in 1848 and 1849, have all three sisters lodging in Grand Place in 1852. The Brontës would at least have been in good company, given that the exiled Victor Hugo was staying in the square that same year. Branwell is not included in the arrangement, which seems rather a pity as the building where Charlotte and her sisters are supposed to have stayed is next to Le

Cygne, a celebrated literary tavern where the one convivial member of the family would have been sure to make himself at home. It was here that Karl Marx convened workers' meetings when writing his *Communist Manifesto* in Brussels in the 1840s.

Just as startling is another frequently-claimed Brontë connection, this time in the leafy outskirts of the city. The suburb of Uccle to the west, today favoured by affluent expatriates and in Charlotte's day an area of country villas on the fringes of the Fôret de Soignes, does not immediately spring to mind as a place that she would have frequented. However, the same guide books that have her penning *Villette* in Grand Place, perhaps in between cosy fireside chats in the square's taverns with Victor Hugo and other literati, also assure us that she spent at least one summer in a country house owned by the Hegers in Uccle, a large tree-screened *château*, in the French sense of the word (country house), used in the summer months by their pupils. This, they claim, was the model for La Terrasse, the 'little château' in *Villette* where Graham and Mrs Bretton make their home.

The usually well-informed Louis Quiévreux was one of those who were convinced that Charlotte spent a summer in Uccle with fellow pupils. In one of his flights of fancy, he tells us that 'We can imagine Charlotte, happy on the edge of the forest, on the road along which the wounded of Waterloo and the victorious Wellington, the hero of her youth, had passed 27 years earlier'[29] (the Waterloo road passes through Uccle).

There is no record of Charlotte ever visiting the Waterloo battlefield, strange as it seems that she did not find an opportunity to do so, as her father did when he accompanied her to Brussels. What is certain is that if she did by any chance make the journey to the site of Wellington's defeat of Napoleon, she did not start out from a country house in Uccle. The Hegers did own a house in Uccle but with a cheerful disregard for dates, the guide-book writers overlook the fact that this was in the 1870s, long after Charlotte's death. This house was not, however, called La Terrasse and there can be no connection with the house of that name in *Villette*. To add to the guide book writers' confusion, Louise Heger inherited another house in Uccle from a painter friend, but that was in the twentieth century in her old age. Surprisingly, even a grandson of the Hegers mentions their country house as the inspiration for Charlotte's La Terrasse.[30]

Many of the places alluded to by Charlotte in *Villette* have been found to refer to real ones, even if some appear to be an amalgam of more than one real-life location. But if La Terrasse was based on an actual place, its origin has always eluded the Brontë scholars and enthusiasts who have combed old Brussels maps and photos for possible manor houses in or around Brussels that Charlotte might have had in mind.

Brussels' revenge?

In his article *Bruxelles, les Brontës et la famille Héger*, Quiévreux described a recent visit he had made to Haworth, a place in which immense efforts had been expended in preserving every last souvenir of the Brontës. The village was relatively unchanged; Branwell's chair had been conserved in the Black Bull; it was not too difficult to imagine yourself back in the 1840s.

> What a place! Everything has been so well preserved that a presence seizes you by the throat as soon as you enter. The sudden appearance of Heathcliff among the tombs wouldn't surprise you any more than that of Catherine's little hand, torn and bleeding, the most tragic cry for help in world literature.

Among the souvenirs lovingly displayed in the Parsonage, Quiévreux told his readers, were mementoes of Charlotte's and Emily's Brussels stay, such as their French *devoirs* and Charlotte's travelling trunk. What a contrast to Brussels, where every memory of her had been effaced. 'The Brontë sisters, on whom Brussels left such a strong impression, have nothing left here to recall their memory ... What cruel destiny, what fatality has turned against every part of the city familiar to the daughters of the Reverend Brontë?' Could it, he wondered, be the city's revenge? Unlike the Belgian commentators who spoke of Charlotte's revenge on Brussels, Quiévreux wrote of the revenge of Brussels on Charlotte. 'Bruxelles-Villette, which Charlotte mocked, has taken its revenge by destroying all the places where her feet trod, all the places where her heart beat.'[31]

The only reparation the city could make was to put up some kind of memorial to the sisters, such as a commemorative plaque, a measure Quiévreux called for repeatedly. 'Would it be too much to ask for a plaque to tell passers-by where the rue Isabelle was and what ghosts may still wander there?' In his view, the city's 'immense stupidity' in razing the Pensionnat, which might have become 'a Mecca of international literature, the Number Two destination for Brontë pilgrims after Haworth', represented one of many mistakes and lost opportunities in its history.

This point had occasionally been made by other journalists. The writer of a 1928 article in a Belgian newspaper recalled an encounter he had had in the streets of Brussels in August 1914, a fortnight after the German invasion of Belgium. The journalist recounted that at a time when a horrified continent was living through the early weeks of the First World War, an 'innocent-looking' young British woman came up to him and asked if he could direct her to the house where Charlotte Brontë had lived (it had of course been demolished four years earlier). The journalist cited the anecdote as a remarkable illustration of the power of literature and the attraction exerted by the literary associations of places.[32]

Quiévreux returned to the subject of a memorial for the Brontës on the occasion of his capital's hosting of the Expo 1958 World Fair. The 1910 World Fair had taken place just after the demolition of the Quartier Isabelle, with King Leopold II and his city planners scrambling desperately to tidy up the area and finish the nearby Mont des Arts in time to receive the influx of visitors. The preparations for Expo 1958, the first universal exhibition after World War Two, brought significant 'Bruxellisation': building works that further transformed Brussels. The city now had a new role as host to many of the main EEC institutions. Modernity was in the air and the urban planners had big ideas. The Atomium was built. High-rise tower buildings started to go up; the 'inner ring' on the site of the boulevards where Charlotte and Emily had walked was modernised to meet growing traffic needs.

The fair could be expected to attract thousands of Anglophone visitors, and this gave Quiévreux a chance to make his call for a Brontë memorial loudly and clearly in an article in *Le Soir* dated 5 January 1958.

Brussels is in danger of disappointing British and American visitors. The reason? 'Wuthering Heights'

Numerous letters from Britain and America about the Brussels World Exhibition indicate that some future visitors will be disappointed by their visit to Brussels. Not, I hasten to add, because Expo 58 will fail to live up to expectations, but because for many of these visitors Brussels is above all the city of the Brontë sisters …

In Great Britain and across the Atlantic, Brontë fans number in their millions. For these Brontëites, any souvenir of Charlotte, Emily, Anne and their brother Branwell is an object of veneration.

Many of these enthusiasts imagine that the Brussels of today has preserved the traces of Emily and Charlotte, who lived in the city in 1842, at No 32 Rue Isabelle.

Only a few days ago I had a telephone call from an American journalist asking me where rue Isabelle was!

'Alas!' I replied, 'it was destroyed in 1909.'[33]

'And the Heger school, where Charlotte taught English and Emily perfected her French?'

'Vanished, along with its lovely street.'

'What? The Belgians have destroyed that shrine to English literature?'

'I'm afraid so ... In 1909, who in Belgium had read *Villette* or *Jane Eyre* or *Wuthering Heights*?'

Many enthusiastic pilgrims will be disappointed in a few months' time. What can we do for these romantic tourists? Take them as close as possible to the atmosphere the sisters breathed, where Charlotte, her heart broken by an impossible love for her teacher Constantin Heger, conceived the novel she was to set in Brussels. We must lead these pilgrims to the foot of the steps down to rue Victor Horta, close to the entrance to the Palais des Beaux-Arts, and tell them:

'You are standing on the site of the refectory in the Pensionnat Heger. A little further on, in rue Ravenstein, was the garden with the *Allée Défendue* and the old pear trees.'

In Brussels, time has effaced a key chapter in the Brontës' story. You must go all the way to Haworth in Yorkshire to visit their house, today a museum, and sense their presence. We went there a few years ago. We did the ritual walk on the moors, gathering heather and bracken. The old graveyard in which they played as children is still there. During our stay we were sad to see that old High Sunderland Hall, used by Emily as the setting of her wild love story about the gypsy Heathcliff, is crumbling into ruins. How many literary pilgrims have searched there for the window through which Cathy's ghostly, bleeding hand came one snowy night?

However, in the Parsonage in Haworth, which has been restored and extended, there is a landing dedicated to Brussels, with memorabilia relating to 1842. What an encounter for Belgians who make the long journey from London to Haworth! Last year, the museum on the wild moors where the wind never stops wuthering had more than 99,000 visitors. If only we had preserved the Pensionnat Heger, what an attraction it would have been for Brontëites!

'Are you telling me there isn't a single plaque, street or building in Brussels with the name Brontë on it?'

'No. No more than there is any memorial to Baudelaire, Voltaire or Rousseau, all of whom stayed here. I'm afraid that's the kind of philistines we are.'

The new Galerie Ravenstein shopping centre, currently being completed, is the place where we should celebrate Brussels' incredible luck in playing host to two of the Brontë sisters. It is there, on the spot closest to the site of the Pensionnat Heger, that a commemorative plaque ought to be placed. It would express our respect for the heights of English literature. It would please foreign visitors, who will be saddened to discover that time and vandalism have swept away all traces of an atmosphere that should have been reverently preserved.

The site of this memorial would be right opposite the steps down to rue Victor Horta. And why not consider also erecting a memorial in the entrance hall of the Palais des Beaux-Arts to these two writers whose fame is steadily growing more than a century after their deaths?

Haworth has paid its tribute to Brussels. Is it not time that Brussels returned the compliment?

Quiévreux's exhortations must have fallen on deaf ears as far as the city authorities were concerned, as had the suggestion of a journalist 25 years earlier that a street be named after Charlotte Brontë. Lamenting the loss of so many picturesquely-named old streets in the path of the *Jonction Nord-Midi* – such as rue du Singe (monkey) and rue Nuit et Jour – the journalist had proposed that if names of famous personages were required for new streets, Charlotte was an obvious candidate.[34]

Despite these occasional calls, Brussels has never commemorated the Brontës either with a street name or a monument of any kind, such as a plaque. Literary plaques in Brussels, however, are often erected not by the city of Brussels but at the instigation of associations or individuals. The plaque to Byron was put up by the writer Edmond Picard in 1896 when he moved to the house in rue Ducale where the English poet stayed. The one commemorating Baudelaire was an initiative of a Belgian writer, the one to Verlaine and Rimbaud was placed by the Belgian francophone community. The fact that there was no memorial to Charlotte and Emily until the Brontë Society placed one late in the twentieth century is likely to be due to the absence of a campaign by a really influential individual or group rather than resentment at Charlotte's anti-Belgian prejudices, though the latter probably played a part. What *is* surprising is that the Brontë Society did not take the initiative sooner.

It was not until 1979 that the Society affixed a commemorative plaque near the entrance to Bozar, one of the spots suggested for the purpose by Louis Quiévreux. Quiévreux did not live to see it. He had died in 1969 at the age of 67. In an article a few months before his death he returned to the attack, writing that the city's biggest mistake was to obliterate rue Isabelle with its Brontë associations, and that 'No Belgian can remain indifferent when the name of the Brontës is spoken.'[35]

It would have been nice if Quiévreux's name had been mentioned at the unveiling of the plaque on 26 June 1980 before assembled worthies both Belgian and British, including the Hegers' great-grandson Paul Pechère. The day of the unveiling 'dawned bright and sunny but by the time we were assembled for the ceremony stormy conditions prevailed and claps of thunder interrupted the proceedings.'[36] Reporting on this 'symbolic' event on 28 June, *Le Soir* referred to the '*Wuthering Heights* weather' (*temps de Hurlevent*) that accompanied it. The weather could be seen as appropriate for both Brontë sisters. 'The name Brontë is that of the Greek god of thunder,' the author of an article on a new translation of *Wuthering Heights* told his readers in 1935, 'the thunder that roars through the souls of the characters in Emily Brontë's novel . . . ',[37] while *Villette* closes with a memorable storm at sea. In 1932, the year the French translation of *Villette* was published, a Flemish journalist described interviewing Heger's grandson, Fernand Héger-Gilbert, in his office high in the law courts building, the massive, brooding Palais de Justice where he worked as a forensic doctor, while a storm raged outside: 'An autumn storm was driving from the South-West, like the one that roared over the ocean when Lucy's M. Paul was due to return from overseas . . .'[38]

As the plaque was unveiled amid the driving rain, was Louis Quiévreux's spirit hovering around the site where he often imagined the

◀ The Brontë Society plaque commemorating Charlotte and Emily's stay in Brussels, placed on the Palais des Beaux-Arts in 1979.

spirits of others? It is easy to imagine with what jubilation he would have reported on the event if he could have been there in the flesh.

'The city where her heart went astray'

An exhibition held at the Musée Charlier from March 1953 to April 1955 for the centenary of Charlotte Brontë's death captured the imagination of many who went to see it and intensified her romantic legacy in Brussels. Along with reproductions of her letters to Heger, one of the exhibits that most moved visitors was the bouquet of dried heather that had mysteriously appeared a few years earlier on Heger's grave, by whose hand no-one knew. Now that the Isabelle quarter and the *allées* and bowers of the Pensionnat garden had disappeared in the great 'hecatomb in which Brussels had lost part of its soul', wrote the writer and critic Paul Caso, the only way to seek Charlotte Brontë's 'plaintive shade' was among documents and mementos such as the ones exhibited. Like many of the visitors, he imagined that the little bunch of heather had been gathered from Charlotte's grave, picturing the grave as a moorland one like Cathy and Heathcliff's (Charlotte is in fact buried in the family vault in the parish church). It was 'a last ray of her great and pure love', the secret she took to her grave, brought to light by the few yellowed letters to Heger now in the British Museum.[39]

In Brussels, as has been seen, the Brontë sisters' romantic image is heightened both by their association with a vanished quarter of the city recalled with nostalgia for its charm, and by the story of Charlotte's 'hopeless love' and the fact that she is supposed to have 'left her heart' in the Belgian capital. But while romantics like Quiévreux have imagined her spirit haunting the sites of the places she knew, another writer, Lucien Christophe, doubted that it would cling to the site of the vanished Pensionnat. Should it be at large in Brussels, he imagined it roaming restlessly through the city unable to find a place where it could be at peace. Christophe, a severe judge of Charlotte Brontë, was considerably less convinced than Quiévreux that she deserved a memorial in the city. His comments were made in 1939 in his article *Le roman bruxellois de Charlotte Brontë*.[40]

> In London's Paternoster Row, a narrow street at the foot of the vast fortress of St Paul's, the English reverently show visitors the place where Charlotte and Emily stayed in 1842 on their way to Brussels. But in Brussels, where Charlotte lived for two decisive years, there is nothing to conjure up her memory ... The house and garden that witnessed her struggle and her rout have vanished, the neighbourhood where she stayed is transformed and unrecognisable. We would search there in vain for her ghost, for ghosts are seen only with their settings.
>
> Brussels has destroyed so many testimonies that would have made our capital into an incomparable and poignant museum of the pain and anguish of exile ... Like a diligent housewife anxious for her house to be worthy of the extensions continually being made to it, tracking down and scrubbing out suspect traces and marks, Brussels has done its best to wipe out or render invisible any trace of the Verlaine stain, the Baudelaire stain, the Brontë stain.
>
> There is also the fact that the name Brontë, like that of Baudelaire, touches a raw nerve ... Charlotte's opinions and judgements about Belgium in general and Brussels in particular are caustic and at times resolutely aggressive.

After a critical discussion of *Villette* as a novel of revenge and of Charlotte's treatment of the Hegers, Christophe concludes: 'I am afraid that these are not arguments that will persuade a Brussels city council to name a street after Charlotte Brontë. And doubtless it is better for her genius to remain for ever wandering, without a refuge, in this foreign city where her heart went astray.'

'A strange and mysterious place': gateway to another world

Whether or not Charlotte's shade can be imagined to continue to haunt the site of the Pensionnat now that the school is buried deep below the Palais des Beaux-Arts, for some imaginative souls there is a section of rue Isabelle that has supernatural associations independent of its Brontë link. Although the street that the Brontës knew disappeared under a twentieth-century redevelopment, it is possible today to walk on the part of it that vanished under an earlier redevelopment – the end that originally led to the old Coudenberg Palace and was buried when Place Royale was built. That stretch of the street was excavated at the turn of the twenty-first century along with the cellars of the Coudenberg; the archaeological site can be visited from the BELvue museum.

Proof of the imaginative appeal of this underground rue Isabelle is its inclusion on a website[41] inspired by the graphic novel series *Les Cités Obscures*, created by the Belgian artist François Schuiten and the French writer Benoît Peeters. The fictional obscure cities or 'Cities of the Fantastic', as they were called in English translation, are located on a 'counter-earth' or parallel universe invisible from our Earth because it is situated exactly oppo-

◀ The underground rue Isabelle in the Coudenberg archaeological site under the Place Royale.

site it on the other side of the sun. It is possible to travel between the two worlds by means of gateways called 'Obscure Passages', and the website contains allegedly factual reports, written in a pseudo-documentary style by a 'network of researchers' called 'Obscurantists', who alert readers to the location of possible points of passage. 'A strong suspicion, well-documented, is quite sufficient.' The buried rue Isabelle is proposed by one of these Obscurantists as a possible place of passage to an obscure city.

The author of the 'report' on rue Isabelle bases his suspicion on the fact that the subterranean street is a 'strange and mysterious place', explaining that it was buried when the site was developed in an early example of 'Bruxellisation'. His main 'evidence' is a document purportedly sent to the Brussels Archaeological Society by one of the authorities on the 'obscure continent' responsible for the 'places of passage', around the time that the Society was proposing to open up the excavations to the public. The document warns that these gateways must remain secret and that only certain privileged individuals are allowed to pass through them.

The author of the website 'report' is not the only person to be intrigued by the vast subterranean labyrinth under Place Royale. Popularly known as 'the catacombs', this labyrinth is said to extend well beyond the square, according to some reports as far as Grand Place. The *Obscurantist* of the rue Isabelle article cites a story of some English families trapped in the Bellevue hotel by the fighting during the 1830 uprising. They were evacuated to safety through these underground passages by a mysterious stranger who then disappeared and was never identified. Could this unknown rescuer have guided his charges to safety via the 'obscure continent'?

The Pensionnat Heger had links with underground passages. A reference to them found its way into Chapter 12 of *Villette* in relation to the ghostly nun who haunts Mme Beck's school:

A vague tale went of a black and white nun, sometimes, on some night or nights of the year, seen in some part of this vicinage. The ghost must have been built out some ages ago, for there were houses all round now; but certain convent-relics, in the shape of old and huge fruit-trees, yet consecrated the spot; and, at the foot of one – a Methuselah of a pear-tree, dead, all but a few boughs which still faithfully renewed their perfumed snow in spring, and their honey-sweet pendants in autumn – you saw, in scraping away the mossy earth between the half-bared roots, a glimpse of slab, smooth, hard, and black. The legend went ... that this was the portal of a vault, imprisoning deep beneath that ground, on whose surface grass grew and flowers bloomed, the bones of a girl whom a monkish conclave of the drear middle ages had here buried alive, for some sin against her vow.

Lucy Snowe tells us that according to tradition there had formerly been a convent on the site of Mme Beck's Pensionnat. Close to the real Pensionnat in medieval times there had in fact been not a convent but a hospice, the Hospice Terarken, housing pauper women. But Frederika Macdonald confirms that there was a slab in the garden of the Pensionnat Heger similar to that in the fictional garden in *Villette*; according to the story she heard, however, it concealed not a vault containing the bones of an erring nun but an underground passage used as an escape route by the crossbowmen when under siege.[42]

Be that as it may, with a sure instinct for seizing on elements of the atmosphere of the real Brussels and transmogrifying them into the Gothic atmosphere of her novel, Charlotte thus hints at the subterranean maze of vaults and galleries that inspired the Obscurantist of the 'Obscure Cities' to view rue Isabelle as a place of passage to another world. And it seems not inappropriate that, as in popular legend in and around Haworth, an aura of the supernatural should also hover around a place associated with the Brontës in Brussels.

As a postscript to this chapter on the destruction of the Brontës' Brussels, we may mention that François Schuiten, the Belgian artist who illustrated the *Cités Obscures* series with detailed drawings of buildings, grew up in the capital and witnessed at close hand the process of 'Bruxellisation' in the 1950s and 60s that destroyed much of his city in favour of modernist office blocks. Schuiten trained to become an architect like his father but opted instead to explore architecture in the world of *Bandes Dessinées*. A graphic album in the *Cités Obscures* series devoted to an imaginary city called 'Brüsel' recounts an adventure set in a counterpart of the Belgian capital located in the other world, a city that, like the real one, has experienced 'devastating urban renewal' at the hands of ambitious urban planners dreaming of an all-new 'Brüsel': 'No more lack of hygiene! No more dusty old buildings! All is razed and enormous new skyscrapers are erected at blistering speed! Never mind the disruptions and uprootings of people's lives! Who needs to preserve and live in history? Hurrah for modernity!'[43]

1   In contrast to 'Joyeuse Entrée', the name used in Belgium for the ceremonial entry of a monarch at the start of a new reign.

2   Quiévreux, *Bruxelles, notre capitale*, p 59.

3   Macdonald, *The Secret of Charlotte Brontë*, p. 9.

4   Gilkin, *Mémoires inachevés: une enfance et une jeunesse bruxelloises*, pp. 384–5.

5   *Villette*, Chapter 12.

6   Open carriage for hire. Brussels *fiacres* are mentioned in *Villette* and *The Professor*.

7   Biebuyck, *Bruxelles: ville en forme de cœur*, p. 173. The title refers to the pentagonal or heart-shaped form of the historical city centre within the 'inner ring' following the line of the old boulevards.

8   Quiévreux, 'Bruxelles, les Brontës et la famille Héger'.

9   De Vries, *Brussels: A cultural and literary history*, p. 91.

10 Tahon, *La Rue Isabelle et Le Jardin des Arbalétriers*, p. 5.

11 *Villette*, Chapter 10.

12 Des Marez, *L'Origine et le développement de Bruxelles: Le quartier Isabelle et Terarken*, p. II.

13 Elizabeth Gaskell, *The Life of Charlotte Brontë* (London: Smith, Elder and Co., 1857), Chapter 11.

14 Nerval, *Œuvres*, p. 812.

15 Addison, *Belgium as she is*, p. 175.

16 Tahon, *La Rue Isabelle et Le Jardin des Arbalétriers*, p. 82.

17 *Ibid.*, pp. 5–6.

18 *Le Soir*, 10 March 1953.

19 Quiévreux, *Bruxelles, notre capitale. Histoire, folklore, archéologie*, pp. 22–4.

20 Des Marez, *L'Origine et le développement de Bruxelles: Le quartier Isabelle et Terarken*, pp. 209–10.

21 T. Wemyss Reid, *Charlotte Brontë: A Monograph* (London: Macmillan, 1877), Chapter 6.

22 Quiévreux, 'Bruxelles, les Brontës et la famille Héger'.

23 Maeterlinck, *La sagesse et la destine*, pp. 275–6.

24 Ruijssenaars, *The Pensionnat Revisited*: p. 28. Cited from a letter from de Knevett to D'Arcy Wentworth Thompson.

25 Preface to Quiévreux, *Bruxelles, guide de la capitale et de ses environs*.

26 *Le soir illustré*, 16 Sept. 1954.

27 Quiévreux, 'Bruxelles, les Brontës et la famille Héger'.

28 Roger Bodart et al, *Guide littéraire de la Belgique, de la Hollande et du Luxembourg* (Paris: Hachette, 1972), p. 9; Piet van Nieuwenhuysen, *Gids voor oud Brussel* (Antwerp, 1988), p. 45.

29 Quiévreux, 'Bruxelles, les Brontës et la famille Héger'.

30 Fernand Héger-Gilbert, in an interview given to *Het Laatste Nieuws*, 3 November 1932.

31 Quiévreux, 'Bruxelles, les Brontës et la famille Héger'.

32 *La Meuse*, 4 May 1928.

33 In fact it was demolished in 1910. Ruijssenaars, *The Pensionnat Revisited*, p. 17.

34 *La Dernière Heure*, 30 August 1933.

35 *Le Soir*, 28 February 1969.

36 'A Plaque is Unveiled in Brussels to Commemorate the Stay of Charlotte and Emily Brontë at the Pensionnat Heger'. *Brontë Society Transactions*, 1980, 17:5, pp. 371–374.

37 *L'Indépendance Belge*, 6 February 1935.

38 *Hat Laatste Nieuws*, 3 November 1932.

39 *Le Soir*, 24 March 1953.

40 *Ibid.*, 3 April 1939.

41 https://passages.altaplana.be/fiches/!cadresF.htm

42 Frederika Macdonald, 'The Brontës at Brussels', *The Woman at Home*, Vol. 2, No. 10, July 1894, pp. 279–91. Reproduced in Ruijssenaars, *Charlotte Brontë's Promised Land*, pp. 70–78.

43 Benoît Peeters and François Schuiten, *Cities of the Fantastic: Brüsel* (New York: Nantier Beall Minoustchine, 2003).

CHAPTER EIGHT

From 'Nobody' to 'Somebody': Charlotte, *Villette* and the Immigrant Experience

IT is not only the streets and buildings of Brussels that have changed beyond recognition since Charlotte Brontë's time. The city's population, too, has been transformed as a result of immigration. The phenomenon did not reach mass proportions until the twentieth century, but even in Charlotte's day the population of the Belgian capital included a considerable percentage of foreign residents.

For Belgian readers, Charlotte Brontë herself and her heroes Lucy Snowe and William Crimsworth provide interesting examples of expatriates/immigrants seeking their fortune in their capital. So much so that Sophie De Schaepdrijver, a Flemish historian, opens her book *Elites for the Capital? Foreign Migration to mid-19th century Brussels* with a discussion of *Villette* and of Lucy's story as that of a woman finding a place and a role for herself in the environment of a foreign town.

Lucy's destiny in Villette/Brussels, and to a lesser extent Charlotte's own stay in Brussels, can be considered, as De Schaepdrijver does, in the context of the city's history of immigration. Located as it is in the heart of Europe, the Belgian capital's tradition of receiving immigrants was established early on. As a buffer state for the conlicts between its bigger neighbours and a region often governed by foreign powers, Belgium has always been at a crossroads of cultures – French, German, Spanish. Reviewing the history of the country in his essay *L'âme Belge* (1897), the writer and politician Edmond Picard saw Belgium as a place with a special attraction not just for invaders but for migrants – 'a seductive place where people like to settle'.[1] Part Germanic, part Latin, the Belgians themselves are a hybrid race, a mix of ethnicities. Today, around two-thirds of the population of Brussels are of non-Belgian origin; after the Second World War there were major waves of immigration both from Europe (notably Spain, Italy and Turkey) and north Africa, particularly Morocco, and the foreign population has been further swelled by staff working at the EU institutions and other international organisations.

The nineteenth century saw population growth and expanding urbanisation throughout Europe, and Belgium experienced a higher rate of urbanisation than any other European country. The Belgian capital became one of the fastest-growing in Europe. From a town of 113,000 inhabitants in the Brontës' time, it had grown to over three-quarters of a million by the start of the First World War. Although much of the expansion was attributable to migrants from other parts of Belgium, foreign immigration was also a significant phenomenon. Even as early as 1842 the foreign population of Brussels accounted for 7% of the total (around 7,000 inhabitants), a higher percentage than in either London or Paris. The largest groups of foreign residents were those from France (who represented almost half), the Netherlands and Germany. The British community in Brussels accounted for 11% of foreign immigration, a sizeable proportion, added to which there were many Britons living in other Belgian towns such as Ostend and Bruges.

Most of the foreign immigrants who came to Brussels in search of work – as opposed to *rentiers*, people of independent means who were attracted to it by the low cost of living – were artisans and middle-class professionals: teachers, businessmen, bankers. Brussels offered them better opportunities than in their own countries, where there was more competition for their skills.

The British flocked to Belgium just after the Battle of Waterloo, when the country became a fashionable destination. Of those who went to tend the wounded, or simply to visit the battlefield, some decided to stay on. Some of these British residents were scared away by the political uncertainty following the 1830 Revolution, but there was still a substantial British population in Brussels when the Brontës arrived there. It included many people who struggled to live on their income in Britain but could get by in Belgium, where, moreover, they could give their children a Continental education at a relatively low cost. The Brontës' friends the Wheelwrights, who had a large family of daughters to maintain, could afford to send all five girls to the Hegers' Pensionnat.

Contemporary guide books note the number of amenities that had sprung up in the city for its British residents. Many of them are catalogued by Henry Robert Addison in the 1843 guidebook, with its account of Belgium's bustling little British community, that so fascinates the writer Leen Huet. Just as *Villette* has its English doctor, Graham Bretton or 'Dr John', so Brussels had an English physician, a Dr Parkinson. If Charlotte, with her perennial dental problems – by the time she was in her thirties she had many missing teeth – had been able to afford it, she might have consulted a Mr Alex, Surgeon Dentist, formerly employed by the Duke of Gloucester, who was to be found in rue de la Madeleine and of whom Addison reported: 'He is the inventor of several improvements in the fabrication of false teeth and professes to stop decayed teeth with a metallic preparation, however far gone they may be.' Had she fallen seriously ill in Brussels and wished to draw up a will she could have called in Mr Bassett, solicitor, in Boulevard du Régent, whose wife kept a girls' school much frequented by the English.

It is not known whether Charlotte ever visited Mr Todd's English circulating library at 45 Montagne de la Cour, which sold 'English stationery, patent medicines, perfumery and fancy articles', but we do know that she bought a book (a goodbye present for one of the Hegers' children) at Edward Browne's English reading room in the same street, where you could read all the English journals and periodicals. British residents could have their coats made by an 'extremely civil' English tailor, Mr Wells in rue des Douze Apôtres, who was 'employed by almost all the respectable English residents', and buy English groceries in rue Montagne de la Cour from Mr Yates, 'one of the most respectable tradesmen on the Continent'. When they wearied of Brussels *pistolets,* they could be supplied with muffins and crumpets by 'Philip', an English baker in the *faubourg de Namur.*

After all this it comes as no surprise to learn that the Upper Town was almost as English in flavour as French. To judge from the description of a Belgian author, describing in 1851 the effect of passing from the lower town to the upper, the latter seems to have been as much a little Britain as a miniature Paris. It was almost as common to hear English spoken as it is in Brussels today and there was evidence everywhere of the vogue for English commodities.

> You have passed from the Flemish colony to the francophone colony; here now, you find yourself in a sort of polyglot exile haven, where, a few years from now, English will be the national language. On a lovely July morning, you could believe that Bond Street or Regent Street had just emigrated and transported their teapots, sole domestic relics of old Albion, to the district of the Park. Dogs, riding tackle and clothing, everything is British.[2]

Crimsworth, in *The Professor,* admires the fluent English of a Belgian gentleman staying in his Brussels hotel, which 'impressed me for the first time with a due notion of the cosmopolitan character of the capital I was in; it was my first experience of that skill in living languages I afterwards found to be so general in Brussels'.[3] Similarly, Lucy Snowe describes *Villette* as a cosmopolitan capital, though she observes this phenomenon principally in the microcosmic world of the Pensionnat, where there are 'girls of almost every European nation', rather than in the streets of the city. Although Lucy's friends in Villette are English, the novel does not quite convey a sense of an English colony or of Lucy as a member of such a colony; at any rate, we do not imagine her as being surrounded by English shops and libraries. Her habitual state of mind in Villette is that of feeling isolated in her Englishness in a foreign culture rather than a member of an expatriate community – even though the English characters Ginevra Fanshawe, the Brettons and Paulina De Bassompierre play a very large part in the novel.

Lucy's experiences are somewhere between those of an immigrant and those of an expatriate. In our own time there is a clear demarcation between the two. In Charlotte Brontë's Brussels, the demarcation line was between foreigners who had to earn their living and the *rentiers* who had private means. Charlotte, middle-class and well-educated but poor, was positioned between the two. Like many other middle-class young ladies she studied languages at a European finishing school; however, to pay for her keep she also gave English classes. Although she inherited some money from her aunt at the end of her first year, her poverty would have distanced her from much of the social life of the British community even if her timidity had not prevented her from seeking it out.

At the beginning of her first year in Brussels, Charlotte arrived as any middle-class girl would have done on a first trip to Europe to study at a boarding school – accompanied by family and friends, including menfolk to protect her on the journey (her father and the brother of her friend Mary Taylor). Her return to Belgium, however, without Emily, to start her second year at the Pensionnat was made in very different circumstances. She travelled alone, arriving in London so late that rather than try to book into a hotel she opted to spend the night on board the Ostend steam-boat or 'packet', a frightening experience in the course of which she was overcharged by the haggling watermen who rowed her out to the ship. She spent the following night in an Ostend hotel before taking the train to Brussels. In all it was a three-day journey, undertaken completely alone. Moreover, her situation at the Pensionnat was no

▲ London Bridge steam wharf, where Charlotte boarded the steam boar ('packet') to Ostend.

longer what it had been in the first year. Although she continued to perfect her French and write essays for M. Heger, she returned as a teacher, an employee.

Without Emily, and with the departure of many of her friends in that second year, Charlotte's situation at the Pensionnat was a lonely one. That of Lucy Snowe is still more challenging. Lucy is an orphan who has no relatives to turn to; before she departs for the Continent she is forced to earn a living as companion to a sick lady. On her employer's death she is left almost destitute. With just fifteen pounds in her pocket, she decides to seek her fortune in London. On her first evening in the metropolis, after booking into an inn, she feels utterly desolate:

> What was I doing here alone in great London? What should I do on the morrow? What prospects had I in life? What friends had I on earth? Whence did I come? Whither should I go? What should I do?[4]

But the following morning, elated by her first sight of London, she feels more emboldened. The idea of seeking her fortune even further afield, in Europe, has been planted in her mind by a foreign nursemaid employed to speak French in a household in her home town. When Lucy learns that Englishwomen can find similar employment teaching English to the children of families on the Continent, she determines to get on the next packet for Europe, which is bound for 'Boue-Marine' (Ostend). 'I had nothing to lose.' At this stage Lucy does not even know which city she will head for once she reaches the Continent.

At Boue-Marine Ginevra Fanshawe, a flighty young thing Lucy encounters in the packet, is whisked off by friends who have come to accompany her to her boarding school in Villette. Lucy, in contrast, makes her way there alone. Having learned from Ginevra that the directress of the school needs a nursery governess for her children, she heads to Villette on the strength of this 'shadow of a project'.[5] On arrival late at night, with very little money and without her trunk, which the conductor of the diligence has left behind in 'Boue-Marine', she is directed to an inn by a fellow traveller who guides her part of the way. When he turns back she gets lost and ends up by chance in front of Mme Beck's door, terrified after being followed by a couple of moustachioed, cigar-smoking men.

Lucy is a poor immigrant starting a new life in a strange place. Unlike Charlotte, she doesn't know a word of French when she arrives and has to learn a new language as well as acclimatise to a different culture. She is armed for the struggle ahead with nothing but her intelligence, courage and her one marketable commodity: as it turns out, she can earn her living teaching English. Lucy's experience is in some ways close to that of a latter-day immigrant of the least fortunate kind, arriving virtually penniless, perhaps after some catastrophe in the home country (she hints at misfortunes that have left her alone in the world) to start life over again in a strange one. Although her first job as a nursery governess bears a resemblance to that of a modern-day *au pair*, and although, at certain points of the novel, she slips out of the day-to-day work routine at the Pensionnat into the moneyed expatriate world of the Brettons and Bassompierres – a world in which she stays in comfortable houses and is taken to concerts and plays – her habitual position in the city is that of a poor employee obliged to work for her living, who ultimately achieves independence by acquiring her own school. The same applies to William Crimsworth, although unlike Lucy he does not stay on permanently in his host country, returning to England as soon as he has saved enough money to become a man of independent means.

To return to Sophie De Schaepdrijver and her book on *Foreign Migration to mid-19th century Brussels,* De Schaepdrijver is interested in *Villette* as the story of how someone who is 'nobody' in her own country, since she has no family or property, is able to become 'somebody' in a foreign town. Before her move to Villette, as a single woman in paid employment – something considered socially demeaning for a middle-class woman – Lucy has no social position. To use a modern term, she suffers from 'social exclusion'. What interests De Schaepdrijver is that Lucy is able to find a social role precisely because she is an immigrant and a foreigner. Although she has no money she has skills, and they are skills that are needed in the thriving city of Villette. Foreign, poor, and single, she starts out there as an outsider in every sense of the word. 'Because of migration and paid work she eventually wins a definite if modest place in society'.

It is not my intention to impose an ill-fitting framework on this complex book by reading it simply as a story of upward social mobility through migration. *Villette* is by no means a rags-to-riches story about an emigrating wage-seeker who becomes a successful business-owner. Brontë did not, as Theodore Dreiser would half a century later in his novel *Sister Carrie,* describe a young woman's move to the city from an emphatically social point of view. But the book certainly deals with finding one's place in society. In this sense, I would like to point out the fact that the social environment of a foreign town makes a difference; the *deus ex machina* in the novel is not Paul Emanuel, but Villette. Lucy Snowe finally has been able to find a position in Villette because she is a foreigner and, as a foreigner, has brought with her skills than can be capitalised on because of local demands (whether or not Brontë considered this course of action suitable for herself, the theme must have been foremost in her mind; in *The Professor,* too, the protagonist starts out as a teacher and ends up opening a school in Brussels). As things turned out, it is by coming to this town that the heroine of *Villette* has found an unequivocal social identity – that she has become 'somebody'.[6]

Another Flemish academic, Daniel Acke, writing in *Écrire Bruxelles/Brussel Schrijven,* also points out that the immigrant may discover a new identity in a strange city. 'Confrontation with a strange, foreign city may give rise to a quest for one's own identity … Contact with a foreign culture engenders a process of reflection about yourself.'[7] From being someone whose identity is indeterminate, as shown by Ginevra's question 'Who *are* you, Miss Snowe?',[8] Lucy can be seen as forging an identity for herself both personally and professionally in the strange town of Villette, not just finding love but achieving success as the mistress of her own school.

Lucy's situation strikes a particular chord with Sophie De Schaepdrijver, who is herself a migrant, having moved to the US and taught at a university there for over two decades. Another reason for the appeal of *Villette* for De Schaepdrijver is that the action takes place in Brussels, a city for which she has a deep affection. Thus, a novel written by a British writer about her experience living in exile in Brussels while homesick for England has a strong attraction for a Belgian writer exiled in the United States and homesick for Brussels.

Brussels in *Villette*, De Schaepdrijver says, is 'a place of exile but also of hope'.[9] For Charlotte herself, the experience of life abroad was overall not a happy one. In *Écrire Bruxelles/ Brussel Schrijven*, Daniel Acke points out that emigrants imagine the city of destination and dream about it before they see it, projecting their desires on to it. The reality may prove to be a disappointment.[10] Charlotte called Brussels her 'Promised Land' when it was still the city of her dreams and ambitions, the place that was to provide her with culture, knowledge, freedom, the means of earning her living and becoming independent. The real Brussels became a city of disappointment and frustration, although these negative experiences were to prove fruitful for her emotional and creative development.

As can be seen from De Schaepdrijver's analysis, Lucy Snowe's encounter with Villette is much more positive than Charlotte's with Brussels, and only reflects Charlotte's in part. At some stage Charlotte may have toyed with the idea of opening a school in Brussels like Lucy Snowe in *Villette* and Frances Henri in *The Professor*; as it turned out, her own destiny was to be very different from theirs, but in *Villette* she tells what is at one level the story of a successful immigrant in a foreign city.

1   Reproduced in Aron, *La Belgique artistique et littéraire*, p. 91.

2   Lesbroussart, *Types et caractères belges contemporains*, p.185. Cited, in English translation, in Michael Hollington (ed.), *The reception of Charles Dickens in Europe* (London; New York: Continuum, 2011), Vol. I, p. 259.

3   *The Professor,* Chapter 7.
4   *Villette,* Chapter 5.
5   *Ibid.,* Chapter 7.
6   De Schaepdrijver, *Elites for the Capital?,* p. 11.
7   Acke and Bekers, *Écrire Bruxelles/Brussel Schrijven,* pp. 36–7.
8   *Villette,* Chapter 27.
9   In an article in which Flemish women discussed their favourite novels, *De Standaard,* 10 November 2004.
10 Acke and Bekers, *Écrire Bruxelles/Brussel Schrijven,* pp. 37–8.

CHAPTER NINE

Education and Hopeless Romantic Love: *Villette* and *The Professor* as a Window on Nineteenth-Century Brussels Boarding Schools

C HARLOTTE Brontë is read all over the world for many reasons: as a compelling storyteller, for the romantic appeal of her novels, for her powers of psychological analysis, added to which is the romantic appeal of the Brontës themselves as figures of literary myth. She is not thought of principally as a source of social history, though her books do not lack information on subjects such as educational institutions for poor orphans (*Jane Eyre*) or industrial unrest in the early nineteenth century (*Shirley*).

One legacy of Charlotte Brontë in Belgium, however, as already seen, is that her novels constitute a source of information on life in Brussels in her time. A recent compilation of passages from nineteenth-century novels reflecting aspects of life in the capital (*Bruxelles: la vie quotidienne au XIXe siècle vue par les écrivains de l'époque*)[1] contains no fewer than eight extracts from *Villette*, which is virtually the only non-Belgian novel cited. The extracts are chosen for Charlotte's impressions of Brussels life and characters. Her portrait of King Leopold I is there and so is that of Rosine, the Pensionnat's pert 'portress' (used to illustrate a section on 'Brussels *concierges*'). Even Lucy's account of her first meal at the Pensionnat is of interest to the author in a chapter about food in Brussels in the period.

Naturally enough, given that Charlotte spent most of her time within the classrooms of the Pensionnat Heger, the aspect of the city's life covered in most detail in both *The Professor* and *Villette* is life inside a Brussels boarding school. Her account of her fictional characters' tribulations as teachers in Belgium – Crimsworth's initial tussles to impose discipline on his intractable pupils at M. Pelet's and Mlle Reuter's schools, Lucy Snowe's struggles, as a *sous-maîtresse*, with Mme Beck's young ladies – make painful reading at times, both for their brutally honest and psychologically revealing analysis of classroom dynamics from the teacher's standpoint and – particularly where Belgian readers are concerned – for her fictional teachers' all too evident dislike and contempt for their charges.

As pointed out in the previous chapter, Charlotte's fictional characters William Crimsworth and Lucy Snowe, unlike Charlotte herself, are examples of successful emigrants making a new life for themselves. These fictional teachers, too, are more successful in the classroom than Charlotte Brontë was herself. Particularly positive is their achievement in setting up their own schools. As directress of her own establishment, Frances Henri, like Mme Heger, combines her professional duties with those of a wife and mother, while Lucy runs the pensionnat set up for her by M. Paul. At the time of her Brussels stay, Charlotte's plan was to start a school with her sisters in the Parsonage back in Haworth, but, as Sophie De Schaepdrijver says, thoughts of opening one in Brussels may have crossed her mind from time to time. Perhaps she occasionally imagined herself, like Zoë Heger, running her own Pensionnat with the support of just such a husband as Constantin Heger – quite possibly, in the world of fantasy, with none other than M. Heger himself! The Hegers' school, run by a married woman, seemed a more attractive model than the ones she had known in England, directed by maiden ladies.

As things turned out, Charlotte opened a school neither in Belgium nor in England. She and her sisters were unable to attract a single prospective pupil to Haworth and she was to find professional fulfilment as a writer, not a schoolteacher. However, little as she relished her teaching duties, in *Villette* and *The Professor* she left an extremely interesting account of her experience in Belgian classrooms.

In addition to recounting the tribulations and triumphs of teachers in the classroom, the two novels, in particular *Villette*, provide a mass of information about girls' boarding schools in Brussels. Few details of life in the Hegers' Pensionnat were omitted by Charlotte in her fictional accounts. We learn about the exact distribution of its rooms and how they were lit, heated and furnished. We learn every particular of the daily routine, as the inmates of the fictional pensionnats move from classroom to refectory, from refectory to oratory. We learn about the religious component of that routine (the *prière du midi* at the start of afternoon lessons, the evening prayer in the oratory, the *lecture pieuse* – lives of the saints – with which the boarders are regaled after the evening study hour, except when M. Paul provides variety by readings of a livelier nature), and about the hours of recreation in the garden, where Charlotte even tells us the kind of swing there was in the play-

▲ The Pensionnat and rue Isabelle in the second half of the nineteenth century.

ground for the younger children. We learn about the rhythm of the school year: the ways in which fête days were celebrated, the cramming for the examination day before the school broke up for the summer vacation. We experience what it was like to listen to a speech by one of the masters of the Athénée Royal, the boys' school next door, at a solemn ceremony to mark a royal birthday. Charlotte heard M. Heger speak on such an occasion, and the event duly made its way into Chapter 27 of *Villette*.

One reason why the compiler of *Bruxelles: la vie quotidienne au XIXe siècle* was grateful for Charlotte's impressions is the lack of information available on the city's boarding schools in the first half of the nineteenth century, particularly *girls'* schools. Private establishments like the Hegers' left few archives. Moreover, in the period immediately following Belgian independence, there was little focus on education or on intellectual life generally.

The second half of the century was to see major improvements in women's education. These had already been campaigned for earlier in the century by a friend of Zoë Heger's, Zoë Gatti de Gamond, who in 1834 wrote a treatise on the importance of female education, *De la condition des femmes au dix-neuvième siècle*. (It was at the house of this friend that Zoë Parent, as she then was, is said to have met her future husband Constantin Heger.) Gatti de Gamond's daughter Isabelle continued her mother's pioneering work, founding the first non-sectarian state secondary school for girls in the 1860s, the period when education for women really took off in

Belgium. For information on girls' schools earlier in the century, were it not for the insider accounts left by Charlotte Brontë, data would mostly have to be gleaned from sources such as census records and prospectuses.

In an article on private girls' schools in the decades after Belgian independence, *Un réseau privé d'éducation des filles. Institutrices et pensionnats à Bruxelles (1830–1860)*, Valérie Piette, a social historian at Brussels University, acknowledges her debt to Charlotte Brontë for data on the subject. She tells us that the school about which most information is available is the Pensionnat Heger, due partly to its prestige and impressive longevity – it was carried on by the couple's daughters – but chiefly to the account of it left by Charlotte Brontë. 'We owe our information on the Pensionnat Heger to Charlotte Brontë's presence there, and to her hopeless romantic love for Constantin Heger'.[2]

Charlotte's novels are not the only source of information on her stay at the Hegers'; researchers also find information in her letters, as when she tells Ellen that her salary as a *sous-maîtresse* was £16 a year, around 400 francs.[3] The interest surrounding the Brontës' attendance at the Pensionnat led, too, to the publication of reminiscences by other pupils at the school which provide further sources.

In the opinion of another chronicler of education in the nineteenth century, John Bartier, 'Charlotte Brontë's testimony is doubtless a little distorted by her unhappy passion for Heger, but nevertheless ... we can extract interesting information'. From the evidence in Charlotte's novels and letters, he writes, we know that a Pensionnat could be a profitable business venture. One reason was the low salaries paid to teachers, to judge from Charlotte Brontë's stipend. Curiously, Bartier attributes a self-interested motive to Heger's kindly letter to Patrick at the end of Charlotte and Emily's first year stressing the desirability of allowing the sisters to study in Brussels for a further year, seeing in it an indication of the Hegers' reluctance to lose income from the Brontës as pupils and Charlotte's services as a teacher.[4]

Another girls' boarding school about which we know a lot thanks to the Brontë connection was the Château de Koekelberg pensionnat where their friends Mary and Martha Taylor studied, run by an Englishwoman, Catherine Goussaert née Phelps. Too expensive for the Brontës themselves, it was more international than the Hegers' school, with a large number of English, German and French pupils. Like the Hegers', it was one of the longest-lived and most prestigious Pensionnats in the capital. Both establishments were included in a list of five schools recommended by the

Baroness Willmar in 1850 to a friend in her collection of letters *Souvenirs de Bruxelles*. She praised the *bon ton* and good manners inculcated at the Koekelberg school, and the quality of the teaching.[5] A Belgian newspaper commended it in 1835 as 'one of the best schools we know in our country'.[6]

A letter to Ellen Nussey written jointly by Charlotte and the Taylor sisters has preserved the Taylors' lively impressions of the school. Mary Taylor's description gives us interesting information on the curriculum and the staff, even if it is difficult to ascertain the real quality of the teaching from her light-hearted account.

> I must now tell you of our teachers Miss Evans is a well educated English woman who has been eight years in France whom I should like very well if she were not so outrageously civil that I every now & then suspect her of hypocrisy. The French teacher we have not yet got so I can tell you nothing of her except that she is coming in a few days (which she has been doing ever since Christmas). Madame Ferdinand the music mistress is a little thin, black, talkative, French woman. Monsieur her husband is a tall broad-shouldered man with a tremendous mouth who is constantly telling his pupils that the voice has but a very little hole to get out at & that there are both tongue and teeth to interrupt it on its road and that the orifice ought by all means to be opened as wide as possible –
>
> Then comes M. Gauné, a little black old Frenchman with his history written on his face and a queer one it is – I speak either of the face or the history – which you please. He has a good appreciation of the literature of his own country and speaks some curious English. I think him a good master – Mons. Huard – the drawing master is a man of some talent, a good judgement, and an intelligible manner of teaching. He would be my favourite if he did not smell so of bad tobacco. Last and least is Mons. Sacré not that he appears to me to want sense and being a dancing master he ought not to want manner – but he has the faults of a French puppy and they make it advisable never to exchange more words with him than the everlasting 'Oui Monsieur – Non Monsieur' – Martha is considerably improved I can't put out my feet – 'Allongez! Plus long! More!' All our awkwardnesses however are thrown into the shade by those of a Belgian girl who does not know right foot from left and obstinately dances with her mouth open. There is also a Mon. Hisard, who

makes strange noises in the back school room teaching gymnastics to some of the girls and I had almost forgotten a grinning, dirty, gesticulating Belgian who teaches Cosmosgraphy and says so often 'Ainsi donc! C'est bien compris! N'est-ce pas?' that he has earned himself the names of ainsi donc and Mr Globes. Amongst all this noise and bustle we have every opportunity of learning – if we choose. I must except French in which we make very little progress owing to the want of a governess. There are more English and Germans than French girls in the school consequently very little French is spoken and that little is bad.[7]

Incidentally, the name of Monsieur Sacré, the dancing master who makes an appearance here as a 'French puppy', pops up regularly in books about Brussels in the nineteenth century; his career seems to have spanned much of it. Mrs Wemyss Dalrymple, in her 1839 guide to Brussels,[8] mentions him as a dancing master and master of ceremonies for court balls. In the 1880s M. Sacré was still going strong, organising and conducting summer concerts at the Vauxhall in the park.[9]

Mary Taylor's account tells us that many of the teachers employed at private schools in Brussels of the period were non-Belgian, a fact confirmed by census information. As William Crimsworth and Lucy Snowe find out, to be one of these nationalities was an asset in the private teaching world. Pelet, the school director who employs Crimsworth, is a Frenchman, and both Crimsworth and Lucy easily find employment in Brussels as English teachers.

Mary's description does not tell us whether the establishment of Mme Goussaert, an Englishwoman, bore out the opinion expressed by Addison that the moral tone in British-run schools was higher than in Belgian ones. He warns his readers against entrusting their children to Belgian-run schools because of the low moral standards of these establishments.[10] This opinion was of course shared by Charlotte Brontë. She would presumably have approved more of schools run by Protestants, of which there were several in Brussels at that time.

Prospectuses of pensionnats in the period, whatever their denomination, stressed the importance of moral teaching even more than of academic standards. At another prestigious establishment for young ladies, Mme Féry's in the *faubourg de Namur*, there was such apparent emphasis on decorous behaviour that the directress had her day pupils brought to the school in a carriage supervised by a teacher. Charlotte Brontë's opinion was that no more than lip service was paid to morality at Catholic schools and that what counted most for directresses like Mme Féry was appearances. She would have viewed such constant surveillance as a demonstration of what was wrong with the methods employed – an indication that pupils were not trusted to behave correctly without supervision.

Her low opinion of the moral climate she observed at the Pensionnat is not borne out by the opinion of the Baroness Willmar, who knew the Heger school well and recommended it unreservedly, writing that she had always found there 'affability, kindness, delicacy, sound instruction and the instilling of good manners.'[11] Nor is it borne out by accounts of the Pensionnat by other ex-pupils such as Frederika Macdonald and Janet Harper, though it might be argued that they were simply more uncritical than Charlotte and did not probe as deeply as she did beneath the surface in order to examine the underlying precepts of a Catholic education.

Moral standards apart, Charlotte was bound to acknowledge the amenities of life at a Belgian Pensionnat compared with the English schools she had known. No-one had too much work and there were frequent diversions, everyone had plenty to eat, and the school was .competently run. Valérie Piette, in her article on girls' pensionnats of the period, observes that however negative Charlotte's portrait of the school directress in *Villette* in some respects, she clearly had a grudging admiration for Mme Beck – and by implication for Mme Heger – as a successful businesswoman. A skilful manager, Mme Beck knows how to get the best out of her teachers, and her school prospers. Piette concludes that we can deduce that these were the qualities that enabled other privately-run schools to survive and flourish.[12]

John Bartier writes that 'from numerous pages of *Villette*, we know that at the Pensionnat Heger the discipline was light and the studies not very demanding.' ('Masters came and went,' Lucy tells us, 'delivering short and lively lectures, rather than lessons, and the pupils made notes of their instructions, or did *not* make them – just as inclination prompted; secure that, in case of neglect, they could copy the notes of their companions.'[13]) One explanation for the success of the Pensionnat Heger, he concludes, was that the shrewd Hegers knew how to keep their pupils happy through a light regime. Charlotte's opinion that academic standards were not very high at *pensionnats de demoiselles* is borne out by Belgian commentators. The nineteenth-century historian Henri Moke, an advocate of women's emancipation and higher educational standards for women, criticised the superficiality of education at girls' *pensionnats*, which, he said, left little trace on women after they left school.[14] Indeed, Belgian girls made haste to forget what they had been taught, since their society did not value learning in women.

The same observation was made by the novelist Caroline Gravière. In Gravière's *Une parisienne a Bruxelles*, the womenfolk of a Brussels bourgeois family are portrayed through the critical eyes of Lydie, a Parisian who has married the son of the family. Gravière tells us that parents sent their daughters to boarding schools not to acquire learning but merely to get them out of the way. Long years 'vegetating' in these establishments taught them next to nothing and they soon forgot the little they did know through a horror of being thought 'blue-stockings'. When Lydie asks her Belgian sisters-in-law their opinion of the Romantic poet Lamartine, she is informed that his poetry was not authorised reading at their pensionnat.[15] The Hegers' school was, intellectually speaking, much more advanced and open-minded than such establishments. Although Lucy Snowe records that novel-reading is frowned on by the pupils' confessors (in Gravière's novel, a young lady is expelled from her pensionnat for this misdemeanour), Charlotte and Emily were encouraged by M. Heger to read the French Romantics. Indeed, Charlotte was instructed by him to read one of Lamartine's 'Harmonies', on 'the Infinite',[16] which probably inspired an essay she wrote for him entitled 'The Immensity of God'.

It is because Charlotte Brontë was a great writer that her novels are read today in Belgium at all, but it is thanks to one of her least subtle qualities as a writer – namely the recording of apparently unimportant details – that *Villette* and *The Professor* constitute such a mine of information on Brussels life, in this case Brussels school life. The daily routine in a Belgian pensionnat had a particular fascination for her as a foreign observer, though she was almost as comprehensive in her recording of day-to-life at Lowood School in *Jane Eyre*, based on the Cowan Bridge school of her own childhood. Thanks to her preoccupation with such minutiae, Belgian readers of *Villette* do not just read a classic of English literature. They also learn every detail of life in a girls' boarding school in mid-nineteenth century Brussels, down to the information that on the directress's birthday it was the custom to collect money by subscription for a gift and that an acceptable offering was a silver cutlery set worth 300 francs, which was almost as much as Charlotte earned in a year, that on outings to the countryside the pupils were treated to waffles and white wine, and that supper each day consisted of rolls and milk 'diluted with tepid water'.[17]

1   Van Wassenhove, *Bruxelles: la vie quotidienne au XIXe siècle vue par les écrivains de l'époque*.
2   Piette, 'Un réseau privé d'éducation des filles. Institutrices et pensionnats à Bruxelles (1830–1860)', p. 159.
3   Stated in a letter to Ellen Nussey of April 1843. Smith, *The Letters of Charlotte Brontë*, Volume I, p. 315.
4   Bartier, *Laïcité et Franc-Maçonnerie*, p. 164.
5   Willmar, *Souvenirs de Bruxelles*, p. 261.
6   *Le Libéral*, 18 Octobre 1835.
7   Letter from Mary and Martha Taylor and Charlotte Brontë to Ellen Nussey, March–April 1842. Smith, *The Letters of Charlotte Brontë*, Volume I, pp. 280–1.
8   Wemyss Dalrymple, *The Economist's New Brussels Guide*, p. 43.
9   Hymans, *Bruxelles à travers les âges*, p. 168.
10 Addison, *Belgium as she is*, p. 176.
11 Willmar, *Souvenirs de Bruxelles*, p. 260.
12 Piette, 'Un réseau privé d'éducation des filles. Institutrices et pensionnats à Bruxelles (1830–1860)', p. 174.
13 *Villette*, Chapter 8.
14 In the 1860 essay 'Du sort de la femme dans les temps anciens et modernes', cited in Bartier, *Laïcité et Franc-Maçonnerie*, pp. 166–7.
15 Gravière, *Une parisienne à Bruxelles*, pp. 45–6.
16 Lonoff, *The Belgian Essays: A Critical Edition*, p. 42.
17 *Villette*, Chapter 28.

CHAPTER TEN

Grande passion and *petite pluie*:
Charlotte and the Hegers

'C'est moi M. Paul'

THE bicentenary of Charlotte Brontë's birth in 2016 brought a crop of books and films, and press articles on both sides of the Channel. A feature of many of these was the interest shown in Charlotte's time in Brussels and in her teacher Constantin Heger. Film crews wanted to film in Brussels as well as Haworth, and perhaps meet an Heger descendant. They wanted to know more about the man whose influence has long been recognised by Brontë scholars but has never registered much with the general public; few of the Brontës' readers are even aware of Charlotte and Emily's Brussels stay.

Claire Harman's biography, which came out for the bicentenary,[1] opens not in Haworth or in Patrick Brontë's home country of Ireland but with Charlotte, depressed and tormented by her feelings for Heger, among other frustrations, driven to confession in the Church of St Gudule during her lonely second summer in Brussels. And the biography also ends in Brussels, in Heger's study in rue Isabelle. It is 1887 and Heger (aged 78) is writing a letter to Meta Mossman, a former pupil at the Pensionnat who had been a favourite of his. Heger, a busy man who disliked writing letters, was often a tardy correspondent, and apparently Charlotte was not the only ex-pupil to take him to task for this. His ingenious excuse for not writing earlier to Meta is that he can be in communication with her without the need for pen or paper:

> Although it is true that I have not written, I have nevertheless answered you frequently and at length, and this is how. Letters and the post are not, luckily, the only means of communication, or the best, between people who are really fond of one another; I am not referring to the telephone, which allows one to speak, to have

conversation, from a distance: I have something better than that. I have only to think of you to see you. I often give myself the pleasure when my duties are over, when the light fades. I postpone lighting the gas lamp in my library, I sit down, smoking my cigar, and with a hearty will I evoke your image – and you come (without wishing to, I dare say) but I see you, I talk with you – you, with that little air, affectionate undoubtedly, but independent and resolute, firmly determined not to allow any opinion without being previously convinced, demanding to be convinced before allowing yourself to submit – in fact, just as I knew you, my dear [Meta], and as I have esteemed and loved you.[2]

It is a letter that has been cited to demonstrate that Heger adopted what is judged to be a flirtatious manner with at least some of his female pupils. It is argued that his playful, affectionate, intimate tone might easily have led the more susceptible of them – and Charlotte Brontë would have been highly susceptible – to become too attached to their charismatic teacher.

The letter is cited by Jolien Janzing as an indication that her novel *Charlotte Brontë's Secret Love* – like Harman's biography, timed to come out for the bicentenary – might be more than a novelistic fantasy about what took place between Charlotte and Heger. In the novel, which is the only such exploration of Charlotte's time in Brussels by a Belgium-based writer, Heger is a flirt whose appreciation of his wife's physical charms does not prevent him from being susceptible to those of other women. He finds himself attracted to Charlotte and the two conduct a heated romance under Madame's nose.

Even when not being charged with flirting, Heger is often accused of being unfeeling. He replied late or not at all to Charlotte's desperate letters, and when he did answer them, admonished her to write no more than twice a year and to confine herself to more impersonal topics. Three of her four extant letters to him were torn into pieces and then repaired; according to the version of events given by Louise Heger to the family's British friend Marion Spielmann, Heger tore them up and his wife repaired them and hid them away as evidence that there had been no impropriety on his side.[3] Worst offence of all, in the margin of the last of the letters is a scribbled note, presumably by Heger, containing the word 'cordonnier' (shoemaker) and an address. This has been taken by many, starting with Spielmann himself, as evidence of Heger's indifference to Charlotte's appeals:

So little real importance did the recipient apparently attach to these letters, so little did he seem to recognize the true ring of their piteous appeal (except righteously, no doubt, to reprove the writer as 'exaltée') that in the margin of the last he has jotted odd pencil notes: still legible on it are the name and address of a Brussels shoemaker.[4]

The Hegers were a highly-regarded family and counted the daughters of some of the best families in Brussels among their pupils. Heger was known not just as a brilliant teacher but as a devout man who devoted much time to good works. Through their six children, he and Zoë founded a distinguished dynasty: the names of their scientist son Paul Heger and artist daughter Louise live on in Belgium today. One might therefore expect Heger to find champions on the Belgian side of the Channel to defend him against slurs on his character concerning his relations with Charlotte Brontë.

◀ Torn and stitched envelope of one of Charlotte's four extant letters to M. Heger

douce joie de voir votre écriture, de lire vos conseils me fait comme une vaine vision, alors, j'ai la fièvre – je perds l'appétit et le sommeil – je dépéris

Puis-je vous écrire encore au mois de Mai prochain? j'aurais voulu attendre toute une année – mais c'est impossible – c'est trop long.

C Brontë

I must say one word to you in English – I wish I could write to you more cheerful letters, for when I read this over, I find it to be somewhat gloomy – but forgive me my dear master – do not be irritated at my sadness – according to the words of the Bible: "Out of the fullness of the heart, the mouth speaketh" and truly I find it difficult to be cheerful so long as I think I shall never see you more. You will perceive by the defects in this letter that I am forgetting the French language – yet I read all the French books I can get, and learn daily a portion by heart – but I have never heard it French spoken but once since I left Brussels – and then it sounded like music in my ears – every word was most precious to me because it reminded me of you – I love French for your sake with all my heart and soul.

Farewell my dear master – may God protect you with special care and crown you with peculiar blessings

Nov. 18th
Haworth Bradford Yorkshire
CB.

▲ Passage in English at the end of Charlotte's last extant letter to Heger, dated 18 November 1845.

There were indeed plenty in Belgium to defend both the Hegers during their lifetimes, in the decades after the publication of *Villette*. The couple were often perceived to have been treated shabbily by Charlotte by being used as characters in the novel – though most of the indignation was on behalf of Madame, for her supposed portrayal as Mme Beck. From accounts of visitors to the Pensionnat, Heger appears to have rather revelled in his own fictional alter ego and to have enjoyed startling literary pilgrims with sudden appearances and declarations of 'C'est moi M. Paul!' Although he always refused to publish Charlotte's letters to him, according to some reports he was indiscreet enough to show them on occasion. The English poet Thomas Westwood claimed that Heger had shown the letters to his wife's cousin, a former pupil of the Pensionnat. Westwood's verdict on Heger was 'He is a finished specimen of a Jesuit, but with all that a worthy and warm-hearted man.'[5]

Thus, although Heger reportedly said that it was 'bien vilain' of Charlotte to portray the inmates of the Pensionnat as she did, he seems to have felt little resentment on his own account. That he pitied rather than blamed Charlotte was clear from a letter written to Ellen Nussey after Charlotte's death urging her not to publish her friend's private letters and expose her 'pauvre coeur malade'[6]. It was for this reason that he refused to allow the publication of the letters he himself had received from Charlotte.

After their parents' deaths, the Hegers' children donated Charlotte's letters to their father to the British Museum in order to scotch rumours that there had been an *intrigue sentimentale* between him and Charlotte; in their view these letters constituted proof that there had been nothing 'dishonourable' on *either* side. Marion Spielmann, who assisted them with the arrangements with the Museum, said that their decision was prompted by 'generosity and magnanimity'.[7]

Charlotte's treatment of the Hegers still aroused indignation in some quarters even after their deaths and the publication of the letters. The writer of an article in *L'Indépendance Belge* in 1926, referring to Charlotte's passion for Heger as a 'bizarre episode' in her life, describes Heger as 'one of the most noble personalities of the Belgian teaching profession' and expresses indignation that the name of 'one of our most justly respected families' was mixed up in such an affair. In his view, Charlotte's letters revealed the unhealthy, pathological nature of her passion. Her fury that it was not returned explained the malevolence of *Villette* and *The Professor*, which novels, moreover, mischievously provided food for the rumours of a romantic attachment between her and Heger.[8]

The publication of the letters prompted mixed reactions. While some Brontë scholars continued hotly to deny that Charlotte was 'in love' with Heger in the romantic, passionate sense of the term, and to affirm the 'innocence' of her feelings, the letters gave ammunition to those who took a more romantic view of things. On both sides of the Channel, biographical accounts tended to be sympathetic towards Charlotte, with Heger often receiving blame for his handling of her. One of the few French biographies of the Brontës was a novelistic one by Emilie and Georges Romieu published in 1929, which proved popular enough to be translated into English. The Romieus' sympathy is for Charlotte, a 'true romantic' who is hopelessly in love yet asks for very little: 'To be with him, to catch his glance, to talk and commune with him spiritually, that was all that she asked'. Heger is berated for not granting her even this little: 'Cruelly he denied her all'. For these French biographers, he was not just cruel but wholly unworthy of her adoration: 'How much one could wish that the absurd little plump black idol before whom she kneels might be worthy of such a tribute. But is not love always inspired by illusion?'[9]

A more sober account was provided in 1939 by the Swiss Robert de Traz in *La Famille Brontë*, a biography that was widely read in Belgium. But in it Heger, again, is taken to task. While he is absolved from deliberately setting out to attract Charlotte, the shoemaker scribble in the margin of her last letter comes back to haunt him. 'He used her last letter to write the name and address of a cobbler; they can still be read, in their utilitarian pettiness, on the sheet of paper where Charlotte's heart had bled.'[10]

Louis Quiévreux painted an unappealing portrait of Heger in his article *Bruxelles, les Brontës et la famille Héger*.[11] In his account, once again it is the fiery and unconventional Charlotte who receives the sympathy, the upstanding bourgeois Heger the criticism. And once again, Heger's shoemaker note is dragged in, with a quote from a recent English biography: 'So shod, he could trample at his ease on the broken heart of a mad governess'.[12]

However, Quiévreux does not see Heger as a deliberate breaker of hearts but rather as a man too limited to be an object worthy of Charlotte's attachment. 'A typical representative of the stuffy, virtuous Brussels bourgeoisie of the time, he would never have guessed the depths of pain of this extraordinary girl ... He liked moderation and placid enjoyments. Tempests and passions were not for him. It's just as well he didn't succumb to Charlotte's passion. By resisting it, he allowed Charlotte to reveal herself.' If he had 'hurled himself with her into the abyss,' says Quiévreux, the scales would soon have fallen from her eyes and she would have seen him for the unromantic being he was. 'Poor girl! To be caught in that way in the trap of the Continent, after mocking the Belgians' manners and vulgarity! To have had her heart ensnared by a papist, a corrector of school essays for whom an adjective had to correspond strictly to a noun, and vice versa!'

Quiévreux also pointed out that had it not been for the Brontës, those 'terribly alive, frail creatures' who died so young, Heger would have been long forgotten. However, Quiévreux concedes, 'he was a good man in the accepted sense of the word. He was faithful to his wife and now they lie side by side in Boitsfort cemetery'.

A view of Heger as mediocre and limited had already been given in the memoir *The Secret of Charlotte Brontë* by his ex-pupil Frederika Macdonald, who had not been particularly impressed by Monsieur. Although she acknowledged he was an inspiring teacher, 'His mind was made up upon most subjects, and as he had got into the habit of regarding the world as his class-room, and his fellow-creatures as pupils, he did not argue; he told people what they ought to think about things', which he did, Macdonald says, through a stock of maxims he kept to hand for every occasion.[13] This is a far cry from the 'mental wealth' of Charlotte Brontë's Paul Emanuel, of whom Lucy tells us that 'his mind was … my library, and whenever it was opened to me, I entered bliss'.[14]

The early French Brontë biographer Ernest Dimnet also saw Heger in terms of his limitations. His book came out in French in 1911 just before the publication of the letters, but he comments on these in the English translation of his biography published in 1927. As a Catholic priest, Abbé Dimnet might have been expected to censure Charlotte for her excessive attachment and to commend Heger, as a married man, for his apparent indifference towards her. He presents Heger, however, as an unimaginative pedagogue, inferior to Charlotte and unworthy of her devotion. Dimnet absolves Charlotte of any 'guilty' or adulterous feelings for her teacher. While not condemning Heger for his unresponsiveness, 'we wish with our whole soul he had not scribbled a bootmaker's address on a corner of the last letter…. But Flemish stolidity does not care for nuances. An admirable husband, an excellent teacher, M. Heger had no romance in him.'[15].

The Belgian writer Robert Goffin did not agree. In an article on the exhibition on Charlotte at the Charlier Museum he took a romantic view not just of her relation with Heger but of Heger himself.[16] He believed that Heger had returned her affection and that Madame had grounds for her jealousy, since she 'guessed his secret'. As seen in an earlier chapter, Goffin was the author of a far-fetched theory that Heger was the anonymous translator responsible for *La Maîtresse d'anglais*, the early French adaptation of *Villette*. Speculating that Charlotte and Heger might well have remained secretly in touch for years after her departure from Brussels, he drew certain conclusions about the characters of both Monsieur and Madame from a family portrait painted by the artist Ange François in 1847. In this painting, Romantic in style, the seated Zoë occupies herself with the couple's six children while a bearded Heger, standing on the margin of the family group, gazes somewhat inscrutably into the distance. In 2016, film-makers who came to Brussels seeking material for their bicentenary documentaries on Charlotte Brontë were excited by the idea that Heger provided inspiration for Rochester as well as M. Paul. Eager to portray the man who supposedly inspired Charlotte's fictional heroes as a romantic figure, they, like Goffin, made much of his solitary and detached stance in this family portrait. Goffin's comment on it was: 'Without wishing to speak ill of Mme Heger, who was undoubtedly – as this picture indisputably shows – a good wife and mother, anyone who sees this portrait will agree that Constantin Heger's look and smile carry him towards horizons that Charlotte Brontë could discern better than her "rival"'.

A newspaper article in 1933 recording the death of Heger's last surviving child, Louise, recalls her father in old age, forty or fifty years after this family group was painted, as a 'little old man with an original turn of phrase and a singularly energetic and authoritarian facial expression' who was still remembered by many old *Bruxellois*.[17] Was the young man Charlotte knew closer to Dimnet's and Quiévreux's stolid Belgian burgher or to the passionate, volatile M. Paul in *Villette*? Many biographers have seen something of the romantic Paul Emanuel in him, and in our own time there has been a preference for seeing him as a man with a romantic and also a flirtatious side.

The novelist Jolien Janzing has taken the idea of a passionate and flirtatious Heger further than ever before. In her novel *De Meester*, Heger is depicted as a man who flirts unabashedly with his wife's pupils. In Janzing's fictional scenario, the attraction between him and Charlotte is mutual and it is physical as well as intellectual. There is no question of his leaving his wife, but he asks Charlotte to be his mistress. Charlotte, who has dreamed of more, rejects the proposal as mere 'crumbs from his table'.

As we saw, Heger's letter to Meta Mossman has been cited as proof of his 'flirtatiousness'. What is not always pointed out is his age when he wrote it (almost 80) and the fact that *both* Madame and M. Heger maintained playful and intimate correspondences with favourite ex pupils. In a letter to one of these, Madame jokes about Monsieur losing his heart to her when she was a child, reminding her correspondent of an occasion when he asked her, 'Who is my favourite girl?' only to receive the dry reply: 'Your wife'.[18] Unlike such favoured pupils, Charlotte was not a child but a woman of 25 when Heger first encountered her, and for much of her time at the Pensionnat she was his colleague, a teacher as well as his pupil. Caution is therefore required when taking the affectionate tone he adopted with a former *pensionnaire* as an indication of how he might have charmed Charlotte Brontë.

In Belgium, however, the novel *De Meester*, in particular, and the media coverage surrounding it in Charlotte Brontë's bicentenary have encouraged the idea that there was 'something between' her and Heger. The Heger family descendants have always objected to any such suggestion, but on another charge, namely that Heger behaved callously, Heger's own great-grand-nephew, Paul Héger, accused his ancestor of coldness and insensibility towards Charlotte in a radio interview in 2008. 'When he read her letters he could have been in no doubt as to her sentiments, yet he remained cold and impervious. Personally, I deplore his attitude. One doesn't react like that when a lady declares her love to you.' And he ended the interview with yet another reference to the scribble in the margin. 'I just hope she never knew about it!'[19]

On the subject of the cobbler scribble, it was not a Belgian but a Brussels-based Irish researcher, Brian Bracken, who recently came to Heger's defence with a novel theory about the scrawled address which, if true, might show him in a better light. The note in the margin is difficult to decipher, but there appear to be in fact two different names and addresses. Using the 1842 census, Bracken identified two possible candidates, both of them men living in slum areas of Brussels, one of whom was a shoemaker. As a member of the charitable St Vincent de Paul Society, Heger often visited the poor in such areas. Bracken suggests that rather than reminding himself of the address of a man who was to make him a pair of boots, Heger could have been noting the names of some of the needy poor he intended to visit. While he could do nothing to relieve Charlotte's suffering, and no doubt judged it best to be cruel to be kind, he could give practical aid to poor *Bruxellois* in need of succour. Should this theory be true, his jottings on her last letter would at least indicate his general benevolence – similar to that displayed by Dr Graham Bretton. Graham is kind to Lucy but blind to her love for him and not always sensitive to her feelings. He is, however, invariably compassionate to the poor patients he visits in the hospitals of Villette.

We will never know the truth about Heger's scribble, but his son Paul, like his father a busy man and a pillar of Brussels society, had this to say about Charlotte's relations with the Hegers when he presented Charlotte's letters to the British Museum: 'Doubtless my parents played an important part in the life of Charlotte Brontë, but she did not enter into theirs as one would imagine ... That is evident enough by the very circumstances of life, so different for her and for them.'[20]

Madame Beck: Charlotte's revenge?

If Heger really flirted with his wife's pupils, it would be understandable if Mme Heger was jealous and suspicious, and yet she has been taken to task for being just that: a jealous wife, a spying Mme Beck.

Yet few of the accounts of Mme Heger handed down by ex-pupils and others who knew her have much in common with Mme Beck, commonly supposed to be intended by Charlotte as a portrait of her. The impressions of Frederika Macdonald and those culled from other former pupils by the Brontë biographer Esther Alice Chadwick recall the Pensionnat's *directrice* as a caring and benign presence rather than the unscrupulous hypocrite depicted by Charlotte. In the opinion of Macdonald's brother the Abbé Richardson, a resident of Brussels who knew the Hegers, 'If we except some superficial resemblances of personal prettiness and neatness, noiselessness of movement, and unvarying placidity of temper, this lady was utterly unlike in every particular the crafty and unprincipled woman described by Charlotte Brontë, nor is it possible to imagine that our authoress ever intended any such resemblance.'[21]

According to Baroness Willmar, who knew Mme Heger and warmly recommended her Pensionnat, Madame was a devout woman who did many kindnesses to the less fortunate and 'whose physiognomy seemed to cast a ray of happiness on all who approached her.'[22] However, the testimony given to Elizabeth Gaskell by another Brussels resident who had once met Zoë Heger was that '[She] has something cold and formal in her demeanour which scarcely predisposes you in her favour. I believe her, however, to be loved and valued by her pupils.'[23]

It is not surprising that Charlotte found Zoë Heger's temperament antagonistic to her own. Madame appears to have been the personification of the Belgian phlegm and placidity that acted as an irritant on Charlotte's own excitable nature. It seems likely that Charlotte put at least some elements of Mme Heger into her portrait of Mme Beck, which bears the stamp of close observation of reality. What is more debatable is whether she was motivated by spite or primarily by her requirements as a creative artist, drawing on real life to create a fictional character. As commented in an earlier chapter, she admitted taking real people as the 'germ' of her fictional ones, but denied ever reproducing literal portraits of them: 'We only suffer reality to *suggest* – never to *dictate*'.

That Mme Heger and her family took Mme Beck to be intended as a portrait, or rather caricature, of herself is clear from her daughter Louise's remark in later years that, as 'the daughter of Mme Beck', she naturally felt some annoyance against Charlotte on her mother's behalf.[24] Frederika Macdonald relates an anecdote which, if true, conveys the depth of Mme Heger's hurt at what she perceived as Charlotte's unjust resentment against her. Frederika, while a pupil at the school, once complained to Madame of an injustice done to her, claiming to have been blamed unfairly for some misdemeanour. As she spoke, she saw Madame suddenly turn 'ashen white'. Visibly shaken, she warned the young Frederika against the dangers of seeing injustice where none was intended, thereby becoming unjust oneself, and of being 'dominated by a fixed idea, and the slave of vain desires'. These were similar to words used by Charlotte of herself in a letter to Heger.[25] The 'fixed idea' Charlotte herself was referring to was her obsessive need for Heger's friendship and approval, but if Macdonald's story is true, Mme Heger also seems to have had in mind Charlotte's supposed enduring grudge against herself.[26]

Post-*Villette*, Charlotte was remembered by Mme Heger and her circle for 'the injustice, the untruthfulness, and the ingratitude' of her portrayal of the school.[27] Marion Spielmann claimed that 'the family and their friends . . . resented the closeness of the portraiture, and they were hurt that, while places were drawn with photographic accuracy, the characters of people were often caricatured, the persons themselves gibbeted, and the names of personages well known and universally esteemed in Brussels – de Hamel, van der Huten, Bassompierre – were allotted to creations of the author's fancy'.[28]

An obituary of Heger by Albert Colin, editor of the Belgian daily *L'Etoile Belge*, may indicate how Charlotte was viewed by those who knew something of her relations with the Hegers. For Colin, *Villette* was a 'defamatory libel', a novel of revenge. In an article full of inaccuracies, he makes much of the probably apocryphal story, handed down in the Heger family, that Charlotte uttered the words 'Je me vengerai' on taking leave of Madame; according to a family anecdote probably just as apocryphal, Madame accompanied the *sous-maîtresse* to Ostend and saw her safely on to the boat when she took her final departure in January 1844. In M. Colin's version of the story, Charlotte's threat of vengeance was made when Mme Heger refused to let her stay on at the school a third year because she had made herself so unpopular. Colin writes that Charlotte was desperate to return to Brussels and the happy, peaceful environment of the Pensionnat to escape from her unhappy home where, he tells us, she was regularly beaten by her drunken brother. Colin even holds Charlotte's lack of physical charms against her, praising Mme Heger's generosity in agreeing to take Charlotte on at the Pensionnat despite the fact that not only was she, Colin claims, 'entirely ignorant of the French language' (this was not true of course) but also 'exceedingly plain'.[29]

Accounts of Charlotte's unpopularity while at the Pensionnat may have had an element of hindsight and been coloured by the reaction to the publication of *Villette*. Proof exists that Charlotte gained the affection of at least some of its inmates. A fellow teacher, Mademoiselle Sophie, in a note accompanying a farewell gift, begged her 'from time to time to turn your thoughts again to "la triste Belgique" where more than one person will be thinking of you', and after leaving Brussels Charlotte was pleasantly taken aback to receive a packet of letters from the pupils of one of her classes, begging her to return, as they disliked their new English mistress.[30]

At least two of Heger's children were magnanimous towards Charlotte, despite the distress she had caused their mother. Resentment against her was felt mainly by the two daughters who took charge of the school in their parents' old age. Louise and Paul Heger had a much more tolerant attitude. Moreover, 'they entertained profound respect for the writer's genius; they were proud that her art had been first trained and nurtured within their circle'.[31] Charlotte never knew Paul, who was born a couple of years after her departure from Brussels, but she had been fond of Louise, four and a half at the time she left. 'She had so much character – so much naïveté – so much *truthfulness* in her little face,' she ended a letter to Heger in July 1844.[32] Louise, in her turn, always had a soft spot for Charlotte. She was gratified at having been supposedly portrayed as one of the most sympathetic of Mme Beck's children, little Fifine in *Villette*[33]. As a creative artist, unconventional like Charlotte herself, Louise felt an affinity with the English writer, enjoyed reminiscing about her and was willing to excuse much of her behaviour. She tended to downplay Charlotte's infatuation for Heger, dismissing it as no more than a pupil's crush on a teacher. Her brother Paul had no personal memories of Charlotte and was so little interested in her and her relations with his parents that according to Spielmann he did not read *Villette* until middle age. When he finally did so, he was not offended but 'amused, recognising everything ... and though a little hurt by the exaggerations and unkindnesses which he rightly attributed in the main to literary exigency, he attached no great importance to that – for he realised that the book claimed to be regarded as fiction'.[34]

If Mme Beck was really based on Mme Heger, Madame at any rate inspired a character that various Belgian commentators judge to be a masterpiece of psychology. In the opinion of the writer Charles Bernard, reviewing *Villette* in the year of the 1932 translation of the novel, 'There is nothing more finely detailed, more finished, in her depiction of each trait, each fibre, each reaction, in the whole of nineteenth-century fiction. She is more pitiless than Balzac. She is as meticulous as a Chinese torturer'.[35] Another article in the same year points out that Charlotte's admiration of the character is as evident as her antipathy; Lucy compares Mme Beck's abilities to those of a police commissioner or prime minister.[36] Before Lucy's rivalry with the directress for M. Paul turns her into a deadly enemy and reveals her fully to Lucy as 'a being heartless, self-indulgent, and ignoble' under her benevolent disguise,[37] Lucy in fact lives on good terms with her employer. Her tone when speaking of her is often one of amused admiration for her skill, if not her motives or moral code, and her observation of Madame's little ways is even affectionate. In turn, Lucy is respected by her employer. 'Madame and I understood each other well'.[38] The directress is intelligent enough to perceive that the English *sous-maîtresse* can be trusted without any need for the system of surveillance she employs with every other inmate of the school. Lucy is allowed her freedom and lives contentedly enough under the regime of the establishment that Mme Beck runs so smoothly.

Paul Heger's view that *Villette* was a fictional work that should not be read too literally as autobiography is also taken by some other Belgian commentators. It was the opinion of a critic writing in 1939 that while Mme Heger was upset and Heger flattered by what they took to be their portraits as Mme Beck and M. Paul, 'in fact the Hegers were no more Mme Beck and M. Paul than Lucy Snowe was Charlotte Brontë. Great writers, even if they start off by taking portraits from life, elevate the characters in their fiction into general human types which are much more than the real people who served as models.'[39] The danger of reading *Villette* literally as autobiography was also pointed out by Ernest Dimnet. 'The woman and the author were two distinct and even opposed beings... Charlotte's subconscious mind... is an ocean upon which one hesitates to venture.'[40]

However, the view that the characters in *Villette* are largely fictional has not often prevailed where the character of Mme Beck is concerned. Even Dimnet, while recognising that many details in the novel do not correspond literally to reality, calls her 'the terrible incarnation of Mme Heger': 'Mme Heger, a good woman to whom Charlotte owed much, is blackened with extraordinary mastery. It never occurred to Charlotte that she was doing wrong.' Charlotte, says Dimnet, would have defended herself from the charge of vilifying Mme Heger. She did not seem to realise how easily the Hegers would be identified by Brussels readers of the novel. She would have protested that M. Paul and Mme Beck were not intended as literal portraits of the Hegers, yet, Dimnet points out, the fact is that everyone takes them to be such. Dimnet's theory was that Charlotte had 'two souls', one in her real-life relations with people and one as a creative artist. As a person, said Dimnet, she was 'naturally good' and tried to act fairly; as a writer, in contrast, she was satirical and bitter, more interested in her characters' faults than their virtues. Moreover, as a writer she claimed the freedom to draw on real life for her characters as she pleased.[41]

Dimnet does not altogether exonerate Mme Heger, however. He surmises that she was jealous of the notice her husband took of Charlotte and the evident pleasure that Charlotte – cultured, original, highly interesting for an intelligent man – took in his company, and that this jealousy showed her in a bad light given that, in Dimnet's view, her suspicions were unfounded. Mme Heger, however, Dimnet claims, must have suspected that 'Charlotte had acted in reality as Lucy acts in the book.'[42]

Madame comes out very badly in Emilie and Georges Romieu's rather melodramatic *Vie des Soeurs Brontë* (1929). In their account, she has become, quite simply, a 'dragon'. She will go to any lengths to keep her husband away from Charlotte, and sets out to make Charlotte's life impossible in the second year of her stay. While she does not call into question her husband's virtue (for one thing, 'The Professor valued his wife's rather opulent beauty and could not have been greatly tempted by Charlotte's depressing flatnesses and her fearful and unexpected asperities'), Madame is acutely aware of the age differences between the three principals in the drama (she was 39, her husband 34 and Charlotte 27) and takes preventive measures. She embarks on a 'long and devious operation' to ensure that Charlotte takes no more private lessons with her husband, for:

> If their elbows should touch or their knees should brush one another – a word, some accident, a mere nothing, a momentary lapse might suffice to throw them into each other's arms. Therefore a complete revision of the teaching schedule in the boarding school became absolutely imperative. To promote her own end Mme Heger did not hesitate to disrupt the whole programme of instruction, to alter the hours of courses, to change the assignments of the different teachers.[43]

There is in fact no evidence that Mme Heger, who was the soul of discretion, went to any such elaborate lengths to achieve her object. Nor is there any indication, as the Romieus claim, that Charlotte's 'secret' was the talk of the school!

Their breathless biography, in which all the sympathy is for Charlotte and the opprobrium for Mme Heger, must, if he read it, have been anathema to the writer Lucien Christophe. He was friendly with Louise Heger in her old age and heard about Charlotte and her relations with the Heger family from Louise's own lips. Louise died in 1933 at the age of 94, and a few months later Christophe, who wrote several articles about Charlotte Brontë, published one entitled *Souvenirs de la Pension Heger: Un amour de Charlotte Brontë.*[44]

Christophe, who was half a century younger than Louise, remembered her as a relic of a vanished era, Queen-Victoria-like in her black silk dress. An hour's conversation with her was like entering another age – 'through the door of the parlour where she was expecting you, rather than through the door of a museum'. Even in conversation about present-day topics, you would be subtly transported, by nuances in her talk you were scarcely aware of, into the world of three-quarters of a century earlier. Louise had the added attraction of being the last living person in Belgium to remember Charlotte Brontë. But although Christophe was fascinated by the link, his fear of treating her like a collector's item made him reluctant to ask direct questions about her memories of the English novelist. Louise would sometimes speak of her own accord of 'Charlotte', as she called her. The name would slip out in the course of conversation as naturally and intimately as if she and Charlotte had only recently been chatting together. This gave the young Christophe more of a *frisson* than any number of anecdotes.

Louise always spoke of Charlotte charitably and without resentment, but without losing sight of the hurt that her mother had suffered through the little *sous-maîtresse*. In his article Christophe explores the nature of this hurt, the differences in temperament between Charlotte and her Belgian hosts, and the difference in the treatment meted out by posterity to Charlotte, the great writer and passionate soul, and to the decorous, circumspect directress of the Brussels Pensionnat. Having sketched in Charlotte's Haworth background – the 'rough' people, the wild windswept hills – he goes on to paint a picture of the bourgeois Brussels of the 1840s, a 'petite grande ville' with an aversion to 'strong emotions', and, finally, of the Heger ménage. 'An exemplary marriage. A couple, a family, an institution . . . It was through all this that the impetuous Charlotte swept in 1842 with her demands, her fiery temperament, the pernicious splendour of her devouring passion.' How could she be restored to reason? There is a French proverb that means that small efforts can go a long way: *petite pluie abat grand vent*. The literal meaning is 'a little rain beats back strong winds'. The little rain of Belgium, however, could not put out the fire of that 'devouring passion'.

Charlotte left Brussels 'distraught, humiliated, annihilated'. Then, some years later, she transformed her experience there into literature. She became famous, a cult figure. The Hegers, powerless to defend themselves against her just as, Christophe says, they had been powerless to defend her from herself, were dragged along in the train of her 'turbulent immortality'.

For Christophe, Charlotte's depiction of Mme Heger in *Villette* was motivated by vengeance and the wish to compensate herself for past hurt. Yet, he says, Charlotte's skill persuades the reader that the portrait of Mme Beck, inspired by hatred, is as real as that of M. Paul, inspired by love. Christophe notes that a Romantic writer's infatuation for a Brussels schoolmaster could easily have made Charlotte look ridiculous had it not been for the dexterity with which she turns the tables so that it is Madame who is the object of sarcasm. Admirers of Charlotte instinctively take the part of genius and passion against formality and convention. Christophe, at the risk, as he says, of appearing stuffy and unimaginative, refuses to go along with this. He dwells instead on the dignity of the victims, the Hegers, dragged into the public arena for evermore by Charlotte's fictional re-enactment of her inner drama. Faced with her distortion of the facts, they opted to remain silent.

Although Christophe cannot help but be moved by Charlotte's letters to Heger, he asks readers to turn their thoughts away from her suffering to the effect of those letters on a peaceful and harmonious household. Charlotte, in his view, was 'one of those elect and privileged beings that are a scourge for families'. If *Villette* is 'Charlotte's longest love letter to Heger', as has been claimed, Christophe observes that unfortunately this love letter is also a letter full of insults.

He concedes that as a character of fiction, Mme Beck is admirably drawn. The problem is that the character is not entirely the creation of its author, since everything in *Villette* is drawn from what Christophe calls 'the other novel' – that is, the novel of Charlotte's actual life. The combat between Mme Beck/Heger and Charlotte is an unequal one. Whereas we, the reader, can never lose sight of Charlotte's humanity and suffering, we see Mme Beck as no more than a satirical representation. It does not occur to us that the other woman, Charlotte's rival, could have known equal suffering in the struggle that pits them against each other. 'They are not on the same plane. The light that bathes them is not the same. Charlotte makes sure that we see her adversary in the light of the world and Charlotte, the loser in the battle, in the light of the soul.' Christophe imagines how, if the situation had been reversed and Mme Heger had possessed Charlotte's novelistic power, she might have depicted her rival. She could have shown Charlotte as someone who, after trying to destroy the peace and honour of a family, turned the couple into objects of derision – since even Heger, the object of Charlotte's adoration, is often ridiculed in the character of M. Paul. While those familiar with the facts of Charlotte the woman's relations with the Hegers may well have sympathy to spare for Mme Heger, Charlotte the author ensures that the sympathy of the reader of *Villette* is with Lucy rather than with Mme Beck.

These days, whenever Charlotte Brontë's name comes up in the Belgian press, the headlines tend to focus on the titivating: her 'hopeless love for' and 'love' letters to Constantin Heger, the Belgian 'love of her life'. Mme Heger is of little interest except for her role in piecing together, keeping and (according to Louise Heger's version of events) hiding the letters after Heger tore them up. Madame's action shows her in a somewhat unfavourable, Mme-Beck-like light: cautious, circumspect and rather cunning. In point of fact Heger seems to have been perfectly well aware of the letters' whereabouts, since he occasionally brought them out and showed them to people, Charlotte's biographer Elizabeth Gaskell among them. This begs the question of whether they were really torn up early in their history as Louise claimed, as it would surely have been awkward to show letters that had been ripped up and then repaired – unless transcripts were used. It casts some doubt on the accuracy of the account given by Louise, who was not always a reliable narrator.

In Jolien Janzing's novel *Charlotte Brontë's Secret Love*, it is Madame who tears up the letters and Monsieur who carefully sews them together again. As far as Mme Heger's character is concerned, however, the novel departs little from the customary view of her, depicting her as a slightly less repulsive, and much more voluptuous, version of Mme Beck but essentially like her: calculating and hypocritical, ruthless under a benevolent mask. Mme Heger and her values have found no-one in Belgium in our own time to defend them as eloquently as Lucien Christophe did in the 1930s in his indictment of Charlotte Brontë.

1   Claire Harman, *Charlotte Brontë: A Life* (London: Penguin Random House, 2015).

2   Edith M. Weir, 'New Brontë Material Comes to Light', *Brontë Society Transactions* (1949), Volume 11, Issue 4, pp. 249–61.

3   Spielmann, *The Inner History of the Brontë–Heger Letters*.

4   Reprinted in M.H. Spielmann, 'The Recently Discovered Letters from Charlotte Brontë to Professor Constantin Heger', *Brontë Society Transactions*, 1914, 5:24, p. 51. Article originally published in *The Times*, 29 July 1913, accompanying the four letters.

5   Thomas Westwood, *A literary friendship: Letters to Lady Alwyne Compton 1869–1881 from Thomas Westwood* (London: John Murray, 1914), pp. 15–16.

6   Dated 16 October 1863. Reproduced in Chadwick, *In the Footsteps of the Brontës*, pp. 276–8.

7   Spielmann, *The Inner History of the Brontë–Heger Letters*, p. 6.

8   *L'Indépendance Belge*, 11 January 1926.

9   Romieu, *The Brontë Sisters*, p. 116.

10   Robert de Traz, *La Famille Brontë*, p. 98.

11   Quiévreux, 'Bruxelles, les Brontës et la famille Héger'.

12   G. Elsie Harrison, *The Clue to the Brontës* (London: Methuen & Co. Ltd., 1948), p. 147.

13   Macdonald, *The Secret of Charlotte Brontë*, p. 175.

14   *Villette*, Chapter 33.

15   Dimnet, *The Brontë Sisters*, p. 251

16   *Le Figaro Littéraire*, 16 May 1953.

17   *L'Indépendance Belge*, 24 July 1933.

18   Letter from Mme Heger written in 1884 to Katie Mossman née Douglas, mother of Meta Mossman. Edith M. Weir, 'New Brontë Material Comes to Light', *Brontë Society Transactions* (1949), Volume 11, Issue 4, p. 253. See also Edith M. Weir, 'The Hegers and a Yorkshire Family', *Brontë Society Transactions* (1963), Volume 14, Issue 3, p. 32, which discloses the identities of the former pupils referred to in this letter and in Heger's 1887 letter to Meta Mossman.

19   Interview on RTBF published in Christine Masuy, *Mon grand-père ce héros* (Brussels: Racine, 2008).

20   Reprinted in M.H. Spielmann, *The Recently Discovered Letters from Charlotte Brontë to Professor Constantin Heger*. Brontë Society Transactions, 1914, 5:24, p. 53.

21   Chadwick, *In the Footsteps of the Brontës*, p. 258.

22   Willmar, *Souvenirs de Bruxelles*, p. 260.

23 Gaskell, *The Life of Charlotte Brontë*, Chapter 11.

24 Letter from Louise Heger to Katie Mossman, 11 May 1912. *Brontë Society Transactions* (1949), Volume 11, Issue 4, p. 258.

25 Letter from Charlotte to Heger of 18 November 1845. Smith, *The Letters of Charlotte Brontë*, Volume I, p. 436.

26 Macdonald, *The Secret of Charlotte Brontë*, p. 259.

27 Theodore Wolfe, 'Scenes of Charlotte Brontë's life in Brussels'. Reproduced in Ruijssenaars, *Charlotte Brontë's Promised Land*, pp. 61–6.

28 Spielmann, *The Inner History of the Brontë–Heger Letters*.

29 Wroot, *Sources of Charlotte Brontë's Novels*, pp. 172–4.

30 Smith, *The Letters of Charlotte Brontë*, Volume I, pp. 337–8 and 346–7.

31 Spielmann, *The Inner History of the Brontë–Heger Letters*.

32 Smith, *The Letters of Charlotte Brontë*, Volume I, p. 359.

33 According to some accounts, Louise was modelled on another of Mme Beck's children, Georgette.

34 Spielmann, *The Inner History of the Brontë–Heger Letters*.

35 *La Nation Belge*, 22 August 1932.

36 *Ibid.*, 25 September 1932.

37 *Villette*, Chapter 38.

38 *Ibid.*, Chapter 26.

39 *La Dernière Heure*, 30 May 1939.

40 Dimnet, *The Brontë Sisters*, p. 99.

41 *Ibid.*, p. 95, pp. 202–3.

42 *Ibid.*, p. 98.

43 Romieu, *The Brontë Sisters*, pp. 118–19.

44 In *Les nouvelles littéraires artistiques et scientifiques*, Paris, 21 October 1933. Also cited here is another article of Christophe's, 'Le roman bruxellois de Charlotte Brontë'.

CHAPTER ELEVEN

'Mon père, je suis protestante':
Charlotte and Catholicism

ONE evening – and I was not delirious: I was in my sane mind, I got up – I dressed myself, weak and shaking. The solitude and the stillness of the long dormitory could not be borne any longer; the ghastly white beds were turning into spectres – the coronal of each became a death's head, huge and sun-bleached – dead dreams of an elder world and mightier race lay frozen in their wide gaping eye-holes. That evening more firmly than ever fastened into my soul the conviction that Fate was of stone, and Hope a false idol – blind, bloodless, and of granite core. I felt, too, that the trial God had appointed me was gaining its climax, and must now be turned by my own hands, hot, feeble, trembling as they were. It rained still, and blew; but with more clemency, I thought, than it had poured and raged all day. Twilight was falling, and I deemed its influence pitiful; from the lattice I saw coming night-clouds trailing low like banners drooping. It seemed to me that at this hour there was affection and sorrow in Heaven above for all pain suffered on earth beneath; the weight of my dreadful dream became alleviated – that insufferable thought of being no more loved, no more owned, half-yielded to hope of the contrary – I was sure this hope would shine clearer if I got out from under this house-roof, which was crushing as the slab of a tomb, and went outside the city to a certain quiet hill, a long way distant in the fields. Covered with a cloak (I could not be delirious, for I had sense and recollection to put on warm clothing), forth I set. The bells of a church arrested me in passing; they seemed to call me in to the *salut*, and I went in. Any solemn rite, any spectacle of sincere worship, any opening for appeal to God was as welcome to me then as bread to one in extremity of want. I knelt down with others on the stone pavement. It was an old solemn church, its pervading gloom not gilded but purpled by light shed through stained glass.

Few worshippers were assembled, and, the salut over half of them departed. I discovered soon that those left, remained to confess. I did not stir. Carefully every door of the church was shut; a holy quiet sank upon, and a solemn shade gathered about us. After a space, breathless and spent in prayer, a penitent approached the confessional. I watched. She whispered her avowal; her shrift was whispered back; she returned consoled. Another went, and another. A pale lady, kneeling near me, said in a low, kind voice:–

'Go you, now; I am not quite prepared.'

Mechanically obedient, I rose and went. I knew what I was about; my mind had run over the intent with lightning-speed. To take this step could not make me more wretched than I was; it might soothe me.

The priest within the confessional never turned his eyes to regard me; he only quietly inclined his ear to my lips. He might be a good man, but this duty had become to him a sort of form: he went through it with the phlegm of custom. I hesitated; of the formula of confession I was ignorant: instead of commencing, then, with the prelude usual, I said:–

'Mon père, je suis Protestante.'

He directly turned. He was not a native priest: of that class, the cast of physiognomy is, almost invariably, grovelling: I saw by his profile and brow he was a Frenchman; though grey and advanced in years, he did not, I think, lack feeling or intelligence. He inquired, not unkindly, why, being a Protestant, I came to him?

I said, I was perishing for a word of advice or an accent of comfort. I had been living for some weeks quite alone; I had been ill; I had a pressure of affliction on my mind of which it would hardly any longer endure the weight.

'Was it a sin, a crime?' he inquired, somewhat startled.

I reassured him on this point, and, as well as I could, I showed him the mere outline of my experience.

He looked thoughtful, surprised, puzzled. 'You take me unawares,' said he. 'I have not had such a case as yours before: ordinarily we know our routine and are prepared; but this makes a great break in the common course of confession. I am hardly furnished with counsel fitting the circumstances.'

Of course, I had not expected he would be; but the mere relief of communication in an ear which was human and sentient, yet consecrated – the mere pouring out of some portion of long accumulating, long pent-up pain into a vessel whence it could not be again diffused – had done me good. I was already solaced.

'Must I go, father?' I asked of him as he sat silent.

'My daughter,' he said kindly – and I am sure he was a kind man: he had a compassionate eye – 'for the present you had better go: but I assure you your words have struck me. Confession, like other things, is apt to become formal and trivial with habit. You have come and poured your heart out; a thing seldom done. I would fain think your case over, and take it with me to my oratory. Were you of our faith I should know what to say – a mind so tossed can find repose but in the bosom of retreat, and the punctual practice of piety. The world, it is well known, has no satisfaction for that class of natures … It is my own conviction that these impressions under which you are smarting are messengers from God to bring you back to the true Church. You were made for our faith: depend upon it our faith alone could heal and help you – Protestantism is altogether too dry, cold, prosaic for you. The further I look into this matter, the more plainly I see it is entirely out of the common order of things. On no account would I lose sight of you. Go, my daughter, for the present; but return to me again.'[1]

My advice to all Protestants who are tempted to do anything so besotted as turn Catholic – is to walk over the sea on to the Continent – to attend mass sedulously for a time – to note well the mummeries thereof – also the idiotic, mercenary, aspect of all the priests – and then if they are still disposed to consider Papistry in any other light than a most feeble, childish piece of humbug let them turn Papist at once that's all – I consider Methodism, Quakerism, and the extremes of High and Low Churchism foolish but Roman Catholicism beats them all.[2]

Much has been made of Charlotte's confession at St Gudule in Brussels, which furnishes a key episode in *Villette*. The scene in the confessional provides a dramatic opening both to Claire Harman's recent biography and Jolien Janzing's novel about Charlotte and Heger, and a connection is generally made between Charlotte's impulse to talk to a Catholic priest and her infatuation with her teacher.

◀ The Church of St
Michael and St Gudule.

Her experiment in confession is certainly startling given the opinion of Catholicism voiced above in a letter to Ellen and spelled out just as unequivocally in *Villette* and *The Professor*. Her condemnation of Catholicism began with her denunciation of the educational methods she observed at the Pensionnat. 'Papists' were discouraged from thinking for themselves or taking responsibility for their actions. An extreme case of this lack of autonomy is Sylvie, the model pupil at Mlle Reuter's who is destined for a convent and has given up all independence of thought and action into the hands of her confessor: 'With a pale, passive automaton air, she went about all day long doing what she was bid; never what she liked or what, from innate conviction, she thought it right to do ... [her] soul had been conjured by Romish wizard-craft.'[3]

The pupils in Charlotte's fictional pensionnats are not, in general, destined for the cloister, and the regimes at her schools appear to have little in common with the soul-searching, mortification of the flesh and preoccupation with eternal punishment described by Antonia White in *Frost in May* (1933), an account of a convent-school education in the early years of the twentieth century. But what the two types of school do have in common are hierarchical systems in which individual responsibility is abdicated:

Sensual indulgence ... was permitted by way of counterpoise to jealous spiritual restraint. Each mind was being reared in slavery; but, to prevent reflection from dwelling on this fact, every pretext for physical recreation was seized and made the most of. There, as elsewhere, the CHURCH strove to bring up her children robust in body, feeble in soul, fat, ruddy, hale, joyous, ignorant, unthinking, unquestioning. 'Eat, drink, and live!' she says. 'Look after your bodies; leave your souls to me, I hold their cure – guide their course: I guarantee their final fate.' A bargain, in which every true Catholic deems himself a gainer. Lucifer just offers the same terms: 'All this power will I give thee, and the glory of it; for that is delivered unto me, and to whomsoever I will I give it. If thou, therefore, wilt worship me, all shall be thine!'[4]

Charlotte's view of the pernicious effects of a Catholic education was common enough in the English Protestant world. An English novel published in 1840, *The School Girl in France*, warns Protestant parents about the dangers of sending their daughters to Continental schools. The novel's two heroines, one of whom is tempted to convert to Catholicism while the other withstands temptation and remains steadfastly Protestant, experience, at both a lay school and a convent school in France, the snares and spells of 'that most dangerous system of false religion, which, appealing with almost irresistible power to the senses, through them prostrates the reasoning faculties.'[5] An 1885 brochure, *Do-the-Girls Hall*, warns parents who are considering sending their daughters to a school run by Ursuline nuns in Belgium to think again, quoting *Villette* on the evils of Belgian schools and setting Charlotte's account of the repression of the mind and indulgence of the body against the wholesomeness of an English education, the 'fresh, pure air which ... English girls habitually breathe in their own land.'[6]

Charlotte's view in *Villette* of the Catholic regime as one based on surveillance and submission to authority, with everyone, from the priests down, spying on everyone else, is echoed in the books for Protestant parents. In *The English Girl in a Convent School* (1874), set in Belgium, the pupils' lives are governed by 'spying and watching'; the narrator catches one of the nuns ransacking her belongings in her desk, just as Lucy observes Mme Beck going through her things.[7] That this feature of a Catholic upbringing was just as prevalent in Catholic schools in England is confirmed by Antonia White in *Frost in May*: 'As in the Jesuit Order, every child was under constant observation.'[8]

When Lucy objects that the method employed by M. Paul for his favourite occupation of 'studying human nature', namely spying on the inmates of the Pensionnat from the window of a room in the Athénée hired for the purpose, is 'not right', his response is: 'It is not right? By whose creed? Does some dogma of Calvin or Luther condemn it? What is that to me? I am no Protestant.'[9] His Jesuit education predisposes him to such covert methods.

In Frances Henri's opinion in *The Professor*, the constant surveillance makes for insincerity and hypocrisy.

> A Romish school is a building with porous walls, a hollow floor, a false ceiling; every room in this house, Monsieur, has eye-holes and ear-holes, and what the house is, the inhabitants are, very treacherous; they all think it lawful to tell lies, they all call it politeness to profess friendship where they feel hatred.[10]

In contrast, in Charlotte's view, a fundamental feature of a Protestant upbringing was trust, openness and autonomy, the importance of being directed by one's own conscience rather than by the kind of surveillance she must have observed, to some degree, even at the benignly-run Pensionnat Heger. The result of this control from above was that Catholic-educated children had no true inner sense of right and wrong. This was an opinion shared by the anonymous author of *The English Girl in a Convent School*, who claims that in the Belgian school she describes, the pupils could not be trusted to behave well of their own volition since 'foreign girls are not used to having their sense of honour appealed to ... The nuns seemed to take it for granted that girls would go wrong if a most severe and arbitrary control was not exercised over them. Human nature was hopelessly corrupt and the roots of this corruption were so deep and strong that it was of no use whatsoever to endeavour to eradicate the plant, the only thing to be done, was to cut off the shoots as soon as they made their appearance.' As in Charlotte's fictional pensionnats, what counted was the *appearance* of morality; the girls' instructors seemed to consider that the most compelling reason for good behaviour was that it was more *convenable* (seemly) than bad.[11]

Charlotte would presumably have agreed with the opinion of foreign schools expressed by Addison in his guide *Belgium as she is* when he told his readers that English-run schools in Belgium were 'a blessing in a foreign land, where many a fair and promising child has been ruined by early vices inculcated in Continental schools, or blighted by want of attention to that system of high morality which English preceptoresses so eminently instil.'[12] One of the 'vices inculcated in Continental schools', in Charlotte's view, was deceitfulness. At Mme Beck's Pensionnat, offences such as untruthfulness are considered less reprehensible than novel-reading; as long as they are duly confessed on Sunday, the state of the perpetrators' soul is no great matter for concern.[13] Another result of Catholic educational methods is discovered by Crimsworth when he becomes a teacher at a girls' school. If the surveillance to which Catholic girls were subjected was supposed to keep them in a state of innocence – modest and pure of thought – his perception is that it has the opposite effect and that his pupils are not just 'arrant coquettes' but 'mentally depraved':[14] 'scarcely one of these girls having attained the age of fourteen could look a man in the face with modesty and propriety' or without 'an air of bold, impudent flirtation'.[15]

Lucy Snowe's invectives against Catholicism in *Villette* draw a rebuke from the novel's first Belgian reviewer in the *Revue Trimestrielle*. 'Religious issues take up quite a considerable part of this book. We will not follow the author on this thorny path, and will merely observe that these matters are not always treated with all the dignity and calm they require.'[16]

Charlotte was writing the novel at a time when the issue of the Catholic church in England was much in the news. There had been a surge of anti-Catholic feeling when John Henry Newman converted to Catholicism in 1845, and in 1850 there were anti-Catholic riots when the Pope set up a hierarchy of dioceses in England and Wales, the first time that the Catholic church had had bishoprics there since the Reformation. The 1851 Ecclesiastical Titles Act, representing an ultimately unsuccessful last effort to repress the Catholic church in England, forbade the use of English place names for episcopal titles outside the Church of England. Charlotte was one of those who saw the Pope's move as an act of 'papal aggression'.

'The tender unction of Catholicism'

And yet on 1 September 1843 she had entered the Church of St Gudule, attended mass – surprising enough in itself – and then joined the penitents waiting at a confessional and persuaded the priest behind the grating, taken aback at this request from a Protestant, to hear her confession. She thus gained first-hand experience of one of the Catholic church's main means of gaining control over its adherents: the 'mystic lattice' of the confessional through which the 'sleepless eye' of Rome keeps watch.

Although, in a letter to Emily the following day, she dismissed her confession as no more than a 'freak', an eccentric impulse born of curiosity as much as depression, it has always been seen as one of the most intriguing episodes of her life.

The incident naturally has piquancy for Belgian readers. It is related in many guide books, and sometimes by tourist guides showing groups round

▲ Confessional in St Gudule.

the Cathedral. As we saw in a previous chapter, the thoughts of the writer
and academic Kristien Hemmerechts turn to Charlotte's confession in St
Gudule whenever she glimpses the cathedral towers from the window of her
university lecture hall. The novelist Jolien Janzing finds in the episode
support for the hypothesis of Charlotte and Heger's 'secret love'. Janzing has
related how she first heard the story of Charlotte's confession from a cathedral guide as she was sitting on the steps of St Gudule one day during her
lunch break. This was also the occasion when she first learned about the
Brontës' stay in Brussels.

Whether or not Charlotte was experiencing the temptations of a
forbidden love, one temptation she was exposed to that day in September
1843 was that of conversion to Catholicism. Like the priest who hears Lucy's
confession in *Villette*, the real-life priest in St Gudule attempted to 'bring her
back' to the 'true church'. Was she ever tempted, if only for a moment? The
confession episode has been seen as proof that her attitude to Catholicism
was ambivalent and that it attracted as well as repelled her. Lucy in fact states
its insidious attraction explicitly in Chapter 15 of *Villette*, giving this as a
powerful reason for rejecting the invitation of Père Silas, the priest who hears
her confession, to visit him the following day.

That priest had arms which could influence me; he was naturally kind, with a sentimental French kindness, to whose softness I knew myself not wholly impervious ... Had I gone to him, he would have shown me all that was tender, and comforting, and gentle, in the honest Popish superstition ... We all think ourselves strong in some points; we all know ourselves weak in many; the probabilities are that had I visited Numero 10, Rue des Mages, at the hour and day appointed, I might just now, instead of writing this heretic narrative, be counting my beads in the cell of a certain Carmelite convent on the Boulevard of Crécy in Villette.

La Maîtresse d'Anglais, the early adaptation of *Villette,* reinforces this point in a typically free translation of the original that enhances Charlotte's references to the appealing side of Catholicism. 'Although born a Protestant, my belief did not go so deep that it could not be uprooted; I felt very accessible to the tender unction of Catholicism, its mystical poetry, its sublime abnegation.'[17]

Similarly, the Romieus' biography imagines Charlotte succumbing totally to the charm of the Catholic mass, from the moment when, passing by St Gudule, she hears the summons of the church bells:

Suddenly a species of benediction fell upon her, drop by drop, like a sweet rain from heaven. A song, a voice, a call pealing down from a neighbouring belfry to summon the faithful to vespers ... Her surprised vision, searching the mystery and the poetry of the high vaults and deep aisles, came to rest on the ... statues, which the flame of the humble votive candles had touched and brought to miraculous life. Her gaze fell on the choir rich with gilding, with flowers, and with lights. A strange emotion ... disturbed her soul. She resisted, refused to yield, but a kind of beneficent numbness invaded her ... Clouds of incense enveloped her like the breath of a friend ... It did not for a moment occur to her to smile at these 'impious and theatrical mummeries' on which in her letters she had formerly heaped her sarcasms. She remained until the end of the ceremony, transfixed, without thought, surrendering herself to that atmosphere of sweetness, serenity, piety.[18]

Even Antonia White, who in *Frost in May* chronicles the more sinister aspects of a Catholic education, acknowledges the seductively tender side

◀ The interior of St Gudule.

of the creed, recounting that as a child, although she found God no more than a distant concept, she could talk to the Virgin and Child and the saints who peopled her convent school world as easily as to friends. For the writer Marie Gevers, the 'gentle tenderness' of Catholicism contrasted with what she saw as the Brontës' harsh and joyless Puritanism.

In *Villette*, Lucy admits that this 'tender' quality of Catholicism might have overcome her resistance to it at her deepest moment of depression. The priest is kind, and Lucy is susceptible to kindness even when it is somewhat intrusive. Like M. Paul in his constant spying on her, Père Silas wishes to 'watch over' as well as 'watch' her, and his benignity might conceivably have obtained its end. Moreover, in a moment of despair, entering a convent, despite the dire fate of the nun in the Pensionnat legend, might appear to offer a solution to the dilemma of an unsatisfied single woman like Lucy

Snowe, seeking a role and a purpose, a life that would fill the void of her current existence.

There is no evidence that Charlotte herself seriously experienced a similar temptation, despite the temporary relief of human contact afforded by the act of confession. Moreover, while those around Lucy lose no opportunity to try and convert her, no such attempt would have been made with Protestant pupils at the Pensionnat Heger – at any rate not by its directors.

In fact, the main seductive power of Catholicism for Charlotte was not any temptation towards conversion but the possibilities that the manifestations of the Catholic faith offered to her writer's imagination. The religion of the city depicted in *Villette* is a potent ingredient of the Gothic atmosphere and imagery that permeate the novel.

'A perfect example of the uncompromising Protestant'

The Catholic culture may have fed Charlotte's imagination, but she found no beauty or spiritual meaning in its rites, and her hostility to them is frequently voiced without much subtlety. Crimsworth arrives at Mlle Reuter's school to take a class in the first hour after lunch just as the midday prayer is ending.

> I heard a rapid, gabbling sound – which warned me that the 'prière du midi' was not yet concluded – I waited the termination thereof – it would have been impious to intrude my heretical presence during its progress. How the repeater of the prayer did cackle and splutter! I never before or since heard language enounced with such steam-engine haste. 'Notre Père qui êtes au ciel' went off like a shot; then followed an address to Marie 'vierge céleste, reine des anges, maison d'or, tour d'ivoire!' and then an invocation to the saint of the day, and then down they all sat, and the solemn (?) rite was over.[19]

Catholic places of worship pleased her no more than Catholic forms of prayer. Used to the simplicity of Protestant churches such as her father's in Haworth, she objected to the 'flowers and tinsel [and] wax-lights'[20] in Brussels churches, despite the Romieus' fantasy that she surrendered herself to the candles and incense of St Gudule. The French observer Gautier similarly describes the profusion of 'tinsel, wreaths, flowerpots' and other accoutrements of devotion cluttering the inside of St Gudule as indicative of

Belgian idolatry,[21] while the Englishman Thackeray was more amused than impressed by its extraordinarily elaborate carved pulpit. Victor Hugo, rhapsodising about this pulpit on one of his visits to Brussels, described it as 'poetry in wood' representing 'the whole of creation, of philosophy'.[22] Thackeray's response was rather different:

> In the matter of sculpture almost all the Brussels churches are decorated with the most laborious wooden pulpits, which may be worth their weight in gold, too, for what I know, including his reverence preaching inside. At St. Gudule the preacher mounts into no less a

place than the garden of Eden, being supported by Adam and Eve, by Sin and Death, and numberless other animals; he walks up to his desk by a rustic railing of flowers, fruits, and vegetables, with wooden peacocks, paroquets, monkeys biting apples, and many more of the birds and beasts of the field ... A priest, however tall or stout, must be lost in the midst of all these queer gimcracks; in order to be consistent, they ought to dress him up, too, in some odd fantastical suit ... But ... it is only bad taste. It may have been very true devotion which erected these strange edifices.[23]

The streets of Brussels were almost as filled with the symbols and rituals of Catholicism as its churches. Gautier noted that practically every Belgian house had a virgin or saint in a niche, with a lamp before it 'as in Spain or Italy'. He marvelled at the number of crucifixes placed at crossroads and in squares. Like the virgins, they were illuminated at night, and Gautier found these livid-faced and blood-streaked Christ figures particularly startling and 'sinister-looking' when stumbled upon in lantern-light in the evening mist.[24]

This religious devotion was not universal in Belgian society at the time. Politically the country was divided between the Catholic and Liberal (secularist) factions, with many adherents of the latter in government and the intelligentsia. This was something Charlotte picked up on: Lucy tells us that by no means all M. Paul's fellow teachers at the Athénée shared his devout Christian faith. 'Most of M. Emanuel's brother professors were emancipated free-thinkers, infidels, atheists.'[25] The Brussels administration was dominated by the liberal, anti-clerical faction; the university had been founded by Liberals, freemasons. There was, however, much religious fervour among the people following the country's separation from the Protestant northern Netherlands. Nerval reported that Brussels was as Catholic as in the times of Spanish rule, that men went to church as well as women and that, unlike men in Nerval's own country, they were not ashamed of being seen to be religious.[26] M. Heger was extremely devout, and Lucy describes M. Paul as 'crossing himself as devoutly as a woman'.[27]

Nerval's fellow Frenchman Edmond Texier enjoyed the spectacles proffered by the Church in the city's streets:

Almost every monument has its legend, and these marvellous legends still live in the people's imaginations. Nowhere can you see finer processions. The civic guard, choral societies, workers' corporations with banners and escutcheons, everybody attends these religious solemnities, which are truly magnificent. In the streets along which the procession passes, the walls of the houses disappear under tapestries of natural flowers. Above the closed shops, the windows and plinths are covered in linden boughs. After Rome, I think that it is in Brussels that you can find, in all their splendid majesty, the ancient pomps of Catholicism.[28]

Thackeray recorded his reaction to a much more modest procession of a kind to be seen everywhere in the streets.

To-day, strolling by the cathedral, I heard the tinkling of a bell in the street, and beheld certain persons, male and female, suddenly plump down on their knees before a little procession that was passing. Two men in black held a tawdry red canopy, a priest walked beneath it holding the sacrament covered with a cloth, and before him marched a couple of little altar-boys in short white surplices, such as you see in Rubens, and holding lacquered lamps. A small train of street-boys followed the procession, cap in hand, and the clergyman finally entered a hospital for old women, near the church, the canopy and the lamp-bearers remaining without.

It was a touching scene, and as I stayed to watch it, I could not but think of the poor old soul who was dying within, listening to the last words of prayer, led by the hand of the priest to the brink of the black fathomless grave. How bright the sun was shining without all the time, and how happy and careless everything around us looked![29]

(It was Thackeray's opinion that 'The priests of the country are a remarkably well-fed and respectable race, without that scowling, hang-dog look which one has remarked among reverend gentlemen in the neighbouring country of France', which is interesting in the light of Lucy's conclusion that Père Silas must be French because he does not have the typically 'grovelling' physiognomy of his Labassecourien counterparts.)

Thackeray is touched by the homely manifestations of Catholic devotion even while noting the 'tawdriness' of its accoutrements. Frances Trollope reports a similar reaction at the sight of a poor old woman kneeling in prayer before an image of the Virgin in a church in Ostend. She found the doll-like wooden statue, dressed in satins and lace, 'childishly grotesque' but was touched by the old woman's 'passionate devotion', which it was impossible to witness 'without losing all inclination to ridicule the source of it'.[30] She felt more reconciled still to Catholicism when she attended high mass in St Bavo's Cathedral in Ghent and enjoyed a service performed with 'dignity and solemn stateliness, which no difference of faith could prevent my feeling to be deeply and religiously impressive.'[31] The guide book writer Mrs Wemyss Dalrymple reported in 1839 that it was fashionable for English visitors and other foreigners to attend mass at the cathedral and other churches.[32]

Twenty years before Charlotte, the English traveller Henry Smithers, in *Observations made during a residence in Brussels*, found Belgian religious pageantry well worth seeing, enjoying it as a spectacle different from anything in his own country. He reported on a procession in Bruges in honour of St Francis Xavier, which was

> preceded by a number of boys ringing bells, and bearing flags; these were followed by different corporate bodies with their appropriate ensigns, carrying long flambeaux lighted; then followed a number of young females dressed in white, and other members of the corpora-tion, next came a priest bearing an image dressed sumptuously in blue and silver, representing the Virgin Mary; more young females and men carrying flambeaux were succeeded by a priest bearing a silver hand, in which is said to have been enshrined part of one of the thumbs of Francis Xavier; this relic was surrounded by priests with flambeaux, incense, and a band of music, the whole terminated by a priest splendidly attired, bearing the host under a canopy of velvet, attended by the military.[33]

One of the aspects of Catholicism that Charlotte most objected to was 'idolatry', the use of images such as that of the Virgin, which, in her view, came between the worshipper and God. The Protestant Smithers, who like her believed that 'the beauty of Christianity is its purity and simplicity', acknowledges the force of Protestant objections to paying homage to images which in Protestantism is paid to God alone but takes care to present the argument on the other side: for a Catholic, the statue or picture is no more than a symbol of the Deity, serving simply to recall Him to remembrance as a picture serves to recollect an absent friend.

Smithers further points out that while it is true that one of the Commandments prohibits bowing down before 'graven images', another command is to 'judge not that we be not judged'. While holding firm to our own beliefs, we ought to show tolerance and goodwill to those who differ from us. '[Christ] forbids us to assume the seat of judgement, which belongs only to himself; and admonishes us against dealing out anathemas against those who differ from us. In such remarks I have to make on the religion of this country, I shall endeavour to pursue this line of conduct.'[34]

Such tolerance of religious differences was not the guide that Charlotte took for her own discussion of Catholicism, and this draws a rebuke from the 1854 Belgian reviewer of *Villette*: 'Devotion to one's own faith does not authorise one to insult that of others'. Lucy Snowe is unrelenting in her hostility to the 'painted and meretricious face' of the church of Rome.[35] 'There was a hollowness within, and a flourish around "Holy Church", which tempted me but moderately.'[36] When taken by M. Paul to witness the most splendid rites of his church in an effort to convert her, she remains frostily unmoved, except to disdain. Charlotte was far from indifferent to lavish spectacles in general, but the most solemn pomp of Catholicism leaves Lucy as unimpressed as Charlotte was by the 'mummery' of the carnival. She acknowledges her inability to 'subjugate her reason to her imagination', finding no pleasure in the spectacles of the Romish church even as spectacle.

> My third temptation was held out in the pomp of Rome, the glory of her kingdom. I was taken to the churches on solemn occasions – days of fête and state; I was shown the Papal ritual and ceremonial. I looked at it.
>
> Many people – men and women – no doubt far my superiors in a thousand ways, have felt this display impressive, have declared that though their Reason protested, their Imagination was subjugated. I cannot say the same. Neither full procession, nor high mass, nor swarming tapers, nor swinging censers, nor ecclesiastical millinery, nor celestial jewellery, touched my imagination a whit. What I saw struck me as tawdry, not grand; as grossly material, not poetically spiritual ...
>
> On the evening of a certain day when ... I had been made to witness a huge mingled procession of the church and the army – priests with relics, and soldiers with weapons, an obese and aged archbishop, habited in cambric and lace, looking strangely like a grey daw in bird-of-paradise plumage, and a band of young girls fantastically robed and garlanded – *then* I spoke my mind to M. Paul.

'I did not like it,' I told him, 'I did not respect such ceremonies; I wished to see no more.'

...I told him I could not look on flowers and tinsel, on wax-lights and embroidery, at such times and under such circumstances as should be devoted to lifting the secret vision to Him whose home is Infinity, and His being – Eternity. That when I thought of sin and sorrow, of earthly corruption, mortal depravity, weighty temporal woe – I could not care for chanting priests or mumming officials...[37]

Charlotte's French biographer Ernest Dimnet was surprised and disappointed that she remained so impervious to the solemn rites of his church.

It is extraordinary that gifted as she was with a rich imagination, fond of ancient things and passionately admiring Walter Scott, Charlotte was not more tolerant of the Catholic ritual as it appeared in a church like Saint Gudule. She always remained inflexible upon this point. In London many years later she was present at a confirmation service in the Spanish chapel conducted by Cardinal Wiseman. She saw nothing in it but 'theatrical impiety.'

Given that Charlotte opened her soul to a Catholic priest in Brussels, it is curious that the first biographer on the Continent to scrutinise her mind and soul was a French Jesuit priest, Abbé Dimnet. Dimnet's *Les Soeurs Brontë* (1911) was the first biography in French available to Belgian readers after Elizabeth Gaskell's, a French translation of which came out in 1877. Abbé Dimnet did not himself take church services or hear confessions. His life was spent teaching, lecturing and writing. His passion for English literature and fascination with the Brontë family went back to his adolescence growing up in a sleepy provincial town in northern France close to the Belgian border. A prolific author, in English as well as French, he lived for many years in the United States; his book *The Art of Thinking* became a best-seller.

Dimnet found Charlotte 'a perfect example of the uncompromising Protestant, not only armed and distrustful but forward and aggressive, a type which the Oxford Movement was in course of suppressing .... Charlotte was perhaps the last Englishwoman to delight in the idea of heresy and to repeat the word "heretic" with a wild and provocative joy.'[38]

◀ The Protestant Chapel in Place du Musée in 1844.

In one sense, however, in *Villette* Charlotte worked her way through to a certain tolerance of the Catholic faith. She remained steadfastly hostile to the Catholic church herself, viewing it as a tyrant that used its followers' faith as a means of increasing its power and wealth rather than cherishing that faith for its own sake. But Lucy does become reconciled to Catholicism in M. Paul, even if, in their debates on religion, she never wavers in asserting the superiority of her own. Despite his subjection to priests and 'priestcraft' she is touched by his child-like faith. 'I thought Romanism wrong ... but it seemed to me that this Romanist held the purer elements of his creed with an innocency of heart which God must love.'[39] 'All Rome could not put into him bigotry, nor the Propaganda itself make him a real Jesuit. He was born honest, and not false – artless, and not cunning – a freeman, and not a slave.'[40]

Similarly, M. Paul, while repelled by the self-reliance of Lucy's 'terrible, proud, earnest Protestantism',[41] becomes reconciled to it in her. 'My little English Puritan, I love Protestantism in you. I own its severe charm. There is something in its ritual I cannot receive myself, but it is the sole creed for "Lucy".'[42]

Despite this, some Belgian readers have seen the ending of *Villette* as an indication that Charlotte saw religion as an unsurmountable barrier to the union of the pair in marriage. In Elisabeth Beker's view, if the marriage of Jane and Rochester was considered subversive by some readers, that of the British Protestant Lucy with the Belgian Catholic Paul Emanuel was too much to contemplate even for Charlotte herself. It was 'a bridge too far'.[43]

1 *Villette*, Chapter 15 'The Long Vacation'.
2 Letter to Ellen Nussey, July 1842. Smith, *The Letters of Charlotte Brontë*, Volume I, pp. 289–90.
3 *The Professor*, Chapter 12.
4 *Villette*, Chapter 14.
5 Preface to Rachel MacCrindell, *The School Girl in France* (London: Seeley and Burnside, 1842).
6 A Parent, *Do-the-Girls Hall, or Conventual Life Unveiled* (London: N. Wilson, 1875(?)), p. 7.
7 *The English girl in a convent school: a record of experience* (London: Frederick Warne and Co, 1874), p. 44.
8 Antonia White, *Frost in May* (London: Desmond Harmsworth, 1933), Chapter 8.
9 *Villette*, Chapter 31.
10 *The Professor*, Chapter 17.
11 *The English Girl in a Convent School*, pp. 25, 28.
12 Addison, *Belgium as she is*, p. 176.
13 *Villette*, Chapter 9.
14 *The Professor*, Chapter 11.
15 *Ibid.*, Chapter 12.
16 *Revue Trimestrielle*, 1854, Vol. 2, pp. 279–83.
17 Charlotte Brontë/Currer Bell, *La Maîtresse d'anglais, ou le Pensionnat de Bruxelles*. Vol II, Chapter 12, p. 17.
18 Romieu, *The Brontë Sisters*, pp. 125–6.
19 *The Professor*, Chapter 14.
20 *Villette*, Chapter 36.
21 Gautier, *Un Tour en Belgique*, p. 89.
22 In a letter from Brussels to his wife dated 18 August 1837.
23 Thackeray, 'Little Travels and Roadside Sketches'.
24 Gautier, *Un Tour en Belgique*. In Zigzags, p. 107.
25 *Villette*, Chapter 33.
26 Nerval, *Œuvres*, p. 814.
27 *Villette*, Chapter 33.
28 Texier, *Voyage Pittoresque en Hollande et en Belgique*, p. 268.
29 Thackeray, 'Little Travels and Roadside Sketches'.
30 Trollope, *Belgium and Western Germany in 1833*, p. 12.
31 *Ibid.*, p. 32.
32 Wemyss Dalrymple, *The Economist's New Brussels Guide*, p. 90.
33 Smithers, *Observations made during a residence in Brussels*, p. 120.
34 *Ibid.*, p. 116.
35 *Villette*, Chapter 36.
36 *Ibid.*, Chapter 34.
37 *Ibid.*, Chapter 36.
38 Dimnet, *The Brontë Sisters*, p. 84–5.
39 *Villette*, Chapter 36.
40 *Ibid*, Chapter 42.
41 *Ibid*, Chapter 36.
42 *Ibid*, Chapter 42.
43 Acke and Bekers, *Écrire Bruxelles/Brussel Schrijven*, p. 133.

CHAPTER TWELVE

In Mr Browne's Shop: Belgian Brontëana

IN March 2012, newspaper headlines all over the world announced the discovery of a hitherto unpublished French *devoir* of Charlotte's, dated 16 March 1842. It is mentioned in Mrs Chadwick's biography *In the Footsteps of the Brontës* (1914), as being in the possession of Paul Heger[1] and is listed in a 1924 bibliography of Charlotte Brontë's early manuscripts,[2] but it could not be traced when a collected edition of Charlotte's and Emily's *devoirs*, in the original French and in translation, was published in 1996.[3] The composition in question, entitled *L'Ingratitude,* had not really been lost, but forgotten. It was spotted by the Brussels-based researcher Brian Bracken in the recently-digitised catalogue of the Musée Royal de Mariemont in southern Belgium.[4] Until the catalogue went online, Brontë scholars had been unaware that the essay was in the museum's collection.

The museum staff were somewhat taken aback by the excitement of the world press. The Mariemont, which stands in the blighted industrial landscape around Charleroi, has a huge collection of manuscripts, whose authors include Erasmus, Galileo and Mozart. Charlotte's little French exercise (the first of the Brontës' Brussels essays to have survived) may not have seemed worth making a fuss about. It forms part of an album of Brontë-related items given by Paul Heger in 1915 to his friend Raoul Warocqué, a wealthy coal magnate whose collection the Musée Mariemont now houses. Written on a single sheet of ruled paper, it is a fable about an ungrateful young rat who perishes when he leaves his home and loving father in search of adventure.

The Mariemont staff doubtless assumed that the *devoir's* location was known to Brontë researchers. The fact that it slumbered undisturbed for a century in their collection indicates that in Belgium, interest in the Brontës does not attain the feverish pitch it can reach in English-speaking parts of the world.

The exercise-book page on which *L'Ingratitude* was written is just one of the items of Brontëana left behind in Brussels. Which other mementos of her stay did Charlotte leave there for future Brontëites? She is known to

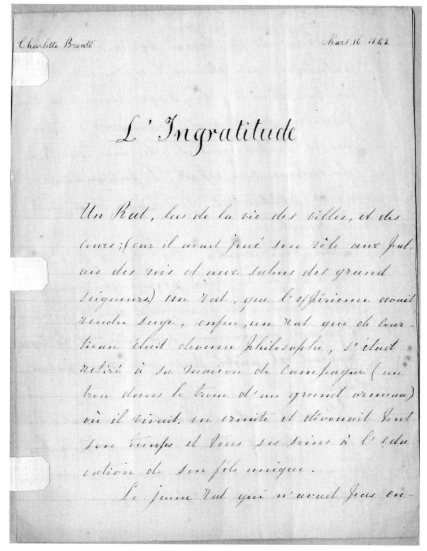

▲ *L'Ingratitude*, a French *devoir* of Charlotte's dated 16 March 1842 which dropped out of sight for almost a century and was rediscovered in 2012 in the Musée Royal de Mariemont.

have treasured those that she herself took back to Yorkshire, mainly gifts from Heger. As well as books, he gave her a more unusual offering: a fragment of the wooden coffin in which Napoleon's remains were returned to France from St Helena in 1840 for burial in the Hôtel des Invalides. Heger had acquired it from his French colleague Joachim-Joseph Lebel, director of the boarding section at the Athénée Royal, thought to be the model for M.

Pelet in *The Professor*. Lebel in turn had it from a member of the French royal family, the Prince de Joinville, a brother of Queen Louise's, who commanded the frigate that brought back Napoleon's remains. Charlotte wrote on the paper in which it was wrapped the time and the date on which Heger had put it into her hand as she sat in class: 1 pm on 4 August 1843, shortly before the start of the desolate summer vacation that drove her to the confession box.

Apart from *L'Ingratitude*, which some of her Belgian critics would consider aptly named in view of her subsequent treatment of the Hegers, a sizeable collection of the Brontës' essays remained with Heger. Most of them were subsequently dispersed owing to his habit of honouring favoured pupils and visitors to the Pensionnat with the gift of a *devoir*. Some of the visitors were American, one reason why several of the essays have ended up in the United States. Today just four remain in the possession of his descendants.

The discovery of a Brontë manuscript in an attic or antiquarian bookshop is a fantasy of many Brontëites, and even today the odd one occasionally surfaces. *L'Amour Filiale*, written in August 1842, another previously unpublished *devoir* of Charlotte's, was discovered in a book in a private library and bought by the Brontë Society in 2013. None of the essays have so far come to light in Belgian attics, but a chance find was made in 1892 when a bound volume containing some juvenilia of Charlotte's was discovered on a Brussels second-hand bookstall by a university professor called Ernest Nys. These were some Angrian tales written by her around the time of her eighteenth birthday: *The Spell: An Extravaganza, High Life in Verdopolis*, and some shorter pieces. It is supposed that Charlotte gave the stories to Heger, possibly when she returned to Brussels for her second year. The manuscripts had been bound in leather, presumably by Heger, and the cover embossed in gold lettering that read 'Manuscrits de Miss Charlotte Brontë (Currer Bell)'. Nys sold the volume to the British Museum for £25.[5]

Heger was still alive, and it is not known how the manuscripts came to leave his possession and end up on a second-hand bookstall. Possibly there was a clearance of some of the Hegers' belongings after Mme Heger's death in 1890. Professor Nys would have known Heger's son Paul, who, like him, taught at Brussels University. Nys was a big name in academic circles whose work is still highly regarded today, an eminent scholar who wrote prolifically on international law and was later nominated for the Nobel prize. When he sold the manuscripts to the British Museum he was already well acquainted with its reading room, having spent entire summer vacations there deep among manuscripts of a rather different kind.

Both novelettes centre around Angria's ruler the Duke of Zamorna, the moody, despotic Byronic hero of Charlotte's youthful fiction. The various heroines in *High Life in Verdopolis*, which has been described as 'a delightful orgy of Bryonism',[6] are all besotted with the Angrian king. Zamorna shares with Constantin Heger the honour of serving as a model for the character of Rochester; Charlotte's fixation on Heger has echoes of the capacity for infatuation of her early fictional heroines.

Another item of Brontëana, a book connected with Charlotte Brontë albeit not one written by her, finished up in the house of Lucien Christophe, a writer who has been cited several times in these pages. He recorded its history in a newspaper article. The little book itself and Christophe's commentary form a touching part of Charlotte's Brussels legacy. In 1926 Louise Heger, then 87, sent the book in question to Christophe's wife as a present for the couple's young daughter. With it she sent a letter, which Christophe and his wife kept reverently. They regarded Louise with affection and veneration as someone from another era who, while taking a keen interest in the present, had many stories to tell of her past in a Brussels they had never known. A past in which Charlotte Brontë had played a part.

> Dear Madam,
>> This book was given to me by Charlotte when she left Brussels. My sister Marie was five. I was only three ...[7]
>> We learned English from this book, which was always lying around in the nursery. There was a dedication (signed by Charlotte) which very much pleased a Russian lady who removed it before my astonished eyes; but I never suspected at that time that I was being robbed of a precious keepsake.
>> Nothing remains of what gave the book its value, but it will amuse your dear little girl, for Charlotte chose well.
>> With my best regards.
>> L.H. 22 November 1926

In the article in which he relates how he came to own a book bought by Charlotte Brontë, *Souvenirs de la Pension Heger: Un amour de Charlotte Brontë*, Christophe described the book in question.

It is an old English book for children, a small book with a romantic binding. It is at the end of its career. It is set out like a catechism and looks like a worn school book. There are loose pages. The cover is stained. It is the kind of book you find in profusion in the boxes on second-hand bookstalls, among odd volumes of Barthélemy's *Travels of Anacharsis* and almanachs with pages torn out of them.

Christophe was writing a few months after Louise's death at the age of 94. 'She was the only living person on the whole Continent who remembered being dandled on the knees of Charlotte Brontë.' Christophe, who knew Louise only as a very old lady dressed in black who reminded him of Queen Victoria, tried to imagine her as a red-cheeked three-year-old who was loved by Charlotte Brontë.

The book was entitled *The Child's Best Friend: A Series of Examples for the Proper Behaviour of Children – with six fine wood engravings*. A yellow label on the back cover, which looked as unworn as if it had been gummed in place only the day before, read: 'Se trouve à la librairie anglaise de Edward Browne, Montagne de la Cour, 80, à Bruxelles.' Beside it, in pencil, was written the year of purchase: 1843. Edward Browne's shop makes an appearance in various Brussels guides of the time; Addison mentions the 'English reading room that takes all English journals and periodicals in Montagne de la Cour, kept by a Mr Browne'.

Christophe had often listened to Louise reminiscing about 'Charlotte'. In the article *Souvenirs de la Pension Heger: Un amour de Charlotte Brontë* he judges Charlotte severely for her treatment of the Hegers – a family for which he had great respect and affection – particularly of Madame. In making this judgement, his sympathies seem to be much more with the Hegers than with the writer who bared her soul in her letters to Brussels – much more with the long-suffering discretion and dignity of the Belgian family than with the heartache, indiscretion and what he saw as the vengefulness of the little English teacher, the viper they had nursed in their bosom.

But in concluding the article Christophe shows that he can feel for the English teacher's suffering too. 'Charlotte' was someone of whom his old friend Louise Heger always spoke not just with forbearance but with affection. Christophe imagines Charlotte Brontë towards the end of her stay in Brussels, at the end of 1843, driven from the city by the impossibly awkward situation that her feelings had created for her at the Pensionnat. She and her employers had agreed to part company. Her berth on the

Ostend–London steamer was perhaps already booked, and she was looking for goodbye presents for her very small circle of acquaintances in the city. Most of her English friends had moved on, but she must buy something for the Hegers and their children. She had a particular interest in Louise, the second eldest child, one of the small and select number of children she encountered in the course of her life for whom she felt real affection. Louise claimed to recognise herself in *Villette* as Fifine, Mme Beck's second child.

> The second child, Fifine, was said to be like its dead father. Certainly, though the mother had given it her healthy frame, her blue eye and ruddy cheek, not from her was derived its moral being. It was an honest, gleeful little soul: a passionate, warm-tempered, bustling creature . . .[8]

The Heger children were taught English and had English nursemaids, and Browne's reading room cum bookshop seemed a good place to look for a gift for Louise. Christophe followed Charlotte in imagination into the shop.

> I can picture her, the little English teacher who has been dismissed,[9] and who knows that this is it, she has to go. I can see her in Edward Browne's bookshop, full of shame and grief, her heart in tumult, touchingly powerless in her attempt to turn her humiliated love towards a three-year-old girl, the child of the man she loved, a child who could have been her daughter. I don't want to know anything about what will come later – without which, however, she would never have taken her place in the gallery of famous lovers of history. The most pathetic moment in Charlotte's life is surely the one when, solitary, unknown, exiled, fleeing her heart, she chose for a three-year-old child, who will deny her like the others, because that's how it has to be, a little book full of messages that will never arrive. Her eyes are swimming with repressed tears. She smiles at Mr Browne, who is bustling around in his shop. She leafs through the book to see whether it will do. She reads the introduction:
> 'Reading, writing, drawing, music and dancing, it is true, are accomplishments fit to adorn the mind, and complete the more important part of education; – but patience, forbearance, industry, generosity, frankness and kindness of heart, are qualities much more

essential to our happiness than any accomplishments we may possess.'

Yes, that's good. She is smiling sadly. 'I'll take this book, Mr Browne.' Mme Heger will approve of these sentiments and when, eighty years later, 'little Loulou' gives *The child's best friend* to a little girl about the same age as she was when she received it, she will say, 'Charlotte chose well.'

How I applaud the action of that very ill-mannered Russian lady who tore the dedication out of this little book! But for that, it would have been destined to be imprisoned under a glass case in a museum among other Brontë memorabilia. How much more touching for it to continue to play a modest, useful role in a family and for a little girl to learn English from it, in memory of a very old lady with a brusque, cordial way of speaking and affable manners, very Queen Victoria in her black silk dress, the old lady who was once little Louise with red cheeks, rather intimidating for a small girl in 1933, but so kind, so attentive. The old lady who, on her deathbed, her eyes already glazed over, said playfully to the young mother who had come to see her, 'Ah! Ah! You're coming to give me news of your little girl. She had her piano examination today. How did she play her Bach?'

---

1   Chadwick, *In the Footsteps of the Brontës*, p. 216.

2   C. W. Hatfield (1924), 'The Early Manuscripts of Charlotte Brontë: A Bibliography'. *Brontë Society Transactions*, 6:34, p. 234.

3   Lonoff, *The Belgian Essays: A Critical Edition*.

4   Brian Bracken, 'L'Ingratitude', *London Review of Books*, 8 March 2012.

5   Introduction by Christine Alexander (ed.) to Charlotte Brontë, *High life in Verdopolis* (London: British Library, 1995).

6   Fannie Elizabeth Ratchford, *The Brontës' Web of Childhood* (New York: Columbia UP, 1941), p. 84.

7   Louise, born on 14 July 1839, was actually four years old at the time Charlotte left Brussels.

8   *Villette*, Chapter 9.

9   In fact Charlotte was not dismissed. Increasingly miserable, she gave her notice to the Hegers in October 1843 but was persuaded by Heger to stay on a little longer. On 19 December she wrote to Emily, 'I have taken my determination. I hope to be home the day after New Year's Day. I have told Madame.' (Smith, *The Letters of Charlotte Brontë*, Vol. 1, p. 449).

CHAPTER THIRTEEN

'The Brontës in Africa' and Charlotte in the Congo

A s we saw in an earlier chapter, in 1955 the author Marie Gevers visited the Congo to give a series of lectures on the poet Émile Verhaeren, in the centenary of his birth. On her flight from Elisabethville (today Lubumbashi) to Albertville (Kalemie), an item in a sheet of newspaper used to protect the cover of her guide to the Congo reminded her that it was also the centenary of Charlotte Brontë's death. During the flight over the vast expanse of Lake Tanganyika she found herself meditating on the Brontës' childhood fantasy world of Angria, based in part on their reading about the continent Gevers was now discovering. As her eyes took in the dazzling vista of the African sky and the lake below, her thoughts were busy in the world of Angria and the sumptuous city of Glasstown or Verdopolis, supposedly located in central west Africa, in which Charlotte and Branwell Brontë (and Emily and Anne before they broke away to found their own country of Gondal) led a tumultuous existence and found the perfect escape from the limitations of life in Haworth Parsonage.

Like Leopold I, the Brontës dreamed of colonies. Unlike the first King of the Belgians they succeeded in establishing one, albeit only in fiction. The siblings' African saga, written over many years, drew inspiration from their readings of accounts of European explorers, such as Mungo Park's expeditions to discover the course of the river Niger. The children named the twelve toy soldiers given to them by their father after heroes and explorers they admired and dispatched them in imagination as adventurers to establish a colony in the west coast of Africa, in an area roughly equivalent to the Gold Coast. The young authors had read about the wars between the British and the Ashanti empire in the 1820s. Their mythical African world included the kingdom of Ashantee; their heroes waged wars against the native Ashantee tribes and their wonderfully named leader Quashia Quamina.

The Brontës famously chronicled their heroes' conquests and love affairs in tiny notebooks, the smallest of which were no more than two inches square. Branwell named one of his soldiers after Napoleon, Charlotte christened one of hers the Duke of Wellington, subsequently replaced in her affections by his son Zamorna. Well into her twenties, she continued to inhabit this 'infernal world', as she called it, of the imagination, located on the Gulf of Guinea: the world of the Glass Town Federation and the neigh-bouring Kingdom of Angria; of Verdopolis, the Federation's splendid capital, established at the mouth of the river Niger; of Adrianopolis, Angria's capital on the banks of the Calabar.

Gevers does not mention the fact that two of the Angrian stories – the novelettes discovered by Professor Nys on a Brussels bookstall – have a Belgian link.

Gevers' musings also led her to consider the privations of Charlotte's adult life, in particular the unrequited love that she took back to Haworth as a result of her visit to Belgium – her love for Constantin Heger. The landing of the plane in Albertville interrupted her Brontëan reverie, but, only momentarily since, as she relates, 'A curious continuation of my mental adventure awaited me when I stepped off the plane'. A pleasant man in his late forties met her at the airport and told her that he was there in place of his wife, who was the president of the *Union africaine des Arts et des Lettres*, an organisation set up by the Belgian administration. She had made the arrangements for Gevers' lecture but was indisposed that day and unable to come to meet her. 'Allow me to introduce myself. I am Jacques Heger.' Gevers almost had to rub her eyes to make sure she wasn't dreaming. 'Jacques Heger? Are you a descendant of Constantin Heger, the Brontës' teacher in Brussels?' 'I'm his great-grandson.'

This member of the Heger family, a civil servant, was the son of Constantin Heger's grandson Fernand, Paul Heger's only son. During her time in Albertville, Gevers spent an evening with him and his wife in their house overlooking the lake with its avenues of coconut trees. Evening falls early in the Congo. On the Hegers' huge terrace under the stars, by the lake made luminous by moonlight, much of the conversation was about the Heger family and Charlotte Brontë. In the dimly-lit sitting-room there were photos of Constantin and Zoë and the Pensionnat. Jacques Heger (born in 1907) spoke of his father's memories of the couple. While Gevers' mind, as always when she thought of the Brontës, was full of compassion for Charlotte, scalded by her unhappy experience, at the Brussels Pensionnat, of falling in love, Jacques Heger spoke of a Pensionnat scorched by the passage of the incendiary English teacher and left 'burning' after the publication of *Villette* and the subsequent incursions by English and American literary pilgrims.

This conversation under the African sky took place amid the perfume of frangipani flowers. The 'nocturnal fairyland', in Gevers' words, of the garden mingled with that of the lake and the moon. It might seem a strange setting in which to be thinking obsessively of the Brontës, but as Gevers had reflected on the plane, the exoticism of far-off colonies had exerted a strong hold on the imaginations of the young Brontës. She might also have reflected that the fascination continued in Charlotte Brontë's adult fiction. Mr Rochester's first bride comes from Jamaica, Jane Eyre's suitor St John Rivers wants her to accompany him as a missionary to India and Paul Emanuel takes himself off to the French West Indian colony of Guadeloupe.

Oddly, Gevers did not confide the thoughts that were occupying her to the Hegers. She did not put them into words until she set them down in an article entitled *Les Brontë en Afrique* and, subsequently, in a memoir of her African trip.[1] Indeed, at times during her evening with these colonial Hegers, neither she nor her congenial hosts felt the need for words at all. They fell silent on the terrace, the better to allow the tropical night and the moonlight to work its spell. 'A sentence from *Villette* came to my mind: "Silence is of different kinds, and breathes different meanings; no words could inspire a pleasanter content than did M. Paul's wordless presence."'[2]

Charlotte Brontë continued to run through Gevers' mind throughout her time in Africa, but she closes her article *Les Brontë en Afrique* with a reference to Emily. On a car journey up into the hills near Usumbura (today Bujumbura), she noted idly the names of the various plantations they passed, the paths to which led off the mountain road they were climbing. The name at the entrance of the last plantation they passed on their ascent, the highest of all of them, lodged in her memory. It was 'Hurlevent': 'Wuthering Heights'.

---

1   Gevers, 'Les Brontë en Afrique', *Revue Générale Belge*, 15 September 1956; *Plaisir des Parallèles: essai sur un voyage*, pp. 88–103.
2   *Villette*, Chapter 29.

CHAPTER FOURTEEN

'Land of Enchantment': Charlotte and the Park

'YOUR shortest way will be to follow the boulevard, and cross the park,' he continued; 'but it is too late and too dark for a woman to go through the park alone; I will step with you thus far.'

He moved on, and I followed him, through the darkness and the small soaking rain. The Boulevard was all deserted, its path miry, the water dripping from its trees; the park was black as midnight. In the double gloom of trees and fog, I could not see my guide; I could only follow his tread. Not the least fear had I: I believe I would have followed that frank tread, through continual night, to the world's end.[1]

It is a late evening in February and Lucy Snowe has just arrived in Villette, alone and friendless. A fellow passenger, a young Englishman, takes pity on her, gives her the name of an inn where she can spend her first night in the city and accompanies her for the first part of the way, across the park. Later in the novel he will turn up again as Graham Bretton, with whom Lucy falls in love before finding a more suitable mate in Paul Emanuel.

Lucy Snowe crosses the park at a time when her fortunes are at their lowest ebb. She does not speak the language of Villette, has no friends there, does not even have the name of a hotel and barely has money enough to pay for one. The park, unlit and dripping in the rain, is practically the first place she sees in the city. At the Pensionnat, Charlotte Brontë lived a stone's throw away from the Parc de Bruxelles and must often have seen it on Sundays when it was all animation. But her own impressions of it in *Villette*, often cited by Belgian readers, are nothing like those in Brussels guide books.

Her first sight of it is at night and in the rain. The park scene most frequently cited is, likewise, a night-time one, which takes place towards the end of the novel. Lucy has now lived in Villette for some time. She has made friends and fallen in love there. But a stifling summer's night finds her wandering in the park as lonely as on her first night in the city. Lonely, but not alone; she is surrounded by people – some of whom she recognises, to some of whom she has formed attachments. To all of them, however, Lucy, imperceptible in her nondescript attire, seems to be invisible.

Lucy is often in mental anguish in *Villette,* and this second park scene follows some of the passages in the novel in which her pain is at its most intense. It has been announced that M. Paul is to set out on a long voyage just as her friendship with him seemed to be evolving into something closer. She doesn't know the reason for his impending departure. She waits for days for a chance to meet him for explanations, but he makes no sign and she fears he will sail without even taking leave of her. In Lucy's agony of solitary waiting Charlotte described one of the torments of her own life. Waiting for love; waiting for Heger's letters, for a sign that he cared for her; and in later years, as her solitude pressed more and more on her after her siblings' deaths, waiting for similar signs from the young man to whom she became attracted, her publisher George Smith, 'Graham Bretton' in *Villette.* Lucy's anguish mounts steadily in the 'weary days' preceding the park scene as her confidence that she had gained Paul Emanuel's affection for life is 'torn by the roots out of [her] riven, outraged heart', like Charlotte's own hope of retaining the friendship of Constantin Heger when her appeals to him met with no response. Her distress becomes intolerable after Mme Beck, by now revealed as a deadly rival, makes sure that Lucy has no opportunity to speak to M. Paul when he comes to take leave of the pupils. The evening of the following day, spent once again in suspense in the hope of a meeting with him, finds Lucy 'untamed, tortured, again pacing a solitary room in an unalterable passion of silent desolation'.[2]

Towards midnight, unable to sleep, having been administered, on Madame's orders, an opium-spiked sleeping draught which has the opposite effect of that intended, Lucy ends up in the park, driven there in the heat and her feverish state by longing thoughts of the cool waters of its stone basin. When she creeps out of the stuffy dormitory and makes her way towards it she imagines herself alone there in the moonlight. Instead, she finds the park illuminated and teeming with crowds of Villette burghers.

Accounts of the Parc de Bruxelles by other visitors also describe it as teeming with joyous crowds, but their descriptions are of a sunny, noonday place. Many visitors found the park enchanting; only Charlotte describes it as being *enchanted,* an other-worldly and almost surreal place. The tourists of the time concurred in extolling the special charm of this public garden, created by the French architect Gilles-Barnabé Guimard and the Viennese landscape gardener Joachim Zinner when the royal quarter was built. It occupies the space between the *Palais de la Nation*, the Houses of Parliament, and the much less elegant royal palace, which gaze at each other through the trees; in the opinion of a French *proscrit*, the respective architectural merit of the two buildings made a statement about the relative importance of parliament and royalty in a constitutional monarchy.[3]

Henry Robert Addison was one of the visitors who was charmed by the park. He wrote about it in his guide *Belgium As She Is*.

> The Park of Brussels is one of the most enchanting gardens imaginable, planted with splendid old trees, arranged in the fashion of the early part of the last century, divided by broad walks, and square cut grass plots; it may seem in mere written description as stiff and unpicturesque, but viewed in reality on a fine day, every vista affording the view of some splendid building at the close of it, dotted here and there with flowers, ornamented with statues, and thronged with a crowd of gay well dressed people: the scene is almost fairylike and strongly reminds one of the old pictures of *al fresco* fêtes when Dames and Knights, stretched along the grass, whiled away the time in telling love tales, or listening to the soft breathings of some dulcet lute. I am aware that such romantic language is ill fitted for the pages of a dry

▲ Hollow or wilderness in the park.

223

guide book, but I have no other terms in which I can properly give an idea of this lovely garden, which is basely wronged in being styled a park.[4]

No wonder that the writer Leen Huet, in her dictionary of Belgium *Mijn België*, marvels at the view of the country presented by the upbeat Addison. In the pages of his guide she sees her 'dull birthplace', Belgium, 'turn briefly into a romantic landscape'. For Addison, she says, 'the wonderful park of Brussels was the heart of Belgium.'[5]

Closeted in the Pensionnat, Lucy hears the band playing and imagines the bright Villette life going on around her, so near and yet so far – and that life centres on the park. It becomes a dark place only when Lucy is walking in it herself in her solitude and despair.

Addison's description of its attractions is borne out by the accounts of other visitors. For Gérard de Nerval, the Haute Ville of Brussels may have been a poor imitation of Paris, but he had praise for its park as a 'judicious mixture of the severe style of French gardens and the picturesque style of English ones, avoiding the coldness of the former and the desultoriness of the latter.'[6] While the avenues were laid out in classical style, a romantic air was provided by the dense clumps of trees and by a deep dell at the south (palace) end, a kind of wilderness still there today, which relieved the classical monotony of the French style. This hollow had been a feature of the garden of the old Coudenberg Palace, whose arbours and grottos excited the wonder of visitors. Less appealingly, in the 1830 Revolution it was used by the Dutch troops stationed in the park as a burial ground for their dead.

Thackeray enjoyed a glass of lemonade under the trees, but found something to sneer at. 'Numbers of statues decorate the place, the very worst I ever saw. These Cupids must have been erected in the time of the Dutch dynasty, as I judge from the immense posterior developments. Indeed the arts of the country are very low. The statues here, and the lions before the Prince of Orange's palace, would disgrace almost the figurehead of a ship.' His tone is very much that of Lucy Snowe, scrutinising the well-fattened curves of the 'Cleopatra' at the Villette art exhibition and forming a low opinion of at least some of the city's art.

For the high society of Brussels, the park was the place of rendezvous at midday, before the four o'clock dinner. Contemporary prints show it at noon, packed with animated crowds. On Sundays the ordinary burghers

▲ The Parc de Bruxelles, with the parliament building in the background.

headed there too, decked in their Sunday best. A satirical Brussels journal observes the Brussels burghers on their Sunday outing from the Flemish quarters in the Basse Ville to the francophone, upper-class Haute Ville in 1853, a weekly foray that seems to have caused the worthy 'Labassecouriens' torments of a different kind from those endured by Lucy.

> The Sunday walk in the Park is Brussels *en toilette*: Brussels in its finery, Brussels in disguise, starched up in clothes too tight for it, prinked and curled. For this is no longer you, my stout burgher from the Basse Ville. Gone is your loud laugh, your ease of manner, your workaday Flemish. Alas, your paunch is imprisoned under a tight frock coat, your crimson cheeks repose between two starched collars, like a bouquet of flowers. You're wearing gloves! You're speaking French!
>
> And this is no longer you, Madame, the shopkeeper from rue de Flandres. To come to the Park, you have donned a new brightly-coloured hat. You are clad in silk from top to toe. A fine cashmere shawl covers your broad shoulders, your huge gold chain makes your

neighbour, the grocer's wife, green with envy. Heaven forgive me, but I do believe you're wearing a hairpiece!

And this is no longer you, Mademoiselle. Oh no! This isn't your usual clear, sparkling look and teasing or languorous expression, your coquettish, graceful casual attire ... To appear on the stage of this theatre that is the Park, you too have disfigured and disguised yourself. You had to have a gown, mantilla and hat of the latest Parisian fashion. The hairdresser has tormented your lovely hair for an hour to give it a new turn, and you have tortured your wits for a week to come up with a ravishing toilette.

But this is still you, Madam Countess! This is your costly, elegant attire, these are your disdainful airs towards at the *petites bourgeoises* who cast envious looks at you as they pass by. This is your face just as it always is, plastered with white and red.[7]

The writer Louis Hymans, a chronicler of Brussels life of the period, noted that despite Belgium's much-vaunted social equality, the social divisions were clearly demarcated; he observed that the Belgians' curious blend of respect for authority and independence of character was much like that to be found in England. Nowhere were these divisions more evident than in the park. Each stratum of society had its own time for frequenting it, and its designated *allées*. The upper class favoured the central avenues. The middle class promenaded after dinner, once the *beau monde* had departed in search of other enjoyments. Similar divisions operated in the boulevards. Boulevard du Régent closest to the park was for the most elegant *flâneurs*, Boulevard du Jardin Botanique for the bourgeoisie, the stretches furthest from the park for the plebeians. The city's most popular promenade, the Allée Verte, which was the place to be seen in the evening, was divided into two social zones. Upper-class strollers walked on the canal side, plebeians on the other.[8]

There is an indication of these social demarcations in Lucy Snowe's description of the crowds on the night of the fête. Only Lucy, floating unnoticed amid the crowd, does not clearly belong to any one of the various social categories she enumerates:

Half the peasantry had come in from the outlying environs of Villette, and the decent burghers were all abroad and around, dressed in their best. My straw-hat passed amidst cap and jacket, short petticoat, and long calico mantle, without, perhaps, attracting a glance ...

> Here [at the *kiosque de musique*] were assembled ladies, looking by this light most beautiful; some of their dresses were gauzy, and some had the sheen of satin; the flowers and the blond trembled, and the veils waved about their decorated bonnets . . . Most of these ladies occupied the little light park-chairs, and behind and beside them stood guardian gentlemen. The outer ranks of the crowd were made up of citizens, plebeians and police.
>
> In this outer rank I took my place. I rather liked to find myself the silent, unknown, consequently unaccosted neighbour of the short petticoat and the sabot; and only the distant gazer at the silk robe, the velvet mantle, and the plumed chapeau.[9]

Contemporary books about Brussels refer to the restrictions in force in the park as well as the social divisions. In her 1839 guide to the city, Mrs Wemyss Dalrymple tells us that there were uniformed park keepers – retired veterans wearing blue capes, cocked hats and chamois gloves – whose job it was to enforce regulations such as the ban on walking on the grass. While she admired the 'beautiful and healthy children sporting in the alleys' ('Belgian children are handsome and well dressed but in a very different manner from ours; foreigners generally dress their children like little epitomes of themselves'), she noted that they were not allowed to use their hoops 'lest people be incommoded'.[10] By the 1850s these restrictions had become too many for one observer of Brussels life. In a country of smokers – M. Paul was not the only Belgian to wreathe himself in cigar smoke at every opportunity – Louis Hymans objected to having to put out his cigar as soon as he passed through the park gate.[11]

The restrictions and security measures did not make the park fool-proof against intruders, a fact indicated in *Villette*. When, in the oppressive heat of the school dormitory, Lucy yearns for the cool of the park, she has a plan for entering it even though the park of Villette – like the real one of Brussels – is locked at nightfall (this is something that Charlotte conveniently ignores when she makes Lucy and Graham Bretton cross it on a dark winter's evening).

> The other day, in walking past, I had seen, without then attending to the circumstance, a gap in the paling – one stake broken down: I now saw this gap again in recollection – saw it very plainly – the narrow, irregular aperture visible between the stems of the lindens, planted orderly as a colonnade.[12]

Charlotte's memory, as so often, had served her well in a minor detail. In 1843 the park did indeed have a wooden paling and was enclosed by a hedge, described as a miserable affair by a visitor who saw it the previous year.[13] There was general agreement that this hedge, which invariably suffered damage during fêtes of the kind described by Charlotte, should be replaced with an elegant iron railing more worthy of the main park of a capital city. But although this project was mooted year after year, the requisite funds were not raised for it (by public subscription) until 1849.

On fine days, the park seems to have been a lively place despite the petty restrictions Hymans complained of. In addition to the regimental bands which played every weekend in summer there was the Vauxhall, where there was a theatre, a café called Velloni's celebrated for its ices, and an assembly room for balls. Mrs Wemyss Dalrymple advises those interested in the latter to apply for details to M. Sacré on Boulevard de Waterloo, master of ceremonies, who also gave dancing lessons – to Charlotte's friends Mary and Martha Taylor, among others.

There were no dancing lessons and no balls for Charlotte Brontë or for Lucy Snowe, who feels daunted when Dr John's mother has a pink dress made for her to attend the concert at the Salle de la Grande Harmonie attended by the King and Queen. Her shrinking appearance in this new dress marks one of the most daring of Lucy's rare forays into the social life of Villette. It is also unlikely that Charlotte, who had to watch her expenses carefully, ever sipped lemonade or enjoyed ices at Velloni's. Lucy Snowe does not eat ices in the park either. She visits it at night, alone and incognita, and in despair at the prospect of losing Paul Emanuel. In this mood of depression, expecting to find the park deserted, she discovers instead that it has become something very different from its usual self.

> I took a route well known, and went up towards the palatial and royal Haute Ville; thence the music I had heard, certainly floated; it was hushed now, but it might re-waken. I went on; neither band nor bell-music came to meet me; another sound replaced it, a sound like a strong tide, a great flow, deepening as I proceeded. Light broke, movement gathered, chimes pealed – to what was I coming? Entering on the level of a Grande Place [the Place Royale], I found myself, with the suddenness of magic, plunged amidst a gay, living, joyous crowd.

Villette is one blaze, one broad illumination; the whole world seems abroad; moonlight and heaven are banished: the town, by her own flambeaux, beholds her own splendour – gay dresses, grand equipages, fine horses and gallant riders throng the bright streets. I see even scores of masks. It is a strange scene, stranger than dreams. But where is the park? – I ought to be near it. In the midst of this glare the park must be shadowy and calm – *there*, at least, are neither torches, lamps, nor crowd? . . .

Lo! the iron gateway, between the stone columns, was spanned by a flaming arch built of massed stars . . . following . . . beneath that arch . . . where was I?

In a land of enchantment, a garden most gorgeous, a plain sprinkled with coloured meteors, a forest with sparks of purple and ruby and golden fire gemming the foliage; a region, not of trees and shadow, but of strangest architectural wealth – of altar and of temple, of pyramid, obelisk, and sphinx; incredible to say, the wonders and the symbols of Egypt teemed throughout the park of Villette.[14]

In his article *La vie bruxelloise dans 'Villette'*, Gustave Charlier identifies many of the details of the concert that Lucy hears in the park. He matches them to an actual concert held on 24 September 1843 as part of the annual four-day festival to commemorate the four days of fighting in the 1830 Revolution (23–26 September), most of which fighting took place in and around the Park. These annual festivities brought out all the Belgian love of pomp and partying. They featured a grand national procession with floats representing each of the nine Belgian provinces, competitive games, much marching in the streets, waving of flags, beating of drums, firing of canon and ringing of church bells, and concerts such as the one Charlier is convinced that Charlotte attended.

'Everything indicates,' Charlier says, 'that on that day [24 September] Charlotte *a promené sa mélancholie passionnée* [literally: 'walked her passionate melancholy'] among the revelling crowd in the Parc de Bruxelles.' An image is conjured up of Charlotte 'walking' her melancholy along the avenues of the park as more fortunate residents of the capital walked their spaniels.

Charlier identifies the 'wild Jäger chorus' that so thrills Lucy, issuing from a choir of singers on the 'kiosque', as a hunting song, one of the items in the concert of 24 September, in which over 300 singers participated.

Fête in September 1848 at the Vauxhall in the Park to commemorate the 1830 Revolution.

Choiring out of a glade . . . broke such a sound as I thought might be heard if Heaven were to open – such a sound, perhaps, as *was* heard above the plain of Bethlehem, on the night of glad tidings.

The song, the sweet music, rose afar, but rushing swiftly on faststrengthening pinions – there swept through these shades so full a storm of harmonies that, had no tree been near against which to lean, I think I must have dropped. Voices were there, it seemed to me, unnumbered; instruments varied and countless – bugle, horn, and trumpet I knew. The effect was as a sea breaking into song with all its waves.

The swaying tide swept this way, and then it fell back, and I followed its retreat. It led me towards a Byzantine building – a sort of kiosk near the park's centre. Round about stood crowded thousands, gathered to a grand concert in the open air. What I had heard was, I think, a wild Jäger chorus; the night, the space, the scene, and my own mood, had but enhanced the sounds and their impression.[15]

Lucy's enthusiasm at this choral performance was echoed by newspaper reviews. Charlier points out, however, that Charlotte exaggerated the magnificence of the park lighting. The *Bruxellois* were, typically, less overwhelmed, one newspaper report grumpily complaining about the poor light given out by the lanterns festooning the trees, which put people in danger of falling over groups of spectators on the grass. Charlier observes: 'Happy Lucy Snowe, for whom this somewhat pathetic lighting became something magical. As she herself remarks, it wasn't in her power to observe calmly. She was excited by the drug and her imagination exaggerated everything.'

Like her fictional heroine Lucy Snowe, it was not in Charlotte's power to observe anything calmly. Her imagination set to work on everything she saw, whether to blight it with her sarcasm or magnify its beauties.

However, whatever the shortcomings of the park illuminations on the night of the concert that may have inspired the one in *Villette*, only a week earlier Brussels had been even more splendidly illuminated for a still more imposing occasion: the passage of Queen Victoria and Prince Albert through the city on a five-day visit to Belgium that sent the country into a fever of excitement. During the few hours the royal couple spent in the capital in the company of King Leopold and Queen Louise, they attended a concert in their honour in the park and then drove through the streets to see the illuminations and be seen by the cheering populace, prior to a banquet at the Royal Palace. In a letter to Emily on 1 October, Charlotte, one of many British residents and visitors present on the occasion, mentioned seeing the Queen's carriage pass by along rue Royale; she must also have witnessed the

▲ A concert in the Park at a wooden *kiosque* used before the iron one was installed in 1841.

▼ Concert in the Park to mark Queen Victoria's visit to Brussels on 18 September 1843.

transformation of the town in honour of the British monarch and her consort.

The city's authorities and residents alike pulled out all the stops for the occasion, in a stunning demonstration of what the capital was capable of in the way of pageantry. Funds may not have been forthcoming for a park railing but no expense seems to have been spared to put on a show to impress the English Queen. Britain had played a key role in supporting Belgium's recent independence, and feelings towards the country were warm. 'The young Belgium was full of joy at the honour paid to it,' in the words of the Brussels newspaper *L'Observateur*. British onlookers were surprised at the freedom the security forces allowed the excited crowds, which thronged close to the royal carriage, a freedom explained by the *Observateur's* opinion that 'Nowhere could Victoria feel more secure than among the Belgians'.[16]

The royal carriage passed along streets lined with buildings flying the British and Belgian flags and crowds waving handkerchiefs and crying 'Vive la reine' and 'Vive le roi'. Most impressively, as dusk fell, the houses and streets of the whole city were lit up for the occasion, from the mansions in the Upper Town to the humblest quarters in the Lower. Chinese lanterns hung from trees and houses. Some of the grander buildings sported 'transparencies' with illuminated words and emblems; passers-by stopped to admire the one adorning the shop of the Frères Jones, carriage-makers to the royal family, bearing the inscription 'Welcome the Pride of Britain, Victoria and Albert' among emblems of Britain and Belgium.

The illuminations were particularly brilliant in the park, the boulevards and the botanical gardens. In the latter, the contours of the vast greenhouses were outlined in fire. The boulevards blazed with a triple line of fire, formed by the lights on the houses, the lanterns on the trees and the rows of gas candelabra. The Brussels newspapers described the illuminations as the most splendid since Leopold I's inauguration on 21 July 1831, a British observer as 'the most complete and perfect display of the kind ever witnessed'.[17] 'All this ensemble' in the opinion of *L'Observateur*, 'was like something out of fairyland.'[18]

A Moorish-style triumphal arch, 'blazing in lamps of all colours',[19] was erected at one of the city gates and another at the entrance to the park, doubtless the 'flaming arch built of massed stars' through which Lucy passes in Charlotte's description.

However, other details, such as her reference to 'pyramids', correspond to press descriptions of the preparations for the park illuminations of 24

September, a week after Victoria's visit, the day of the concert that Charlier identifies:

> In the two side allées, two great lines of pyramids have been erected, and in the central one two lines of candelabra ... the illuminations promise to be brilliant this year.[20]

It seems likely that Charlotte fused elements of both festivities in her description of the fête in the park. If the newspaper reports are to be believed, her account of Villette being 'one blaze, one broad illumination', and of the park being changed into 'a land of enchantment', is not far from the reality of what Brussels was capable of in terms of illuminations.

Only four years after Charlotte absorbed the impressions that provided the setting for the park scene in *Villette*, Bernard De Smedt, author of *Le Parc de Bruxelles ancien et moderne*, complained about the devastation caused by the annual September revelries. Each year the illuminations, always the most popular element of the festivities, were splendid on the night, but the following day the park's avenues would be littered with broken branches and the trees blackened by the lanterns nailed to them. As a result, by 1847, when De Smedt's book was published, the authorities had decided that the illuminations for the September fête would henceforth be in the nearby boulevard rather than in the park.

If this decision had been taken before 1843, the result might have been a loss to literature given that Charlotte's account of Lucy's night in the park is one of the most memorable in *Villette*. It is a scene often described as having elements of surrealism. In a discussion of surrealistic writing featuring Brussels, Daniel Acke, in *Écrire Bruxelles/Brussel Schrijven*, discusses how one's sense of identity can change in a strange city and how contact with that city 'can lead to an enlargement of identity; the impulses of the unconscious are given free rein and projected on the urban environment.'[21] A suggestion of this process, typical of the surrealist literature of later periods, can perhaps be seen at work in the account of Lucy in the park, with its blurring of the lines between reality and the imagination, its transformation of a familiar environment into a dream-like and unrecognisable one.

Given the importance of surrealism in Belgian art and literature in the twentieth century, it is not surprising that the surrealistic elements in the scene are picked up on with particular interest by more than one Belgian reader. For the historian Sophie De Schaepdrijver, the dreamscape of the park can be characterised in terms of the Freudian concept of the uncanny',[22] a concept that was significant for the Surrealists. Leen Huet, in *Mijn België*, is haunted by the dark side of Lucy's experience in *Villette* and is particularly mesmerised by her opium-induced hallucinatory perceptions in the park. In the crowds of Brussels burghers among whom Lucy floats, Huet observes, 'Every Belgian will recognise the future masks of James Ensor'. The half Belgian, half English surrealistic painter Ensor, born in 1860, often depicted carnival-type revellers in grotesque masks.

For Huet, though, what gives *Villette* its enduring power is something that goes well beyond the fascination of the surreal. Strongest of all is the novel's ability to convey something very real: the pain of mental suffering.

While Lucy is in the park, she sees Paul Emanuel surrounded by the 'junta' of her enemies, the people who are trying to keep him from her. She witnesses a scene that not only explains his sudden decision to travel to the West Indies but convinces her he cares nothing for her and intends to marry someone else on his return. It is the end of hope, or so Lucy believes. The sensation that this conviction has released her from the bondage of love and the illusion of hope makes her feel temporarily stronger, but the familiar torture soon returns. Jealousy tears her like 'a vulture' and the next day she is back on the 'old rack of suspense' as she lives once again in hope of a last interview with M. Paul before he departs for 'Basseterre in Guadaloupe'.[23]

In the penultimate chapter of the novel M. Paul does come at last, and clarifications and explanations ensue in the course of a long walk on the boulevards, culminating with a visit to a certain little house in a *faubourg* where, as it turns out, Lucy's future in Villette lies. What follows are years of waiting for Paul Emanuel's return, but they are also years of joyous antic- ipation of reunion. But then, in the final chapter, the reader is denied that happy reunion just as it seems to be within reach.

Charlotte put all her pain into *Villette*, and in Leen Huet's opinion she bequeathed to her readers something more important than the gratification of a happy ending. Lucy does not live happily ever after, but what she feels continues to resonate with each generation of readers.

> Every reader will be grateful to Charlotte Brontë because she left us this book showing us how people suffered in bygone years – so we know that our ancestors were not machines who ate, slept, procreated and died in order to lead finally to our own sensitive generation, but living people …'.[24]

One of Charlotte Brontë's greatest legacies to Brussels was her power to transmute into literature what she felt there so powerfully that the reader not only sees the city's park transformed into a land of enchantment through Lucy Snowe's eyes, but experiences Lucy Snowe's suffering.

1   *Villette.*, Chapter 7.

2   *Ibid.*, Chapter 38.

3   Saint-Férreol, *Les proscrits français en Belgique*, p. 98.

4   Addison, *Belgium as she is*, pp. 102–3.

5   Huet, *Mijn België*, p. 13.

6   Nerval, *Oeuvres*, p. 918.

7   *Crocodile*, 3 July 1853.

8   Hymans and Rousseau, *Le diable à Bruxelles*, pp. 47–9, 95–7, 107.

9   *Villette*, Chapter 38.

10   Wemyss Dalrymple, *The Economist's New Brussels Guide*, p. 65.

11   Hymans and Rousseau, *Le diable à Bruxelles*, Vol. 3, p. 41.

12   *Villette*, Chapter 38.

13   Dubreucq, *Bruxelles 1000: une histoire capitale*, Volume 7, p. 283.

14   *Villette*, Chapter 38.

15   *Ibid.*, Chapter 38.

16   *L'Observateur*, 20 September 1843.

17   *The progresses of Queen Victoria and Prince Albert in France, Belgium and England in 1843* (London: William Frederick Wakeman).

18   *L'Observateur*, 20 September 1843.

19   *The progresses of Queen Victoria and Prince Albert in France, Belgium and England in 1843.*

20   *L'Observateur*, 24 September 1843.

21   Acke and Bekers, *Écrire Bruxelles/Brussel Schrijven*, p. 37.

22   *De Standaard*, 10 November 2004.

23   *Villette*, Chapter 41.

24   Huet, *Mijn België*, p. 308.

Conclusion:
Charlotte Brontë's Brussels Legacies

BRUSSELS has not celebrated the name of Charlotte Brontë in a visible way by erecting memorials to her in its streets. Nevertheless, she has an important legacy in the capital, a legacy that takes various forms.

Villette immortalises, in a world classic, a city that has inspired few great works of literature. Disparaging though Charlotte's account of Belgian society is at times, the novel has nevertheless been described in Belgium as 'one of the books in which both the physical city and the soul of Brussels are most sensuously evoked'. Transformed by Charlotte's imagination into an atmospheric backdrop to Lucy Snowe's emotional development, it is at the same time fully recognisable as the Brussels of the 1840s.

Both *Villette* and *The Professor* are valued by Belgian readers as a rare picture of their capital at a period when it was little portrayed in home-grown fiction. It is, moreover, a snapshot captured at an interesting point in the country's history, shortly after Independence. Although Charlotte Brontë's portrait of Brussels life has been described as 'bitter' and 'caustic' and even spiteful, and although *Villette* has been seen as a novel of revenge for her disappointment in love, the portrait is a vivid one. It was her first experience of life abroad and in a city, and her impressions, as Gustave Charlier pointed out, were fresh and lively.

As Charlier also pointed out, her descriptions were astonishingly accurate, providing Belgian readers with a mine of detailed information on aspects of Brussels life. They have proved a useful source for historians researching, for example, Belgian boarding schools in the first half of the nineteenth century, cultural events in the capital, or the character of Leopold I, first King of the Belgians.

'The strange daughters of the pastor of Haworth were endowed with a kind of gift of divination; they read people's secrets in their eyes ... In order to form an idea of what the moral climate in Brussels was around 1840, we must – paradoxically – refer to the impressions of a young Englishwoman who spent a few months there at that period.'[1] This astounding claim is a testimony both to the paucity of accounts of 1840s Brussels and the importance of that left by Charlotte Brontë. It is made by an historian and biographer of Leopold I who was staggered by the perspicacity of Charlotte's psychological analysis of the King, seen by her at a concert. Her comments on Belgian life and manners were equally penetrating.

While readers in Belgium may resent some of her attacks on the country's inhabitants, religion and arts, at the same time they find it piquant to view themselves through her eyes. She was a shrewd observer, and a common assessment is to acknowledge that her observations were preceptive even while deploring the unkindnesses, exaggerations and distortions of her portrayal.

Charlotte Brontë is one of several foreign writers who are read with interest for their comments on Belgium. Belgian readers have a taste for viewing their country through foreign eyes. In the literary history of Brussels, a city of invasion and occupation, of passage and exile, the non-Belgian writers who have lived there have played an important part. Charlotte Brontë's name is often coupled with that of Charles Baudelaire, like her a ferocious critic of Belgian society, leading one commentator to dub her 'Miss Baudelaire'. Their jaundiced view of their host country is considered to have a similar cause – the disappointments and frustrations they experienced in Belgium – and is often excused on those grounds, with Belgian commentators expressing pity rather than resentment towards the two writers.

In Charlotte's case, allowances are made for her as a visitor from a very different culture, northern, Protestant and provincial, who suffered in Belgium from what would today be termed 'culture shock'. Compassion is felt for her more generally for the tragedies of her life and the privations of what is seen as the grim Puritanism of her remote Haworth existence, contrasting starkly with the culture and amenities offered by a city like Brussels.

The comparison with Baudelaire is of limited application, for unlike his, in many ways Charlotte Brontë's Brussels legacy is a positive one. Baudelaire's time in Brussels took place at the end of his life when he was sick and disillusioned, with his best work behind him; Charlotte was setting out in life, gathering impressions and honing skills for the novels that were soon to bring her fame. Baudelaire's stay in the city was a sterile and negative one which produced little more than notes for a book (*Pauvre Belgique*) inspired by hatred. Charlotte's was a fertile, if traumatic, time of emotional and intellectual growth which ultimately produced a novel inspired primarily by love

(*Villette*, with its hero Paul Emanuel based on Constantin Heger; her other novels and fictional heroes also owe part of their inspiration to her feelings for Heger). One of her legacies among Belgians is pride that her time in the country was so important for her personal and artistic development.

Unlike Baudelaire's, too, her association with Brussels is a romantic one, and this goes a long way towards offsetting the negativity of her anti-Belgian remarks. Her name usually comes up in connection with Heger and her 'hopeless love' for him. She has been described as having 'left her heart buried' in the city. The story of this unrequited love further enhances the already romantic and tragic popular image of the Brontë sisters.

The romanticism of that image is heightened further still by the fact that in the literary history of Brussels, the memory of Charlotte Brontë is closely associated with a picturesque part of the city, a quarter with an engaging history, which disappeared under the brutal redevelopment of the early twentieth century. Brussels continues its tradition of self-destruction to this day, and Charlotte and Emily Brontë's passage through the capital is bound up with the nostalgia for the swathes of the city that have been allowed to vanish almost without trace.

Looking at Charlotte Brontë and her works through Belgian eyes thus provides a variety of fresh and intriguing perspectives. Ultimately, of course, while her time in Brussels and the observations on Belgian life in *Villette* and *The Professor* give these novels a particular interest for Belgian readers, she is read in Belgium for the same reason that she is read everywhere else. Most Belgian readers come to *Villette* only after first discovering Charlotte Brontë's voice in *Jane Eyre* and identifying emotionally with the orphan Jane.

If they identify so closely with the narrators of *Jane Eyre* and *Villette*, it is because of what Jane and Lucy suffer. Belgian readers may feel that Charlotte's frustrations and unhappiness sometimes vented themselves in unwarranted attacks on their country; as Thackeray, who admired her and her work, once wrote, 'Miss Brontë is unhappy and that makes her unjust'.[2] But that frustration and unhappiness were also the driving force that gives her novels their power, ensuring that her voice continues to speak across the centuries just as it does across geographical boundaries.

---

1   Bronne, *Belles étrangères en Belgique*, pp. 148, 143.
2   In a letter to Mary Homes, 10 August 1852.

Chronological summary of events that have shaped Belgian views of Charlotte Brontë

As seen in earlier chapters, while *Jane Eyre* has been popular in Belgium from the time of its publication, *Villette* had to wait for the twentieth century to be known to Belgian readers outside a small circle.

In the late nineteenth and early twentieth century it was often Emily rather than Charlotte Brontë who aroused most interest in Belgium, particularly after the publication in 1892 of a French translation of *Wuthering Height*, under the name of *Un Amant*, by Théodore de Wyzewa, an exponent of the Symbolist movement. Critical attention had begun to focus on Charlotte's younger sister with the publication of Swinburne's and Mary Robinson's studies in 1883, though the view of Emily rather than Charlotte as the genius of the Brontë family had been suggested on the Continent as early as 1857 by the French critic Émile Montégut, in an article on Charlotte in the *Revue des Deux Mondes* in 1857.[1] In his biographical introduction to *Un Amant*, De Wyzewa relates how his interest in Emily was first awakened by a young Englishwoman he met who could practically recite *Wuthering Heights* by heart, clearly a member of a new cult. De Wyzewa was one of the worshippers, claiming to have seen Emily's ghost when he visited the parish church in Haworth where she is buried ('a pale, sweet ghost with a scent of heather'). He emphasised the harshness of life in Haworth and painted a highly negative portrait of Patrick Brontë and the Brontës' childhood, repeating discredited stories (from the first edition of Gaskell's *Life*) such as the children being reared by their father on a diet of potatoes. This was the prevailing view of the Brontës among Belgian readers. It was echoed by Emily's best-known admirer in Belgium, Maurice Maeterlinck, like de Wyzewa a proponent of Symbolism.

De Wyzewa claimed that Charlotte, along with other Victorian novelists such as George Eliot, was gradually being forgotten, while her sister was 'gaining popularity by the day'. Clearly, time has not borne out this claim, and today both Brontës are widely read in Belgium. *Jane Eyre* has always been popular there, while the Brussels setting of *Villette* and *The Professor* has always aroused interest, as has Charlotte's stay in the capital.

There have been surges of increased interest in Charlotte Brontë and the Brontë family at regular intervals as a result of events such as new translations of the novels, new biographies, and films or plays. 1877 saw the publication of a French translation of Elizabeth Gaskell's *Life of Charlotte Brontë*. In the early years of the twentieth century interest was generated in Charlotte by the Frenchman Ernest Dimnet's *Les Soeurs Brontë* (1911), and the publication of Charlotte's letters to Heger in 1913. This interest came too late for Belgian Brontëites wishing to see the Pensionnat Heger, which had disappeared in 1910.

The publication of the first complete translation of *Villette* into French in 1932 prompted a spate of reviews and press articles about the novel and Charlotte's years in Brussels. The following year, Gustave Charlier's essay *La vie bruxelloise dans 'Villette'* highlighted an aspect of the novel of particular interest to Belgian readers: the descriptions of actual events attended by Charlotte during her stay in the city. Also in 1933, articles marking the death of Louise Heger, the last surviving child of the Hegers and the last person living in Belgium to have known Charlotte Brontë, drew attention to Brussels' Brontë link.

The decade of the 1930s was also a time when interest in Emily Brontë was at a peak, with a new French translation of *Wuthering Heights* in 1935 (Dutch speakers had to wait until 1941 for the first Dutch translation), a stage adaptation of the novel, *Les Mauvais Anges*, which was performed in Brussels, and above all the 1939 film starring Merle Oberon and Laurence Olivier. Also in 1939, a new biography by Robert De Traz, *La Famille Brontë*, presented a sober and balanced account of the family. In the same year the Belgian author Charles Plisnier wrote that the Brontës had now become cult figures: 'almost every day a new book comes out about them'.[2]

Interest was maintained in the 1940s with the 1944 film of *Jane Eyre* with Joan Fontaine and Orson Welles and the highly fictionalised biographical film *Devotion* (1946), which had scenes set in Brussels. In the 1950s, an exhibition to mark the centenary of Charlotte Brontë's death that ran for two years (1953–1955) at the Musée Charlier in Brussels did much to publicise her stay in Brussels; the exhibits included photos of the letters to Heger. Throughout the decade the Brontëite writer and journalist Louis Quiévreux drew the attention of readers of *Le Soir* and other newspapers to the destruction of the remaining places associated with the Brontës' stay as a result of the construction of the Central Station near the Pensionnat site.

In the succeeding decades, films and televised adaptations of the novels have kept up interest in Belgium in the Brontës' lives and works. A notable example was Téchiné's *Les Soeurs Brontë* (1979). Viewers in Belgium were able to watch the 1983 BBC TV adaptation of *Jane Eyre,* which introduced a new generation of Belgians to the novel. More recently, media interest in the bicentenary of Charlotte Brontë's birth in 2016 focused attention on her Brussels novels and the story of her time in Belgium.

1   Montégut, Emile, 'Miss Brontë: sa vie et ses oeuvres', *Revue des Deux Mondes,* 1 July 1857.
2   *L'Indépendance Belge,* 18 February 1939.

Timeline

1849   Publication of the first French translation of *Jane Eyre*, an abridged adaptation entitled *Jane Eyre: memoires d'une gouvernante*. It first came out in serial form in the *Revue de Paris* and also in *L'Indépendance Belge*, both starting in April 1849. The translator was the Frenchman Émile Dauran-Forgues ('Old Nick'). The first Dutch translation of *Jane Eyre* was published the same year.

1850   First French translation of *Shirley*.

1851   First Dutch translation of *Shirley*.

1854   Publication of the first complete French translation of *Jane Eyre*, by Noëmi Lesbazeilles-Souvestre.

1855   Death of Charlotte Brontë on 31 March.

          First French translation of *Villette*, an abridged adaptation entitled *La Maîtresse d'anglais ou le Pensionnat de Bruxelles*.

          A dramatisation of *Jane Eyre* by the Belgian writers Victor Lefèvre and Pierre Royer, based on Charlotte Birch-Pfeiffer's *Die Waise aus Lowood* (1853), was staged in Brussels at the end of the year.

1856   First Dutch translation of *Villette*.

1858   First French translation of *The Professor*

1859   First Dutch translation of *The Professor*.

1877   French translation of Elizabeth Gaskell's *Life of Charlotte Brontë*.

1892   First French translation of *Wuthering Heights* under the name *Un Amant* by the French critic, translator and admirer of Emily Brontë, Théodore de Wyzewa.

1898   Publication of Maurice Maeterlinck's *La sagesse et la destinée*, a section of which was devoted to Emily Brontë. It was instrumental in increasing interest in Emily in Belgium.

1911   Publication of the Frenchman Ernest Dimnet's biography *Les Soeurs Brontë*.

1913   Publication of Charlotte's four extant letters to Constantin Heger in *The Times* on 29 July, after Heger's children donated them to the British Museum.

1929   Publication of the biography *Les Soeurs Brontë* by the French authors Emilie and Georges Romieu.

1932   The publication of the first complete French translation of *Villette* focused attention on the novel and it was the subject of many press articles.

1933   Publication of Gustave Charlier's *La vie bruxelloise dans 'Villette'* in the *Revue de l'Université de Bruxelles*. In 1947 it was republished in a collection of essays, *Passages*, about the passage through Brussels of various foreign writers. The article, which identifies the cultural events described in Villette as real ones attended by Charlotte, is one of the most important studies to come out of Belgium.

        The death of Louise Heger on 21 July 1933 led to press articles further focusing attention on Charlotte and *Villette*. Louise, who died at the age of 94, was the last person living in Belgium to have known Charlotte.

1938   The play *Les Mauvais Anges*, an adaptation of *Wuthering Heights* by M. Vanderic, was staged in the Théâtre des Galeries in Brussels.

1939   The screening of Wyler's film of *Wuthering Heights* starring Merle Oberon and Laurence Olivier marked a peak in Emily's popularity.

        Publication in France of the biography *La Famille Brontë* by Robert De Traz.

1941   Publication of the first Dutch translation of *Wuthering Heights*.

1944   Release of the film of *Jane Eyre* with Joan Fontaine and Orson Welles.

1946   The film *Devotion,* which has scenes set in Brussels, kept interest focused on the Brontë family.

1949   Publication of a new Dutch translation of *Villette,* the first since 1856.

1951   The play *Survivre: Un épisode de la vie de Charlotte Brontë* by Michel Phillipot was performed in Brussels. It dealt with Charlotte's relationship with Arthur Nicholls and gave a negative portrayal of Nicholls. It was the last role of the actress Ludmilla Pitoeff, whose performance as Charlotte made a great impact on audiences.

1953   Exhibition on Charlotte Brontë at the Musée Charlier in Brussels from 21 March 1853 to 25 April 1855 to mark the centenary of her death. The exhibits that made most impact were reproductions of Charlotte's letters to Heger and a bunch of dried heather from the Haworth moors that had been laid on Heger's grave.

1979   Screening of André Téchiné's film *Les Soeurs Brontë.*

1980   On 26 June the Brontë Society unveiled a plaque near the entrance to the Palais des Beaux-Arts ('Bozar') commemorating Charlotte and Emily's stay in Brussels in 1842–43. The ceremony took place amid a thunderstorm and torrential downpour, described in *Le Soir* as 'un temps de Hurlevent'.

2016   The bicentenary of Charlotte Brontë's birth led to numerous press articles which drew attention to her time in Brussels.

Select Bibliography

The works listed are those that are specifically relevant to the theme of this book. I have not included standard reference works on the Brontës such as Elizabeth Gaskell's or Juliet Barker's biographies.

Acke, Daniel, Bekers, Elisabeth (eds), *Écrire Bruxelles/Brussels Schrijven* (Brussels: VUB Press, 2016).

Addison H.R., *Belgium as she is* (Brussels and Leipzig: C. Muquardt, 1843).

Allott, Miriam, *The Brontës: The Critical Heritage* (London: Routledge & Kegan Paul Ltd, 1974).

Aron, Paul (ed.), *La Belgique artistique et littéraire: Une anthologie de langue française 1818–1914* (Brussels: Editions complexe, 1997).

Baron, A. (ed.), *La Belgique monumentale, historique et pittoresque* (Brussels: A. Jamer and Ch. Hen., 1844).

Bartier, John, *Laïcité et Franc-Maçonnerie* (Brussels: Editions de l'Université de Bruxelles, 1981), p. 164

Baudelaire, Charles, *Pauvre Belgique*. Paris: Conard, 1953.

Biebuyck, Jacques (ed.), *Bruxelles: Ville en forme de cœur* (Brussels: Editions universitaires, 1957).

Britse Sporen in Brussel. Self-guided walk produced by Onthaal en Promotie Brussel.

Bronne, Carlo, *Belles étrangères en Belgique* (Brussels: Didier Hatier, 1986).

Bronne, Carlo, *Léopold Ier et son temps* (Brussels: Goemaere, 1942).

Brontë, Charlotte ('Currer Bell'), *Jane Eyre: Mémoires d'une gouvernante, imités par Old Nick* (Brussels: Alp. Lebègue, 1849).

Brontë, Charlotte/Currer Bell, *La Maîtresse d'anglais, ou le Pensionnat de Bruxelles* (Brussels: A Labroue, 1855).

Chadwick, Ellis H., *In the Footsteps of the Brontës* (London: Pitman and Sons, 1914).

Charlier, Gustave, 'La vie bruxelloise dans "Villette"', *Passage: Essais* (Brussels: La Renaissance du Livre, 1947). (First published in 'Revue de l'Université de Bruxelles', 4, May–July 1933.)

Christophe, Lucien, 'Le Roman Bruxellois de Charlotte Brontë', *Le Soir*, 3 April 1939.

Christophe, Lucien, 'Souvenirs de la Pension Heger: Un amour de Charlotte Brontë', *Les nouvelles littéraires artistiques et scientifiques*, Paris, 21 October 1933.

De Pradt, *De la Belgique depuis 1789 jusqu'à 1794* (Paris: Béchet, 1820).

De Schaepdrijver, Sophie, *Elites for the Capital? Foreign Migration to mid-nineteenth-century Brussels* (Amsterdam: Thesis Publishers, 1990).

De Smedt, Bernard, *Le parc de Bruxelles ancien et moderne* (Brussels, 1847).

De Traz, Robert, *La Famille Brontë* (Paris: Michel, 1939).

De Vries, André, *Flanders, a cultural history* (Oxford, New York: Oxford University Press, 2007).

Defrance, Olivier, *Léopold Ier et le clan Cobourg* (Brussels: Racine, 2004).

Demoor, Marysa, *The fields of Flanders: alles, of bijna alles wat Engelse auteurs ooit schreven over Vlaanderen en België... en waarom* (Groot-Bijgaarden: Globe, 2002).

Des Marez, G., *L'Origine et le développement de Bruxelles – Le quartier Isabelle et Terarken* (Paris-Brussels: Librairie d'Art et d'Histoire, 1927).

Dimnet, Ernest/Sill, Louise Morgan, *The Brontë Sisters* (New York: Harcourt, Brace & Company, 1927). First published as *Les Soeurs Brontë* (Paris: H. Didier, 1910).

Dominkovits, Delinka, *Charlotte Brontë and Brussels* (university dissertation) (Brussels: Université Libre de Bruxelles, 1982).

Dubreucq, Jacques, *Bruxelles 1000: une histoire capitale* (Brussels: Jacques Dubreucq). 9 volumes published 1996–2000.

Dumas, Alexandre, *Excursions sur les bords du Rhin.* (Brussels: Meline, Cans et Cie, 1842).

Duquenne, Xavier, *Parc de Bruxelles* (Brussels: CFC Editions, 1993).

English Girl in a Convent School, the: A Record of Experience (London, Warne, 1874).

François, Pieter, 'A Little Britain on the Continent': British perceptions of Belgium, 1830–1870* (Pisa: Edizioni Plus, Pisa University Press, 2010).

Gautier, Théophile, *Un Tour en Belgique, in Zigzags* (Paris: Victor Magen, 1845).

Gevers, Marie, 'Les Brontë en Afrique', *Revue Générale Belge*, 15 Septembre 1956, pp. 1812–1818.

Gevers, Marie, *Plaisir des Parallèles: essai sur un voyage* (Paris: Stock, 1958).

Gilkin, Iwan, *Mémoires inachevés: Une enfance et une jeunesse bruxelloises 1858–1878* (Brussels: Labor, 2000).

Gilsoul, Robert, *Les influences anglo-saxonnes sur les lettres françaises de Belgique 1850 à 1880* (Brussels: Palais des Académies, 1953).

Goffin, Joël, *Sur les pas des écrivains à Bruxelles* (Brussels: Éditions de l'Octogone, 2001).

Gravière, Caroline, *Une parisienne a Bruxelles* (Brussels: Weissenbruch, 1875).

Henne, Alexandre. *L'Étranger dans Bruxelles: guide historique, statistique et descriptif de la capitale* (Brussels, 1846).

Huet, Leen, *Mijn Belgie* (Amsterdam, Antwerp: Atlas, 2004).

Hymans, Louis, Rousseau, J.B, *Le diable a Bruxelles: étude de mœurs locales* (Brussels: Librairie Polytechnique d'Aug. Decq., 1853).

Hymans, Paul, Hymans, Henri, *Bruxelles à travers les âges*, Volume III (Brussels: Bruylant-Christophe et Cie, 1884).

Janzing, Jolien/Vincent, Paul, *Charlotte Brontë's Secret Love* (London: World Editions, 2015). First published in Dutch as *De Meester* (Utrecht: De Arbeiderspers, 2013).

Jottrand, Lucien, *Londres au point de vue belge* (Brussels, Ghent: C Muquardt, 1852).

Lemonnier, Camille, *La Belgique* (Paris: Hachette, 1888).

Lesbroussart, Philippe et al., *Types et caractères belges contemporains* (Brussels: Lemaire et soeur, imprimeurs-libraire, 1851).

Lonoff, Sue, ed., *The Belgian Essays: A Critical Edition* (New Haven, London; Yale University Press, 1996).

Macdonald, Frederika: *The Secret of Charlotte Brontë: followed by some reminiscences of the real Monsieur and Mme Heger* (London, Edinburgh: Jack, 1914).

MacEwan, Helen, *The Brontës in Brussels* (London: Peter Owen, 2014).

Maeterlinck, Maurice, *La sagesse et la destine* (Paris: Eug. Fasquelle, 1898).

Nerval, Gérard de, *Oeuvres*, ed. Albert Béguin and Jean Richer. Paris: Gallimard, 1960–61, Vol. 2.

Noens, Tina, *Love vs Xenophobia in the works of Charlotte Brontë* (university dissertation) (Ghent: University of Ghent, 2012).

Piette (Valérie), 'Un réseau privé d'éducation des filles. Institutrices et pensionnats à Bruxelles (1830–1860)', *Femmes de culture et de pouvoir. Liber amicorum André Despy-Meyer*, n° spécial de *Sextant*, Vol. 13–14, 2000, pp. 149–77.

Quiévreux, Louis, 'Bruxelles, Les Brontës et la famille Héger', *La Lanterne*, Brussels, April 1953.

Quiévreux, Louis, *Bruxelles, guide de la capitale et de ses environs* (Brussels: A. de Boeck, 1948).

Quiévreux, Louis, *Bruxelles, notre capitale. Histoire, folklore, archéologie* (Brussels, Liège: Editions PIM, 1951).

Quiévreux, Louis, *Dictionnaire anecdotique de Bruxelles* (Brussels: Nelis, 1966).

Roegiers, Patrick, *La spectaculaire histoire des rois des Belges* (Paris: Editions Perrin, 2007).

Romieu, Emilie and Georges/Tapley, Roberts, *The Brontë Sisters* (London: Skeffington & Son, 1931). Originally published as *La vie des soeurs Brontë* (Paris: Librairie Gallimard, 1929).

Roscoe, Thomas, *Belgium: In a picturesque tour* (London: Longman, 1841).

Ruijssenaars, Eric, *Charlotte Brontë's Promised Land: The Pensionnat Heger and Other Brontë Places in Brussels* (Haworth: Brontë Society, 2000).

Ruijssenaars, Eric, *The Pensionnat Revisited: More Light Shed on the Brussels of the Brontës* (Leiden: Dutch Archives, 2003).

Saint-Férreol, Amédée, *Les proscrits français en Belgique ou la Belgique contemporaine vue à travers l'exil* (Paris: Librairie universelle et Bibliothèque démocratique, 1875).

Smith, Margaret, ed., *The Letters of Charlotte Brontë*, Volume I, 1829–1847 (Oxford: Clarendon Press, 1995).

Smith, Margaret, ed., *The Letters of Charlotte Brontë*, Volume II, 1848–1851 (Oxford: Clarendon Press, 2000).

Smith, Margaret, ed., *The Letters of Charlotte Brontë*, Volume III, 1852–1855 (Oxford: Clarendon Press, 2004).

Smithers, Henry, *Observations made during a residence in Brussels* (Brussels: The British Press, 1820).

Spielmann, M.H., *The Inner History of the Brontë–Heger Letters* (London: Chapman and Hall, 1919).

Stengers, Jean (ed.), *Bruxelles croissance d'une capitale* (Antwerp: Fonds Mercator, 1979).

Tahon, Victor, *La Rue Isabelle et Le Jardin des Arbalétriers* (Brussels: Rossignol & Van Den Bril, 1912).

Tennent, James Emerson, *Belgium in 1840* (London: Bentley, 1841).

Texier, Edmond, *Voyage, Pittoresque en Hollande et en Belgique* (Paris: Morizont, 1857).

Thackeray, William Makepeace, 'Little Travels and Roadside Sketches', *Fraser's Magazine*, May 1844.

Trafton, Adeline, *An American Girl Abroad* (Boston: Lee and Shepard, 1872).

Trollope, Frances Milton, *Belgium and Western Germany in 1833* (Brussels: Wahlen, 1834).

Van Nieuwenborgh, Marcel, *Literaire wandelingen door Brussel* (Leuven: Davidsfonds, 1990).

Van Wassenhove, Joseph, *Bruxelles: La vie quotidienne au XIXe siècle vue par les écrivains de l'époque* (Brussels: Samsa, 2016).

Wemyss Dalrymple, Mrs, *The Economist's New Brussels Guide* (Brussels: W. Todd, Brussels, 1839).

Wiertz, Antoine, *Salon de 1842, Bruxelles: Un mot* (Brussels: Parys, 1842).

Willmar, Baronne Anaïs, *Souvenirs de Bruxelles* (Brussels: Devroye, 1862).

Index

Brussels in the 1840s. Copyright © Selina Busch.

Greater Belgian
autor

Trollope

how old Lucy Snowe